Software Containers: The Complete Guide to Virtualization Technology. Create, Use and Deploy Scalable Software with Docker and Kubernetes. Includes Docker and Kubernetes.

Jordan Lioy

Published by Jordan Lioy, 2023.

SOFTWARE CONTAINERS: THE COMPLETE GUIDE TO VIRTUALIZATION TECHNOLOGY. CREATE, USE AND DEPLOY SCALABLE SOFTWARE WITH DOCKER AND KUBERNETES. INCLUDES DOCKER AND KUBERNETES.

First edition. March 15, 2023.

ISBN: 979-8215099186

Written by Jordan Lioy.

Also by Jordan Lioy

Docker & Kubernetes

Docker: The Complete Guide to the Most Widely Used Virtualization Technology. Create Containers and Deploy them to Production Safely and Securely.

Kubernetes: Build and Deploy Modern Applications in a Scalable Infrastructure. The Complete Guide to the Most Modern Scalable Software Infrastructure.

Standalone

Software Containers: The Complete Guide to Virtualization Technology. Create, Use and Deploy Scalable Software with Docker and Kubernetes. Includes Docker and Kubernetes.

Table of Contents

Introduction to Docker

Dockers is a command line program, a background daemon, and a suite of remote services that take a logistical approach to solve common software problems and simplify your installation, execution, publishing, and removal software. To do this, use a UNIX technology called containers.

Historically, UNIX-based operating systems have used the term prison to describe a modified execution time of a program that prevents that program from accessing protected sources. Since 2005, after the launch of the Sun Solaris 10 and Solaris 10 tanks, the tank has become the preferred term for such runtime. The goal, which was only to prevent access to protected resources, was to isolate the process from all resources unless explicitly authorized. The use of containers has been a recommended practice for a long time. But the manual construction of a container can be difficult and just plain wrong. This challenge put them out of reach of some, and misconfigured containers inspired others to have a false sense of security. We need a solution to this problem, and Docker helps. Any software that works with Docker runs in the container. Docker uses existing tank motors to ensure consistent tanks are built in accordance with best practices. This puts greater certainty in the reach of everyone. With Docker, customers get low-cost containers. As Docker and his tanks improve, you get the best and latest jailbreak features. Instead of following the fast-paced and highly technical world of building powerful prison prisons, you can let Docker do it for you. This will save you time, money and give you peace of mind.

Containers are not virtualization

Without Docker, organizations often use hardware virtualization (also known as virtual machines) to provide isolation. Virtual machines provide virtual hardware into which the operating system and other programs can be installed. It takes a lot of time (often minutes) to create and require a significant overload of resources as they run a full copy of the operating system except the software you want to use. Unlike virtual machines, Docker containers do not use hardware virtualization. Programs running in Docker containers communicate directly with the Linux host kernel. As there is no additional layer between the program running inside the container and the computer's operating system, resources are not wasted by using redundant software or simulating virtual hardware. This distinction is important. Docker is not virtualization technology. Instead, it helps you use container technology that is already integrated into your operating system.

Running software in insulation tanks

As mentioned earlier, containers have been around for decades. Docker has used namespaces and Linux control groups, which have been part of Linux since 2007. Docker does not offer container technology but makes it easier to use. To understand what containers look like in your system, first establish a baseline. The following illustration shows a basic example that works in a simplified computer system architecture. Note that the command line interface or CLI works in so-called user space memory, as well as other programs running on the operating system. Ideally, programs running in user space cannot alter the memory space of the kernel. In general, the operating system is the interface between all utility programs and the hardware on which the computer runs.

The first is the Docker demon. If installed correctly, this process must always be started. The other is Docker CLI. This is a Docker program that users interact with. If you want to start, stop, or install the software, you will issue a command using Docker. The image below also shows three containers. Each is executed as a secondary process by the Docker daemon, surrounded by a container, and the delegation process is performed in its own user space. Applications running in a container can only access their own memory and resources, as defined by the containers. The containers built by Docker are isolated in eight respects. This section covers each of these aspects through exploring the functionality of the Docker container. The specific aspects are as follows:

- PID namespace: process and feature identifiers
- UTS namespace: host and domain name.
- MNT namespace: access to the file system and structure
- IPC namespace: processing communication in shared memory
- NET site space: network access and structure
- USR namespace: usernames and identifiers
- chroot (): controls the root location of the file system
- Groups: resource protection

Linux namespaces and management groups support runtime containers. Docker uses another set of technologies to secure containers for files that act as shipping containers.

Shipping containers

You can think of a Docker container as a physical shipping container. This is the box where you store and run the application and all its dependencies. Just as cranes, trucks, trains and ships can easily handle shipping containers, so Docker can also easily manage copy and deliver containers. Docker complements the traditional container metaphor by including ways to package and distribute software. The component that serves as the shipping container is called an image. A Docker image is a pooled snapshot of all the files that should be available to a program running in the container. You can create as many image containers as you want. But when they do, the containers running from the same image do not share the changes in their file system. When you distribute software with Docker, you distribute those images to target computers, creating containers. Images are units that can be sent in the Docker ecosystem. Docker provides a set of infrastructure components that simplify Docker image distribution. These components are records and indexes. You may use publicly available infrastructure provided by Docker Inc., other hosting companies, or your records and indexes.

What problems does Docker solve?

• The use of the software is complex. Before installation, you must determine the operating system you are using, the resources required by the software, other installed software, and other software that depends on it. You have to decide where to install it. Then you'll need to know how to install it. Unsurprisingly, installation procedures vary considerably today. The list of considerations is long and ruthless. Software installation is inconsistent and complicated at best. Most computers have several applications installed and running. And most applications depend on other software. What happens when two or more apps you want to use don't work well together? Disaster. Things only get complicated if two or more applications share dependencies:

• What happens if one application requires an updated dependency and the other does not?

• What happens when you delete an application? Is it gone?

• Can old addictions be removed?

• Can you remember the changes you had to make to install the software you want to remove now?

The truth is, the more software you use, the harder it will be to manage it. Even if you can devote the time and energy it takes to install and run applications, how much can you trust for your safety? Open-source and closed-source programs are constantly releasing security updates and it is often impossible to be aware of any issues. The more software you run, the more likely you are to be attacked.

All these problems can be solved with careful accounting, resource management and logistics, but these are everyday and annoying things. Your time would be better spent using the software you are trying to install, update or publish. The people who built Docker have recognized this, and thanks to their hard work, you can easily find a solution as soon as possible. Most of these problems may seem acceptable today. They may feel trivial because you are used to it. After reading how Docker makes these issues accessible, you can find a change in your opinion.

What is Docker for?

Some key practical questions arise: why would you use Docker and for what? The short answer to the "why" is that, with minimal effort, Docker can quickly save your business.

VIRTUAL MACHINE REPLACEMENT (VMS)

Docker can be used to replace virtual machines in many situations. If you're only interested in the application, not the operating system, Docker can replace the virtual machine and let the operating system take care of someone else. Not only does it boot faster than a virtual machine, but it moves more easily, and thanks to a layered file system, you can share changes easier and faster. It is firmly rooted in the command line and is highly programmable.

PROTECTION SOFTWARE

If you want to experiment quickly with the software without disrupting your existing configuration or going through the tedious task of providing a virtual machine, Docker can provide you with an environment much like a sandbox in milliseconds. It is difficult to understand the liberating effect before experiencing it yourself.

PACKAGING SOFTWARE

Since the Docker image doesn't really depend on Linux users, it's a great way to package the software. You can build your own image and ensure that it can run on any modern Linux computer; Think Java, without the need for a JVM.

MICROSERVIC ARCHITECTURE ACTIVATION

Docker makes it easy to decompose a complex system into a number of constituent elements, allowing you to discuss your services more discreetly. This can allow you to restructure your software so that its components are easier to manage and connect without affecting the whole.

NETWORK MODELING

Since you can create hundreds (if not thousands) of isolated containers on one machine, modeling the network is very easy. This can be useful for testing actual scenarios without breaking the bank.

IMPROVES PRODUCTIVITY IN A FULL BATTERY WHEN OUT OF CONNECTION

Because you can group all parts of your system into Docker containers, you can orchestrate them to work on your laptop and work on the go, even offline.

Reduce cleaning costs

The complex negotiation of different teams over the software delivered is a common place in the sector. We have personally experienced countless discussions about damaged libraries. Problematic addictions; updates were applied incorrectly or in the wrong order or were not made at all; non-reproducible insects; et cetera You probably have one too. Docker allows you to clearly indicate (even as a script) the steps you need to follow to solve a problem in a system with known properties, which greatly simplifies the reproduction of errors and environments, which are normally separate from the system. Secured host environment.

Reduce cleaning costs

The complex negotiation of different teams over the software delivered is a common place in the sector. We have personally experienced countless discussions about damaged libraries. problematic addictions; updates were applied incorrectly or in the wrong order or were not made at all; non-reproducible insects; et cetera You probably have one too. Docker allows you to clearly indicate (even as a script) the steps you need to follow to solve a problem in a system with known properties, which greatly simplifies the reproduction of errors and environments, which are normally separate from the system. Secured host environment.

Documentation of software labels and contact points

When you design your images in a structured and ready way for transfer to different environments, Docker asks you to document dependencies on your software explicitly. Even if you to not use Docker everywhere, this documentation can help you install the software elsewhere.

CONTINUED DELIVERY ACTIVITY

Continuous Delivery (CD) is a paradigm for delivering pipeline based software that with every change reconstructs the system and then goes into production (or "live") through an automated (or partially automated) process. Because it can more accurately control the state of the compilation environment, Docker's constructions are more reproducible and more reversible than traditional software compilation methods. This greatly facilitates the implementation of the CD. Standard CD techniques, such as blue/green implementations (where "real" and "latest" implementations are still active) and Phoenix implementations (where complete systems are updated in each version), are trivial with the application of the game version focused on Docker. process.

Organise

Without Docker, your computer may look like an unwanted tray. Apps have all kinds of dependencies. Some applications rely on system-specific libraries for common tasks such as sound, network, graphics, etc. Others may depend on standard libraries for the language in which they are written. Some others depend on other applications, such as how a Java application depends on a Java virtual machine or a web application may depend on a database. Typically, running a program requires exclusive access to scarce resources, such as a network connection or file. Today, Docker-free applications extend to the entire file system and create a complex network of interactions. Docker keeps things organised by isolating everything with pots and paintings.

Improve portability

Another software issue is that application dependencies typically involve a particular OS. Portability between OSs is a major issue for software users. Although Linux and Mac OS X software compatibility is possible, using the same software on Windows can be more difficult. This may require the creation of full versions of the software. Even this is only possible if there are alternative dependencies that are suitable for Windows. This is a huge effort for application administrators and is often overlooked. Unfortunately for users, a lot of powerful software is difficult, if not impossible to use on your system.

Currently, Docker runs Linux natively and comes with a single virtual machine for OS X and Windows environments. This convergence in Linux means that software running in Docker containers only needs to be written once in a consistent dependency set. You may have thought to yourself, "Wait a minute. You just told me Docker is better than virtual machines." It is true, but these are complementary technologies. Using a virtual machine to contain a unique program is a waste of time. This is especially true of running multiple virtual machines on the same computer. In OS X and Windows, Docker uses one small virtual machine to run all the containers. By adopting this approach, the overhead of running a virtual machine is corrected, while the number of containers can be expanded.

This new portability helps users in many ways. First, open up a world of previously inaccessible software. Second, it is now possible to run the same software, exactly the same software, on any system. This means that the desktop, development environment, business server, and business cloud can run the same programs. Running in harmony with the environment is important. This minimizes any learning curve associated with the adoption of new technologies. This helps software developers better understand the systems that will run their programs. So fewer surprises. Third, when software developers can focus on writing their programs for a single platform and a set of dependencies, this saves them a lot of time and a lot of money for their customers.

Without Dockers or virtual machines, portability is usually achieved at the individual program level by making the software based on a common tool. For example, Java allows developers to write one program that will primarily work on multiple operating systems because they depend on a program called the Java Virtual Machine (JVM). While this is a convenient approach to writing software, other people, other companies have written most of the software we use every day. For example, if there is a popular web server we may want to use but it is not written in Java or any other similar portable language, I suspect that the authors have taken the time to re-write it. With this drawback, language interpreters and software libraries are exactly what creates addiction problems. Docker enhances the portability of each program, regardless of the language in which it was written, the operating system for which it was designed, or the state of the environment in which it is run.

Protect your computer

Most of what I have mentioned so far concerns software usage issues and the benefits of doing things outside the tank. But tanks also protect us from software running inside the container. The program may behave badly or pose a security risk in various ways:

- The program may have been written specifically by the attacker.
- Well-meaning developers could write a program that contains harmful errors.
- The program might inadvertently cause an attacker to handle errors while processing maps.

Running the software compromises the security of your computer. Since the use of software is the most important purpose of a computer, it is wise to apply practical risk mitigation measures. Like physical prison cells, any object contained in a container can access only those contents. There are exceptions to this policy, but only when explicitly created by the user. Containers limit the impact that a program can have on other running programs, data it can access, and system resources. Figure 1.5 shows the difference between running software outside and inside the container. This means for you or your business that the scope of any security threat associated with executing a specific request is limited to the scope of the application itself. Creating powerful application containers is a complex and essential part of any defense strategy in depth. Too often it is ignored or timidly pursued.

Why is Docker important?

Docker provides what is called abstraction. Abstractions let you handle complicated things in a simplified way. So in the case of Docker, instead of focusing on all the complexities and specifics associated with installing an application, we only need to consider the software we want to install. Like a crane that loads a container ship, installing any software with Docker is the same as installing any other software. The shape or size of things inside the shipment may be different, but the way the crane grips the tank will always be the same. All tools can be reused for any container. This goes for eliminating the request as well. When you want to remove the software, simply tell Docker what software to remove. There will be no permanent artifacts as they are all carefully contained and counted. The computer will be as clean as it was before the software was installed.

The abstraction of tanks and tools provided by Docker for working with containers will change the landscape of system administration and software development. Docker is important because it makes containers accessible to everyone. Its use saves time, money and energy.

Another reason why Docker is important is that the software community has a strong incentive to accept container and Docker. The attempt is so strong that companies like Amazon, Microsoft and Google have collaborated to contribute to its development and adopt it in their own cloud offerings. These companies, which mostly disagree, have partnered to support an open source project instead of developing and publishing their own solutions.

The third reason why Docker is important is because it did for the computer what the app stores did for mobile devices. Installing, sharing and removing software are very easy. Better yet, Docker does this openly and across multiple platforms. Imagine all the major smartphones sharing the same app store. That would be a big problem. With this technology implemented, it is possible that the lines between operating systems will finally begin to fade and that third-party vendor offerings play a less important role in operating system selection.

Fourth, we are finally starting to better adopt some of the most advanced features of operating system isolation. This may seem small, but many people try to further protect their computers by isolating them at the operating system level. Too bad his hard work took so long to be mass-adopted. Containers have been in one way or another for decades. It's great that Docker helps us make the most of these features.

Where and when to use Docker

Docker can be used on most computers at work and at home. In particular, how far does it go? Docker can work almost anywhere, but that doesn't mean you want to do it. For example, Docker can currently only run applications that can run on the Linux operating system. This means that if you want to execute native OS X or Windows, you still can't do it through Docker. For example, by restricting the conversation to software that typically runs on a Linux server or workstation, it is possible to create a solid scenario for running most applications in the container. This includes server applications such as web servers, mail servers, databases, proxy servers, etc. Desktop software like web browsers, word processors, email clients or other tools is also very useful. Even trusted programs are just as dangerous to run as programs you download from the Internet if they interact with user-provided data or online data.

Running in the tank and as a user with reduced privileges will help protect your system from attack. In addition to the added benefits of defense, using Docker for everyday tasks helps keep your computer clean. Keeping your computer clean will help prevent common resource issues and make it easier to install and remove software. This same ease of installation, removal and distribution simplifies IT management and can drastically change the way organizations think about maintenance. The most important thing to remember is when the containers are inappropriate.

The tanks will not help much for the safety of the programs that have to work with full access to the machine. At the time of writing, this is possible but complicated. Containers are not a complete solution to security issues, but they can also be used to prevent many types of attacks. Remember, you must not use software from unreliable sources. This is especially true if this software requires administrator privileges. This means that it is a bad idea to blindly manage the containers delivered by the customer in a jointly implanted environment.

Installation / Installation Programs

Installers are, of course, one of the first pieces you need to use Docker on your local computer as well as in server environments.

First, in what environments can you install Docker:

- Linux (various types of Linux)
- Apple macOS
- Windows 10 Professional

In addition, you can launch them in public clouds such as Amazon Web Services, Microsoft Azure and DigitalOcean. With the different types of installers listed, Docker operates in different ways in the operating system. Docker runs natively on Linux; therefore, if you are using Linux, the way Docker runs directly on your system is very simple. However, if you're using MacOS or Windows 10, it works a little differently because it is Linux based.

Linux Installation (Ubuntu 16.04)

As mentioned earlier, this is the simplest installation of the three systems we will test. To install Docker, simply run the following command from a Terminal session:

$ curl -sSL https://get.docker.com/ | sh

$ sudosystemctl docker

These commands will download, install, and configure the latest version of Docker from Docker. At the time of writing the version of the Linux operating system installed with the official software

The installation script is 5/17/05.

Running the following command should confirm that Docker is installed and running:

$ docker version

MacOS installation

Unlike the Linux command line installation, Docker for Mac has a graphical installer.

Before downloading, be sure to use ApplemacOS Yosemite 10.10.3 or later. If you use an older version, there is no lost; You can still run Docker.

You can download the Docker Store installer at http://store.docker.com/editions/community/docker-this-desktop-mac

Just click on Get Docker. After downloading, you will get a DMG file. Mount the image, and opening a desktop-mounted image should show you something like this:

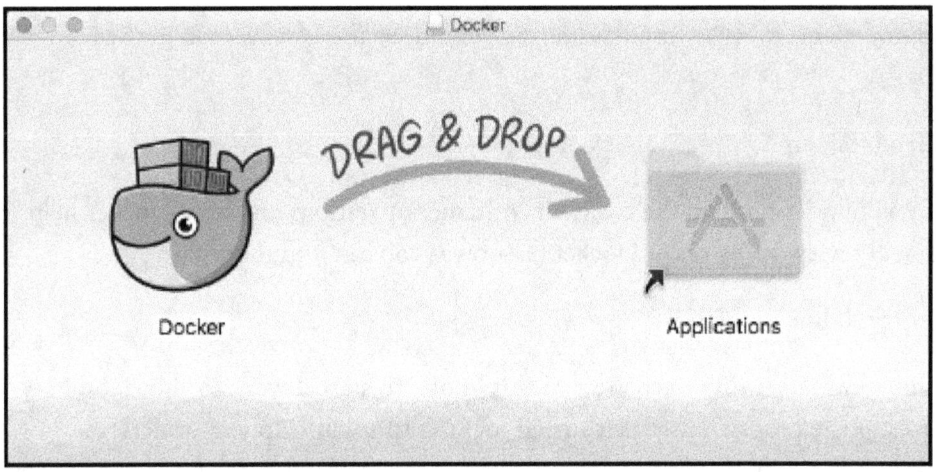

When you have hauled the Docker icon to your Applications folder, double tap on it and you will be asked whether you need to open the application you have downloaded. Saying yes will open the Docker installer:

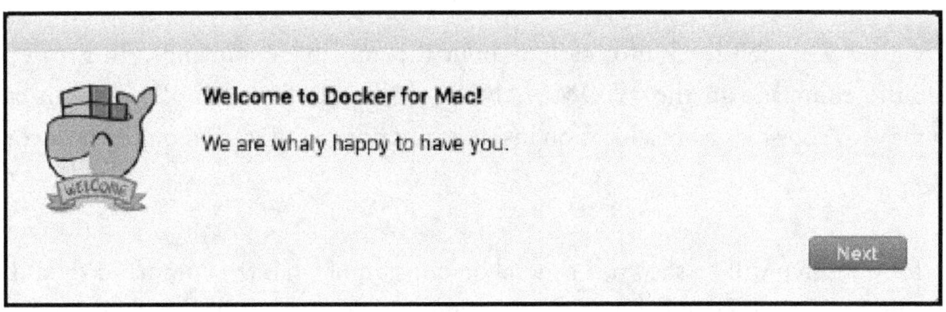

Click Next and follow the on-screen instructions. Once installed and running, you should see the Docker icon in the icon bar in the upper left corner of the screen.

Installation in Windows 10 Professional

Like Docker for Mac, Docker for Windows uses a graphical installer. Before downloading, be sure to use Microsoft Windows 10 Professional or 64-bit Enterprise. If you are running an older version or unsupported edition of Windows 10, you can still run Docker. See Other legacy operating systems in this chapter for more information.

Docker for Windows has this requirement due to Hyper-V dependency. Hyper-V is a native Windows hypervisor and allows you to run x86-64 guests on your Windows PC, either Windows 10 Professional or Windows Server. It's even part of the XBox One operating system.

You can download Docker for Windows from the Docker Store at https://store.docker.com/editions/community/docker-th- desktop-windows /; Simply click the Docker button to download the installer. After downloading, start the MSI package.

Click Install, and then follow the instructions, which will not only work during Docker installation but will enable Hyper-V if you did not enable it. After installation, you should see the Docker icon in the icon bar in the lower right corner of the screen.

Run the software in containers

In this chapter, you will understand all the basics of container operations and how Docker helps resolve clutter and conflict issues. You will review examples of Docker features as you can find them daily.

See the Docker command line for help

Use the Docker command line utility in the rest of this book. To start, I want to show you how to get information about the commands of the program itself with fixed menus. This will help you understand how to use the correct version of Docker on your computer. Open a terminal or command prompt and execute the following command:

the help of docker

Running Docker Help shows basic syntax information for using the Docker command line program, as well as a complete list of commands for your version of the program. Try it and take a moment to admire all the interesting things you can do.

Docker's help only gives you high-level information about the available commands. To get detailed info about a command, include the command in the <COMMAND> argument. For example, you can enter the following command to learn how to copy files from a location inside a container to a location on the host computer:

help docker cp

The usage pattern for dockercp will be shown, a general description of what the command should do, and a detailed overview of its arguments. I'm sure you will have a great time executing the order in the rest of this book, now that you know how to seek help if you need it.

Container control: Creating a monitor for a site

Most of the examples in this book will use real software. Practical examples will help you introduce Docker features and illustrate how you will use them in your daily activities. In this first example, you will install a web server called

NGINX. Web servers are programs that make the files and programs of the site available to web browsers through the network. Do not create a site, but you will install and run a web server using Docker. If you follow these instructions, the web server will only be available for other programs on your computer.

Suppose a new customer enters your office and makes a scandalous offer to create a new website. They want a strictly monitored website. This individual customer wants to perform their own operations. Therefore, you want the solution you provide to be emailed to your computer when the server is down. They have also heard about this popular web server software called NGINX and have specifically asked you to use it. After learning about the benefits of working with Docker, he decided to use it for this project.

Create and run a new container

When we install software with Docker, we say we install the image. There are several methods to install an image and several sources. In this example, we will download and install an image for NGINX from Docker Hub. Please note that the Docker Hub is a public recording provided by Docker Inc. The NGINX image comes from what Docker Inc. calls the approved repository.

Usually, the person or foundation that publishes the software controls the secure repositories for that software. Executing the following command will download, install, and run a container running NGINX:

Docker Run - Add \

—name web nginx: last

After you run this command, Docker will install nginx: last from the NGINX repository located on the Docker Hub and run the software. After Docker installed and started NGINX, a line of apparently random characters is written to the terminal. It will look like this:

7cb5d2b9a7eab87f07182b5bf58936c9947890995b1b94f412912fa822a9ecb5

This character line is a unique container identifier just created to run NGINX. Whenever you run Docker and create a new container, this container will receive a similar unique identifier. It is common for users to capture this output with a variable they use with other commands. You don't need to do this for this example. Once the ID is displayed, it may appear that nothing has happened. This is because he used the—detach option and started the program in the background. This means that the application has started but is not connected to your device. It makes sense to run NGINX this way because we will run some different programs.

Running separate containers is ideal for background programs. This type of program is called a daemon. A demon usually communicates with other programs or people through a network or other communication tool. When launching a daemon or other program in the container that you want to run in the background, be sure to use the—detach flag or its abbreviated form, -d.

Another demon your client needs is advertising. The sender is waiting for the caller's connection and sending the email. The following command will install and run an email application that will work for this example:

docker run -d \

—name mailer \

This command uses the truncated flag form—detach to run a new mailbox called mailer in the background. At this point, he made two orders and provided two-thirds of the systems his client wanted. The last component, called the agent, is perfect for the interactive container.

Executing interactive containers

Programs that can interact with users tend to feel more interactive. A good example is a text editor on a terminal. The Docker command line tool is a perfect example of an interactive terminal program. These types of programs can receive input from users or show output at a terminal. To run interactive programs in Docker, you need to connect parts of your device to the input or output of the bootable container. To get started using interactive containers, run the following command:

Docker Run - interactive - tty \

- internet connection: web \

- Web_test name \

busy: last / bin / sh

The command uses two flags in the execution command: - interactive (or -i) and -ttty (or -t). First, the—interactive option tells Docker to keep the standard input sequence (stdin) open for the container, even if the terminal is not connected. Second, the—tyty option tells Docker to assign a virtual terminal to the container, which will allow it to send a signal to the container. This is usually what you look for in an interactive command line program. You will usually use them when you run the interactive program as a shell in an interactive container.

As important as the interactive metrics are, when you started this container, you specified the program to run inside the container. In this case, he ran a shell program called sh. You can run any available program in the container. The interactive container sample command creates a container, starts a UNIX shell, and is associated with a container that runs NGINX. From this shell, you can execute the command to check that your web server is working properly:

wget -O- http: // web: 80 /

This uses a program called wget to send an HTTP request to a web server (a NGINX server that was previously run in the container) and then display the contents of the web page on your device. There may be a message like "Welcome to NGINX!" at this point.

Everything is working properly and you can continue and stop this interactive container by typing the output. This will interrupt the shell program and stop the tank. You can create an interactive container, manually start the process inside that container, and then disconnect the device. You can do that holding the Crtl (or Control) key and pressing P, then Q. This will only work if you used the—tty option. To complete a client job, you need to run an agent. What does this mean?

This is an agent that will test the web server as in the previous example and send a message to the sender if the web server stops. This command is triggered by an agent in an interactive container using abbreviated indicators:

docker run -it \

- agent's name \

- web link: insideweb \

- Email link: Insidemailer \

dockerinaction / ch2_agent

When done, the mailbox will test the web mailbox every second and print a message like this:

System in place.

Now that you know what you are doing, detach the terminal from the tank. Specifically, when you start the tank and start typing "System On," press and hold the Ctrl (or Control) key, then press P, then Q. Then you will return to the shell of your computer. the host. Don't stop the program; otherwise, the monitor will stop checking the web server. Although you usually use separate containers or daemons for software you deploy to network servers, interactive containers are very useful for running software on your desktop or for manual work on a server. At this point, you have launched all three applications in the mailboxes that your client needs. Before you can rightly pretend to complete, you need to test the system.

List, shut down, restart, and view the production of the container.

The first thing you need to test your current configuration is to check which containers are running with the dockerps command:

dockerps

Executing the command will show the following information about each container being executed:

- container identifier
- the image used
- command executed in container
- the time elapsed since the tank was created
- the duration of the tank
- Network ports exposed by tank.
- container name

At this point, you must have three mailboxes named: Web, Email, and Agent. If one is missing but you have followed the example so far, it may have stopped by mistake. This is not a problem as Docker has a command to restart the container. The following three commands restart each container using the container name. Select the appropriate ones to restart the missing containers in the mailbox list.

restart the web

docker resets mail

Restart Agent

Now that all the containers are running, you should check that the system is working properly. The best way to do so is to review the records of each container. Get started with the web container:

Docker blogs

This should show long records with several lines containing this subpage:

"GET / HTTP / 1.0" 200

The web server is up and running and the agent is testing the site. Each time an agent tests a site, one of these lines is entered in the registry. The dockerlogs command may be useful in these cases, but it is dangerous to believe in it. Anything written by the program in the output string stdout or stderr will be recorded in this register. The problem with this model is that the record is never rotated or truncated, so the data written in the container record remains and expands as long as the container contains indexes. This long-term persistence can be a problem for long-term processes.

You may know that the agent controls the web server by examining only the web logs. To complete, you must examine the registry and mail agent exit log:

Docker commercial

Docker Registration Agent

Mail-order newspapers should look like this:

The CH2 Mailer example is running.

Agent records must contain several lines, such as the one you looked at when you started the container:

System in place.

Now that you have verified that the mailboxes are running and that the agent is able to reach the web server, you should check that the web server notices that the web container has stopped. When this happens, the agent must activate the call to the sender and the event must be recorded in the agent and sender records. The stop docker command tells the program with PID # 1 in the container to stop. Use it in the following system test commands:

docker stop web

Docker commercial

Look for the line at the end of the mail record that says the following:

"Send an email to admin @ work Message: service shut down!"

This line indicates that the agent has successfully detected the NGINX server interrupt on the named web site. Congratulations. Your client will be happy and will build their first real container and Docker system.

Learning the basic features of Docker is one thing, but understanding the reasons to use them and build them for more complete systems is another. The best place to start learning is the namespace of the process identifier provided by Linux.

Fixed issues and PID namespace

Each program or process running on a Linux computer has a unique number called the Process Identifier (PID). A PID namespace is a set of possible numbers that identifies processes. Linux provides the ability to create multiple PID namespaces. Each namespace has a full set of available PIDs. That means that each PID namespace will contain its own PID, like 1, 2, 3, etc. From a process standpoint in one namespace, the PID 1 startup process can be called runit or supervisor. In another namespace, PID 1 may call the shell command bash. Creating a PID with namespaces for each container is a key feature of Docker. Do the following to see it in action:

docker run -d - namespaceA \ busybox: last / bin / sh -c "sleep 30000"

docker run -d - nameBB \

occupied: last / bin / sh -c "nc -l -p 0.0.0.0:80"

docker exec namespaceA ps docker exec namespaceB ps

The command above should generate a list of processes similar to this:

PID USER COMMAND

1 root / bucket / sh -c sleep 30000

5 roots of sleep 30000

6 roots ps

The command above should generate a slightly different list of processes:

PID USER COMMAND

1 root / bin / sh -c nc -l -p 0.0.0.0:80

7 root nc -l -p 0.0.0.0:80

8 ps root

In this example, use the dock exec command to perform additional processes in the current container. In this case, the command you are using is called ps. Displays all current processes and their PIDs. On departure, it is clear that each container has a PID 1 process.

Without the PID namespace, processes running in the container would share the same identifier as those in other containers or the host. The container can determine what other processes took place on the main machine. Even worse, namespaces turn many licensing decisions into domain decisions. This means that processes in one container can control the processes of other containers. A docker would be much less useful without the PID namespace. Linux features used by Docker, such as namespaces, help you solve all kinds of software issues.

Like most Docker features, you can optionally create containers without your own PID space. You can test it yourself by configuring the—pid flag to create a Docker or run the Docker and set the value as the host. Try it yourself with the container running BusyBox Linux and the ps Linux command:

Docker - Busy Host Host: Last ps

Take the previous example of network monitoring. Let's say you don't use Docker and simply run NGINX directly on your computer. Let's say you forgot that you already started NGINX for another project. When you restart NGINX, the second process will not be able to access the required resources because the first process already has them. This is an example of a basic software conflict. You can see it in action when trying to run two copies of NGINX in the same container:

docker run - d - name webConflict nginx: last

docker registers webConflict

docker executive webConflict nginx - g 'daemon off;'

The last command should display the output as follows:

03/29/2015. 04/22/35 [emerg] 10 # 0: connection () to 0.0.0.0:80 failed (98:

Address already used

nginx: [popup] bind () in 0.0.0.0:80 failed (98: address already used)

The subsequent methodology doesn't begin accurately and demonstrates that the necessary location is as of now being utilized. This is called port clash and is a typical issue in genuine frameworks where numerous procedures run on a similar PC or a few people add to a similar situation. This is an incredible case of a contention of issues that Docker rearranges and explains. Run every one out of an alternate compartment, for example, this one:

To make speculations regarding potential clashes between programs, think about the illustration of stopping. Paid stopping has some fundamental highlights: an installment framework, some saved parking spots, and numbered spaces.

By associating these capacities to a PC framework, the installment framework is a mutual asset with a particular interface. The installment framework can acknowledge money or Mastercards, or both. Individuals who convey just cash won't have the option to utilize the carport with an installment framework that acknowledges just Mastercards, and individuals without cash who pay charges won't have the option to stop in the carport.

Likewise, programs that rely upon a typical segment, for example, a specific form of a programming language library, can't run on PCs with another rendition of this library or without this library. Like two individuals utilizing if another installment technique needs to be stopped in a similar carport that acknowledges just a single strategy, a contention happens when you need to utilize two programs that require various forms of the library.

The held spaces in this similitude speak to uncommon assets. Envision a leaving chaperon apportioning a similar space for two autos. Albeit just a single driver needs to utilize the carport at once, no issue. Be that as it may, if both need to utilize the space simultaneously, the previous successes and the last can't stop. As you will see from the case of contention in Section 2.7, this is a similar kind of contention as when two projects endeavor to associate with a similar system port.

Ultimately, consider what might occur on the off chance that somebody changed their leaving numbers while the vehicles were left. At the point when proprietors return and attempt to find their vehicles, they will most likely be unable to do as such. While this is a strange model, it is an incredible representation to recognise what occurs in programs when basic natural factors change. Projects frequently use condition factors or library sections to discover different assets they need. These assets might be libraries or various projects. At the point when projects conflict, these factors may change conflictingly.

Here are some normal issues with strife:

- Two projects need to interface with a similar system port.
- Two projects utilize a similar impermanent document name, which keeps the record from being bolted.
- Two projects need to utilise various renditions of the all around introduced library.
- Two duplicates of a similar program need to utilise the same PID record.
- Another program you introduced changed nature variable utilised by the other program. Presently the primary program has been ended.

These contentions happen when at least one projects share a typical reliance; however, can't acknowledge sharing or have various needs. As in the past port clash model, Docker settles programming clashes with apparatuses, for example, Linux namespaces, the foundation of the document framework, and virtualised arrange segments. These devices are utilised to disengage every compartment.

Container state and dependencies

Eliminating metaconflicts: building a website farm

In the last area, you perceived how Docker causes you to maintain a strategic distance from programming clashes with process disengagement. Be that as it may, in case you're not cautious, you can wind up building frameworks that make metaconflicts, or clashes between compartments in the Docker layer.

Consider another model where a customer has requested that you manufacture a framework where you can have a variable number of sites for their clients. They'd likewise prefer to utilize a similar observing innovation that you manufactured before in this section. Basically growing the framework you constructed before would be the most straightforward approach to complete this activity without redoing the design for NGINX. In this model, you'll fabricate a sys-tem with a few holders running web servers and an observing operator (specialist) for each web server.

One's first intuition may be to just begin more web holders. That is not as sim-ple as it sounds. Recognizing compartments gets confused as the quantity of holders increments.

Adaptable holder distinguishing proof

The most ideal approach to discover why essentially making more duplicates of the NGINX holder you utilized in the last model is a poorly conceived notion is to attempt it for yourself:

dockerrun-d- - namewebidnginx

dockerrun-d- - namewebidnginx

The second order here will fall flat with a contention mistake:

FATA[0000] Error reaction from daemon: Conflict. The name "webid" is as of now being used by holder 2b5958ba6a00. You need to erase (or rename) that holder to have the option to reuse that name.

Utilizing fixed holder names like the web is helpful for experimentation and documenta-tion, however in a framework with different compartments, utilizing fixed names like that can make clashes. Of course, Docker appoints a one of a kind (human-accommodating) name to each con-tainer it makes. The - name banner essentially abrogates that procedure with a known worth. If a situation rises where the name of a holder needs to change, you can, by and large, rename the compartment with the docker rename course:

dockerrenamewebid webid-old

dockerrun - d- - name webid nginx

Renaming compartments can help ease one-off naming clashes yet does little to help keep away from the issue in any case. Notwithstanding the name, Docker doles out an interesting identifier that was referenced in the primary model. These are hex-encoded 1024-piece numbers and look something like this:

7cb5d2b9a7eab87f07182b5bf58936c9947890995b1b94f412912fa822a9ecb5

At the point when compartments are begun in isolates mode, their identifier will be printed to the terminal. You can utilize these identifiers instead of the compartment name with any com-mand that necessities to distinguish a particular holder. For instance, you could utilize the previ-ous ID with a stop or executive order:

docker executive \

7cb5d2b9a7eab87f07182b5bf58936c9947890995b1b94f412912fa822a9ecb5 \

ps

docker stop \

7cb5d2b9a7eab87f07182b5bf58936c9947890995b1b94f412912fa822a9ecb5

The high likelihood of uniqueness of the IDs that are produced implies that it is improbable that there will ever be an impact with this ID. To a lesser degree, it is additionally impossible that there would even be a crash of the initial 12 characters of this ID on a similar PC. So in most Docker interfaces, you'll see holder IDs truncated to their initial 12 characters. This makes produced IDs more easy to use. You can utilize them any place a compartment identifier is required. So the past two directions could be composed this way:

docker executive 7cb5d2b9a7ea ps

docker stop 7cb5d2b9a7ea

Neither of these IDs is especially appropriate for human use. In any case, they work very well with contents and computerisation systems. Docker has a few methods for getting the ID of a compartment to make computerisation conceivable. In these cases, the full or truncated numeric ID will be utilized.

The primary method to get the numeric ID of a compartment is to begin or make another one and relegate the aftereffect of the order to a shell variable. As you saw before, when another compartment is begun in disconnected mode, the holder ID will be kept in touch with the terminal (stdout). You'd be not able to utilize this with intelligent holders if this were the best way to get the compartment ID at creation time. Fortunately, you can utilize another direction to make a holder without beginning it. The docker makes direction is fundamentally the same as docker run; the essential distinction is that the holder is made in a halted state:

docker make nginx

The outcome ought to be a line like:

b26a631e536d3caae348e9fd36e7661254a11511eb2274fb55f9f7c788721b0d

In case you're utilizing a Linux order shell like sh or slam, you can essentially appoint that outcome to a shell variable and use it again later:

CID=$(docker make nginx: latest)

reverberation $CID

Shell factors make another open door for strife, yet the extent of that contention is constrained to the terminal session or current handling condition that the content was propelled in. Those contentions ought to be effectively avoidable in light of the fact that one utilize or program is dealing with that condition. The issue with this methodology is that it won't help if various clients or robotized forms need to share that data. In those cases you can utilize a holder ID (CID) document.

Both the docker run and docker make directions give another banner to compose the ID of another holder to a known document:

docker make - cidfile/tmp/web.cid nginx

Like the utilization of shell factors, this element builds the open door for struggle. The name of the CID record (gave after - cidfile) must be known or have some known structure. Much the same as manual holder naming, this methodology utilizes known names in a worldwide (Docker-wide) namespace. Fortunately Docker won't make another holder utilizing the gave CID record if that document as of now exists. The direction will bomb similarly as it does when you make two holders with a similar name.

One motivation to utilize CID documents rather than names is that CID records can be imparted to holders effectively and renamed for that compartment. This uses a Docker include called volumes, which is shrouded in part 4.

TIP One technique for managing CID document naming crashes is to parcel the namespace by utilizing known or unsurprising way shows. For instance, in this situation, you may utilize a way that contains all web compartments under a known index and further segment that registry by the client ID. This would bring about a way like/holders/web/customer1/web.cid or/contain-ers/web/customer8/web.cid.

In various cases, you can use various headings like docker ps to get the ID of a con-tainer. For example, if you have to get the truncated ID of the last made holder, you can use this:

CID=$(docker ps - most recent - calm)

reverberation $CID

CID=$(docker ps - l – q)

reverberation $CID

TIP If you need to get the full holder ID, you can utilize the - no-trunc choice on the docker ps direction.

Robotization cases are secured by the highlights you've seen up until this point. In any case, despite the fact that truncation helps, these holder IDs are once in a while simple to peruse or recollect. For this rea-child, Docker additionally produces comprehensible names for every holder.

The naming show utilizes an individual descriptor, an underscore, and the last name of a compelling researcher, architect, creator, or another such idea pioneer. Instances of produced names are compassionate_swartz, hungry_goodall, and distracted_turing. These appear to hit a sweet spot for meaningfulness and memory. At the point when you're working with the docker apparatus legitimately, you can generally utilize docker ps to look into the human-accommodating names.

Compartment recognizable proof can be precarious, yet you can deal with the issue by utilizing the ID and name-age highlights of Docker.

Container state and dependencies

With this new information, the new framework may looks something like this:

MAILER_CID=$(docker run-d dockerinaction/ch2_mailer)

WEB_CID=$(docker createnginx)

AGENT_CID=$(docker make - connect $WEB_CID:insideweb \ - interface $MAILER_CID:insidemailer \ dockerinaction/ch2_agent)

This piece could be utilized to seed another content that dispatches another NGINX and operator example for every one of your customer's clients. You can utilize docker ps to see that they've been made:

docker ps

The explanation neither the NGINX nor the operator was incorporated with the yield has to do with holder state. Docker holders will consistently be in one of four states and transi-tion by means of order

Neither of the new holders you began shows up in the rundown of compartments since docker ps shows just showing holders to default. Those compartments were specifi-cally made with docker make and never began (the left state). To see every one of the holders (counting those in the left state), utilize the - an alternative:

docker ps - a

Since you've checked that both of the holders were made, you have to begin them. For that, you can utilize the docker start direction:

docker start $AGENT_CID

docker start $WEB_CID

Running those directions will bring about a mistake. The holders should be begun the backward request of their reliance chain. Since you attempted to begin the specialist con-tainer before the web compartment, Docker revealed a message like this one:

Mistake reaction from daemon: Cannot begin holder 03e65e3c6ee34e714665a8dc4e33fb19257d11402b151380ed4c0a5e38779d0a: Cannot connection to a non running compartment:/clever_wright AS/modest_hopper/insideweb

FATA[0000] Error: neglected to begin at least one compartments

In this model, the operator holder has a reliance on the web compartment. You have to begin the web compartment first:

docker start $WEB_CID

docker start $AGENT_CID

This bodes well when you think about the mechanics at work. The connection system infuses IP addresses into subordinate compartments, and holders that aren't running don't have IP addresses. On the off chance that you attempted to begin a holder that has a reliance on a compartment that isn't running, Docker wouldn't have an IP address to infuse. Compartment connecting is shrouded in part 5, yet it's valuable to show this significant point in beginning holders.

Regardless of whether you're utilizing docker run or docker make, the subsequent holders should be begun in the turn around the request of their reliance chain. This implies circular conditions are difficult to assemble utilizing Docker compartment connections.

Now you can assemble everything into one succinct content that resembles the accompanying:

MAILER_CID=$(docker run - d dockerinaction/ch2_mailer)

WEB_CID=$(docker run - d nginx)

AGENT_CID=$(docker run - d \

- connect $WEB_CID:insideweb \

- connect $MAILER_CID:insidemailer \

dockerinaction/ch2_agent)

Presently you're sure that this content can be run no matter what each time your cli-ent necessities to arrangement another site. Your customer has returned and expressed gratitude toward you for the web and checking work you've finished up until this point, however things have changed.

They've chosen to concentrate on building their sites with WordPress (a prevalent open source content-administration and blogging program). Fortunately, WordPress is bar lished through Docker Hub in a store named wordpress:4. All you'll have to

convey is a lot of directions to arrangement another WordPress site that has a similar checking and cautioning highlights that you've just conveyed.

The intriguing thing about substance the executive's frameworks and other stateful systems is that the information they work with makes each running system particular. Adam's WordPress blog is unique in relation to Betty's WordPress blog, regardless of whether they're running similar programming. Just the substance is extraordinary. Regardless of whether the substance is the equivalent, they're diverse because they're running on various destinations.

On the off chance that you construct frameworks or programming that know a lot about their condition—like locations or fixed areas of reliance benefits—it's hard to change that condition or reuse the product. You have to convey a framework that limits environment reliance before the agreement is finished.

A significant part of the work related to introducing programming or keeping up an armada of PCs lies in managing specializations of the registering condition. These specializations come as worldwide perused conditions (like realized host document framework areas), hard-coded sending structures (condition checks in code or configura-tion), or information region (information put away on a specific PC outside the organization design). Knowing this, if you probably manufacture low-support frameworks, you ought to endeavor to limit these things.

Docker has three definite highlights to help construct condition rationalist frameworks:

▪Read-just document frameworks

▪Environment variable infusion

▪Volumes

Working with volumes is a major subject and the theme of part 4. So as to gain proficiency with the initial two highlights, consider necessities change for the model circumstance utilized in the remainder of this section.

WordPress utilizes a database program called MySQL to store a large portion of its information, so it's a smart thought, to begin with ensuring that a compartment running WordPress has a perused just record framework.

Peruse just document frameworks

Utilizing read-just record frameworks achieves two positive things. In the first place, you can have con-fidence that the holder won't be specific from changes to the documents it contains. Second, you have expanded certainty that an assailant can't bargain records in the holder.

To begin chipping away at your customer's framework, make and start a compartment from the WordPress picture utilizing the - read-just banner:

docker run - d - name wp - read-just wordpress:4

At the point when this is done, watch that the compartment is running. You can do so utilizing any of the strategies presented already, or you can examine the holder metadata

straightforwardly. The accompanying direction will print genuine if the holder named wp is running and bogus generally.

docker review - group "{{.State.Running}}" wp

The docker review order will show all the metadata (a JSON record) that Docker keeps up for a holder. The organization choice changes that metadata, and for this situation, it channels everything with the exception of the field demonstrating the running condition of the holder. This order should yield bogus.

For this situation, the compartment isn't running. To decide why inspect the logs for the holder:

docker logs wp

That should yield something like:

error: missing WORDPRESS_DB_HOST and MYSQL_PORT_3306_TCP condition factors

Did you neglect to - interface some_mysql_container:mysql or set an outer db with - e WORDPRESS_DB_HOST=hostname: port?

WordPress has a reliance on a MySQL database. A database is a star gram that stores information so that it's retrievable and accessible later. Fortunately, you can introduce MySQL utilising Docker simply like WordPress:

docker run - d - name wpdb \

- e MYSQL_ROOT_PASSWORD=ch2demo \

mysql:5

When that is begun, make an alternate WordPress holder that is connected to this new database compartment:

dockerrun-d - name wp2 \

- linkwpdb:mysql \

- p80 - read-just \

wordpress:4

Check once again that WordPress is running effectively:

docker assess - group "{{.State.Running}}" wp2

You can advise that WordPress neglected to begin once more. Inspect the logs to decide the reason:

docker logs wp2

There ought to be a line in the logs that is like the accompanying:

... Peruse just record framework: AH00023: Couldn't make the revamp map mutex (document/var/lock/apache2/revise map.1)

You can advise that WordPress neglected to begin once more, yet this time the issue is that it's attempting to compose a lock record to a particular area. This is a necessary piece of the startup

Make explicit volumes for writeable space

Process and isn't a specialization. It's proper to make a special case to the read-just document framework for this situation. You have to utilize a volume to make that exemption. Utilize the accompanying to begin WordPress with no issues:

#Start the compartment with explicit volumes for read just exemptions docker run - d - name wp3 - connect wpdb:mysql - p 80 \

- v/run/lock/apache2/\ - v/run/apache2/\ - read-just wordpress:4

A refreshed form of the content you've been dealing with should resemble this:

SQL_CID=$(docker make - e MYSQL_ROOT_PASSWORD=ch2demo mysql:5)

docker start $SQL_CID

MAILER_CID=$(docker make dockerinaction/ch2_mailer)

docker start $MAILER_CID

WP_CID=$(docker make - interface $SQL_CID:mysql - p 80 \ - v/run/lock/apache2/ - v/run/apache2/\ - read-just wordpress:4)

docker start $WP_CID

AGENT_CID=$(docker make - connect $WP_CID:insideweb \ - interface $MAILER_CID:insidemailer \ dockerinaction/ch2_agent)

docker start $AGENT_CID

Congrats, now you ought to have a running WordPress holder! By utilising a read-just document framework and connecting WordPress to another compartment running a database, you can be certain that the holder running the WordPress picture will never show signs of change. This implies if there is consistently some problem with the PC running a customer's WordPress blog, you ought to have the option to fire up another duplicate of that holder somewhere else without any issues.

Be that as it may, there are two issues with this structure. To start with, the database is running in a con-tainer on a similar PC as the WordPress holder. Second, WordPress is utilising a few defaults esteems for significant settings like database name, authoritative client, secret managerial phrase, database salt, etc. To manage this issue, you could make a few adaptations of the WordPress programming, each with an extraordinary setup for the customer. Doing so would transform your straightforward provisioning content into a beast that makes pictures and composes documents. A superior method to infuse that arrangement would be using condition factors.

Condition variable infusion

Condition factors are key-esteem matches that are made accessible to programs through their execution setting. They let you change a program's arrangement without altering any records or changing the direction used to begin the program.

Docker utilizes condition factors to convey data about ward holders, the host name of the compartment, and other helpful data for expert grams running in chambers. Docker likewise gives a component to a client to infuse condition factors into another holder. Projects that know to expect significant data through condition factors can be designed at compartment creation time. Fortunately for you and your customer, WordPress is one such program.

Before jumping into WordPress points of interest, take a stab at infusing and survey condition vari-ables all alone. The UNIX direction env shows all the earth factors in the present execution setting (your terminal). To see condition variable infusion in real life, utilize the accompanying order:

docker run - env MY_ENVIRONMENT_VAR="this is a test" \

busybox:latest \

env

The - env banner—or - e for short—can be utilized to infuse any condition variable. On the off chance that the variable is as of now set by the picture or Docker, at that point the worth will be abrogated. Along these lines, programs running inside holders can depend on the factors continually being set. WordPress watches the accompanying condition factors:

- WORDPRESS_DB_HOST
- WORDPRESS_DB_USER
- WORDPRESS_DB_PASSWORD
- WORDPRESS_DB_NAME
- WORDPRESS_AUTH_KEY
- WORDPRESS_SECURE_AUTH_KEY
- WORDPRESS_LOGGED_IN_KEY
- WORDPRESS_NONCE_KEY
- WORDPRESS_AUTH_SALT
- WORDPRESS_SECURE_AUTH_SALT
- WORDPRESS_LOGGED_IN_SALT
- WORDPRESS_NONCE_SALT

TIP This model dismisses the KEY and SALT factors, yet any genuine creation framework should completely set these qualities.

To begin, you should address the issue that the database is running in a compartment on a similar PC as the WordPress holder. As opposed to utilizing connecting to fulfill WordPress' database reliance, infuse an incentive for the WORDPRESS_DB_HOST variable:

docker make - env WORDPRESS_DB_HOST=<my database hostname> wordpress:4

This model would make (not begin) a compartment for WordPress that will attempt to interface with a MySQL database at whatever you determine at <my database hostname>.

Since the remote database isn't likely utilizing any default client name or secret word, you'll need to infuse esteems for those settings too. Assume the database head is a feline sweetheart and detests solid passwords:

docker make \

- env WORDPRESS_DB_HOST=<my database hostname> \ - env WORDPRESS_DB_USER=site_admin \

- env WORDPRESS_DB_PASSWORD=MeowMix42 \

wordpress:4

Utilizing condition variable infusion along these lines will assist you with isolating the physical ties between a WordPress holder and a MySQL compartment. Indeed, even for the situation where you need to have the database and your client WordPress locales all on a similar machine, regardless you'll have to fix the subsequent issue referenced before. Every one of the destinations are utilizing a similar default database name. You'll have to utilize condition variable infusion to set the database name for every free site:

dockercreate - connect wpdb:mysql \

- eWORDPRESS_DB_NAME=client_a_wp wordpress:4For customer A

dockercreate - interface wpdb:mysql \For customer B

- eWORDPRESS_DB_NAME=client_b_wp wordpress:4

Since you've tackled these issues, you can change the provisioning content. To begin with, set the PC to run just a solitary MySQL compartment:

DB_CID=$(docker run - d - e MYSQL_ROOT_PASSWORD=ch2demo mysql:5)

MAILER_CID=$(docker run - d dockerinaction/ch2_mailer)

At that point the site provisioning content would be this:

on the off chance that [! - n "$CLIENT_ID"]; at that point reverberation "Customer ID not set" leave 1

fi

WP_CID=$(docker make \

```
- interface $DB_CID:mysql \
- name wp_$CLIENT_ID \
- p 80 \
- v/run/lock/apache2/ - v/run/apache2/\
- e WORDPRESS_DB_NAME=$CLIENT_ID \
- read-just wordpress:4)
docker start $WP_CID
AGENT_CID=$(docker make \
- name agent_$CLIENT_ID \
- connect $WP_CID:insideweb \
- connect $MAILER_CID:insidemailer \
dockerinaction/ch2_agent)
docker start $AGENT_CID
```

This new content will begin a case of WordPress and the checking operator for every client and associate those holders to one another just as a single mailer star gram and MySQL database. The WordPress compartments can be wrecked, restarted, and updated with no stress over loss of information.

The customer ought to be satisfied with what is being conveyed. However, one thing may be annoying you. In prior testing, you found that the checking operator accurately advised the mailer when the site was inaccessible, however restarting the site and specialist required manual work. It would be better if the framework attempted to recuperate when a disappointment was identified consequently. Docker furnishes restart strategies to help manage that, yet you may need something increasingly vigorous.

Building strong holders

There are situations where programming bombs in uncommon conditions that are brief in nature. Despite the fact that it's imperative to be made mindful when these conditions emerge, it's for the most part in any event as critical to reestablishing the administration as fast as could be expected under the circumstances. The checking framework that you worked in this section is a fine start for keeping framework proprietors mindful of prob-lems with a framework, however it does nothing to help reestablish administration.

At the point when every one of the procedures in a compartment has left, that holder will enter the left state. Keep in mind, a Docker holder can be in one of four states:

▪Running

▪Paused

▪Restarting

▪Exited (likewise utilized if the compartment has never been begun)

A fundamental procedure for recouping from brief disappointments is naturally restarting a procedure when it exits or fizzles. Docker gives a couple of alternatives to checking and restarting holders.

Automatically restarting containers

Docker furnishes this usefulness with a restart approach. Utilizing the - restart banner at holder creation time, you can advise Docker to do any of the accompanyings:

▪never restart (default)

▪Attempt to restart when a disappointment is identified

▪Attempt for some foreordained time to restart when a disappointment is identified

▪Always restart the compartment paying little heed to the condition

A docker doesn't generally endeavor to promptly restart a holder. On the off chance that it did, that would mess more up than it understood. Envision a compartment that sits idle however print the time and exit. On the off chance that that compartment was arranged to consistently restart and Docker in every case quickly restarted it, the framework would sit idle yet restart that holder. Rather, Docker utilizes an exponential backoff methodology for timing restart endeavors.

A backoff procedure decides how much time should go between progressive restart endeavors. An exponential backoff methodology will accomplish something like twofold the past time spent looking out for each progressive endeavor. For instance, if the first run through the compartment should be restarted Docker holds up 1 second, at that point on the second endeavor it would hold up 2 seconds, 4 seconds on the third endeavor, 8 on the fourth, etc. Exponential backoff systems with low introductory hold up times are a typical assistance reclamation method. You can see Docker utilize this methodology yourself by building a holder that consistently restarts and prints the time:

docker run - d - name backoff-indicator - restart consistently busybox date

At that point following a couple of moments, utilise the trailing logs highlight to watch it back off and restart:

docker logs - f backoff-indicator

The records will show every one of the occasions it has just been restarted and will hold up until whenever it is restarted, print the present time, and afterward exit. Adding this single banner to the observing framework and the WordPress holders you've been taking a shot at would explain the recuperation issue.

The main explanation you might not have any desire to embrace this straightforwardly is during backoff periods, and the compartment isn't running. Compartments holding back to be restarted are in the restarting state. To illustrate, attempt to run another procedure in the backoff-locator holder:

docker executive backoff-indicator reverberation Just a Test

Running that order should bring about a mistake message:

Can't run executive direction in the compartment: No dynamic holder exists with ID ...

That implies you can't do whatever requires the compartment to be running, as execute extra directions in the holder. That could be an issue on the off chance that you have to run symptomatic projects in a messed up holder. A progressively complete methodology is to utilize holders that init or boss forms.

A supervisor procedure, or init process, is a program that is utilized to dispatch and keep up the condition of different programs. On a Linux framework, PID #1 is an init procedure. It begins the various framework forms and restarts them if they bomb startlingly. It's a typical practice to utilize a comparable example inside containers to begin and oversee forms.

Utilizing a supervisor procedure inside your container will keep the container running if the objective procedure—a web server, for instance—fizzles and is restarted. There are a few projects that may be utilized inside a container. The most prevalent incorporate init, systemd, runit, upstart, and supervisord. For the time being, investigate a container that utilizations supervisord.

An organization named Tutum gives programming that delivers a full LAMP (Linux, Apache, MySQL PHP) stack inside a solitary container. Containers made along these lines use supervisord to ensure that all the related procedures are continued running. Start a model container:

docker run - d - p 80:80 - name light test tutum/light

You can perceive what procedures are running inside this container by utilizing the docker top direction:

docker top light test

The top subcommand will show the host PID for every one of the procedures in the con-tainer. You'll see supervisord, mysql, and apache remembered for the rundown of running genius grams. Since the container is running, you can test the supervisord restart usefulness by physically halting one of the procedures inside the container.

The issue is that to slaughter a procedure within a container from inside that con-tainer, you have to know the PID in the container's PID namespace. To get that rundown, run the accompanying executive subcommand:

docker executive light test ps

The procedure list produced will have recorded apache2 in the CMD segment:

PID TTYTIME CMD

1 ?00:00:00 supervisord

433 ?00:00:00 mysqld_safe

835 ?00:00:00 apache2

842 ?00:00:00 ps

The qualities in the PID segment will be diverse when you run the order. Discover the

PID on the column for apache2 and afterward embed that for <PID> in the accompanying order:

docker executive light test murder <PID>

Running this direction will run the Linux slaughter program inside the light test container and advise the apache2 procedure to close down. When apache2 stops, the supervisord procedure will log the occasion and restart the procedure. The container logs will plainly show these occasions:

...

... left: apache2 (leave status 0; anticipated)

... brought forth: 'apache2' with pid 820

... achievement: apache2 entered RUNNING state, the process has kept awake for > than 1 second (startsecs)

A common alternative to using init or supervisor programs is to use a startup script that checks at least the prerequisites for running content software. Sometimes used as a default container command. For example, the WordPress repositories you created start executing the script to check and set the default environment variables before running the WordPress process. You can view this script by canceling the default command and using the command to view the contents of the run script:

docker runs wordpress: 4 cats /entrypoint.sh

Executing this command will generate error messages such as:

error: missing WORDPRESS_DB_HOST and MYSQL_PORT_3306_TCP environment

variables

...

This failed because, although you configured the command to run as cat /entrypoint.Sh, Docker containers execute what is known as an entry point before executing the command. Entry points are the perfect place to place code that confirms the prerequisites of the container. Although this is discussed in detail in Part 2 of this book, you need to know how to specifically replace or define a tank entry point on the command line. Try to execute the last command again, but this time uses the—entrypoint flag to specify the executable and use the command section to pass the arguments:

docker run—entrypoint = "cat" \

wordpress: 4 /entrypoint.sh

If you research the script shown, you will see how you validate environment variables according to software dependencies and set defaults. After the script confirms the execution of WordPress, run the requested or default command.

Boot scripts play an essential role in building durable containers and can always be combined with Docker restart strategies to reap the benefits of others. Because MySQL and WordPress repositories already use scripts to run, it is convenient to set a restart policy for each in an updated version of the sample script.

With this latest change, he created a complete WordPress web site provisioning system and learned the basics of container management using Docker.

A significant experiment. Your computer is probably full of containers that you no longer need. To restore the resources used by these containers, you must stop and remove them from your system.

Cleaning up

Ease of cleaning is one of the main reasons for using the cartridge and Docker. The isolation provided by the containers simplifies the steps to stop the process and delete the files. With Docker, the entire cleaning process comes down to one of several simple commands. In any cleaning task, you must first identify the container that you want to stop and dispose of. Remember to use the docker ps command to list all the containers on your computer:

docker ps - a

Since the containers you made for the models in this part won't be utilized once more, you ought to have the option to stop and expel all the recorded containers securely. Ensure you focus on the containers you're tidying up if there are any that you made for your very own exercises.

All containers use hard drive space to store logs, container metadata, and records that have been kept in touch with the container document framework. All containers likewise devour assets in the worldwide namespace like container names and host port mappings. By and large, containers that will never again be utilized ought to be evacuated.

To expel a container from your PC, utilize the docker rm command. For instance, to erase the halted container named wp you'd run:

docker rm wp

You ought to experience every one of the containers in the rundown you created by running docker ps - an and evacuate all containers that are in the left state. If you attempt to expel a container that is running, stopped, or restarting, Docker will show a message like the fol-lowing:

Error reaction from daemon: Conflict, You can't evacuate a running container. Stop the container before endeavoring evacuation or use - f

FATA[0000] Error: neglected to evacuate at least one containers

The procedures running in a container ought to be halted before the records in the container are evacuated. You can do this with the docker stop command or by utilizing the - f banner on docker rm. The key contrast is that when you stop a procedure utilizing the - f banner, Docker sends a SIG_KILL signal, which promptly ends the accepting procedure. Conversely, utilizing docker stop will send a SIG_HUP signal. Beneficiaries of SIG_HUP have the opportunity to perform conclusion and cleanup undertakings. The SIG_KILL signal offers for no such lenient gestures and can bring about record defilement or unfortunate system encounters. You can give a SIG_KILL straightforwardly to a container utilizing the docker murder command. Be that as it may, you should utilize docker kill or docker rm - f just if you should stop the container in under the standard 30-second most extreme stop time.

Later on, in case you're trying different things with fleeting containers, you can keep away from the cleanup trouble by determining - rm on the command. Doing so will naturally expel the container when it enters the left state. For instance, the accompanying command will compose a message to the screen in another BusyBox container, and the container will be evacuated when it exits:

docker run - rm - name auto-leave test busybox: latest reverberation Hello World docker ps - a

For this situation, you could utilize either docker stop or docker rm to appropriately tidy up, or it is suitable to utilize the single-step docker rm - f command. You ought to likewise utilize the - v banner for reasons that will be shrouded in part 4. The docker CLI makes it is anything but difficult to create a speedy cleanup command:

docker rm - vf $(docker ps - a - q)

Summary

The essential focal point of the Docker venture is to empower clients to run programming in contain-ers. This section shows how you can utilize Docker for that reason. The thoughts and highlights secured incorporate the accompanying:

▪Containers can be run with virtual terminals appended to the client's shell or in segregated mode.

▪By default, each Docker container has its very own PID namespace, segregating process data for every container.

▪Docker recognizes each container by its created container ID, abridged container ID, or its human-accommodating name.

▪All containers are in any of four unmistakable states: running, delayed, restarting, or left.

▪The docker executive command can be utilized to run extra procedures inside a running container.

▪A client can pass enter or give extra design to a procedure in a container by indicating condition factors at a container-creation time.

▪Using the - read-just banner at container-creation time will mount the container record framework as read-just and forestall specialization of the container.

▪A container restart strategy, set with the - restart banner at container-creation time, will help your frameworks naturally recuperate in case of a disappointment.

▪Docker makes tidying up containers with the docker rm command as basic as making them.

Software installation simplified

We have presented every new idea and reflections gave by Docker. This part jumps further into container document frameworks and programming establishment. It separates programming establishment into three stages,

The initial phase in introducing any product is distinguishing the product you need to introduce. You realize that the product is dispersed utilizing pictures. However, you have to realize how to tell Docker precisely which picture you need to introduce. I've just referenced that archives hold pictures, yet in this part, I show how stores and labels are utilised to identify pictures to introduce the product you need.

This section broadly expounds on the three fundamental approaches to introduce Docker pictures:

- Docker Hub and different libraries
- Using picture documents with docker spare and docker load
- Building pictures with Dockerfiles

Throughout perusing this material, you'll figure out how Docker separates introduced the delicate product, and you'll be presented to another term, layer. Layers are a significant idea when managing pictures and importantly affect programming clients

Identifying software

Assume you need to introduce a program called TotallyAwesomeBlog 2.0. How might you disclose to Docker what you needed to introduce? You would require an approach to name the program, determine the adaptation that you need to utilize, and indicate the source that you need to introduce it from. Figuring out how to recognize explicit programming is the initial phase in programming establishment, You've discovered that Docker makes containers from pictures. A picture is a document. It holds records that will be accessible to containers made from it and metadata about the picture. This metadata contains data about connections between pictures, the com-mand history for a picture, uncovered ports, volume definitions, and that's just the beginning.

Pictures have identifiers, so they could be utilized as a name and form for the delicate product, however by and by it's uncommon to work with crude picture identifiers. They are long, exceptional groupings of letters and numbers. Every time a change is made to a picture, the picture identifier changes. Picture identifiers are hard to work with on the grounds that they're eccentric. Rather, clients work with storehouses.

What is a repository?

A repository is a named basin of pictures. The name is like a URL. A repository's name is comprised of the name of the host where the picture is found, the client account that possesses the picture, and a short name. For instance, later in this part, you will introduce a picture from the repository named quay.io/dockerinaction/ch3_hello_registry.

Similarly, as there can be a few adaptations of programming, a repository can hold a few pictures. Every one of the pictures in a repository is distinguished extraordinarily with tags. If I somehow happened to discharge another variant of quay.io/dockerinaction/ch3_hello_registry, I may label it "v2" while labeling the old adaptation with "v1." If you needed to download the old rendition, you could explicitly recognize that picture by its v1 tag.

You introduced a picture from the NGINX repository on Docker Hub that was related to the "most recent" tag. A repository name and label structure a composite key, or a special reference made up of a blend of non-novel segments. In that model, the picture was recognized by nginx: latest. Despite the fact that identifiers worked in this style may infrequently be longer than crude picture identifiers, they're unsurprising and convey the aim of the picture.

Utilizing tags

Tags are both a significant method to remarkably distinguish a picture and an advantageous method to make valuable monikers. While a tag must be applied to a solitary picture in a reposi-tory, a solitary picture can have a few tags. This enables repository proprietors to make use-ful forming or include tags.

For instance, the Java repository on Docker Hub keeps up the accompanying tags: 7, 7-jdk, 7u71, 7u71-jdk, openjdk-7, and openjdk-7u71. Every one of these tags is applied to a similar picture. In any case, as the present minor form of Java 7 increments, and they discharge 7u72, the 7u71 label will probably leave and be supplanted with 7u72. In the event that you care about what minor adaptation of Java 7 you're running, you need to stay aware of those label changes. In the event that you simply need to ensure you're continually running the latest variant of Java 7, simply utilize the picture labeled with 7. It will consistently be allocated to the most up to date minor update of Java 7. These tags give clients incredible adaptability.

It's additionally normal to see various tags for pictures with various programming configura-tions. For instance, I've discharged two pictures for an open source program called free-geoip. It's a web application that can be utilized to get the harsh land area related to a system address. One picture is designed to utilize the default configu-proportion for the product. It's intended to run without anyone else with an immediate connect to the world. The second is designed to run behind a web load balancer. Each picture has a particular label that enables the client to effectively recognize the picture with the highlights required.

TIP When you're searching for programming to introduce, consistently give cautious consideration to the tags offered in a repository. In case you don't know which one you need, you can download all the labeled pictures in a repository by just discarding the label qualifier when you pull from the repository. I incidentally do this unintentionally, and it very well may be irritating. Be that as it may, it's not difficult to tidy up.

This is everything to distinguishing programming for use with Docker. With this information, you're prepared to begin searching for and introducing programming with Docker.

Finding and installing software

You can identify the software by the name of the repository, but how do you find the repositories you want to install? Finding reliable software is complex, and the second step is learning how to install software with Docker.

To find repositories, keep guessing until you are lucky or use the index. Indexes are engines that catalog repositories. There are a lot of public Docker indexes, but by default, Docker is integrated into an index called the Docker Hub.

The Docker Hub is a registry and index of sites maintained by Docker Inc. This is the default registry and index that Docker uses. When you run a docker command or docker command without specifying a replacement record, Docker searches for storage in the Docker Hub by default. The Docker Hub makes Docker instantly more useful.

Docker Inc. worked to make Docker an open ecosystem. Post a public image to run your record, and the Docker command line tool can be easily configured to use other records. Other tools for installing and distributing images that came with Docker will be presented later in this chapter. But first, the following section explains how to utilize the default set of tools with Docker Hub fully.

Docker Hub from the command line

You can do nearly anything you can with Docker from the command line. This incorporates scanning for archives at the Docker Hub.

The Docker command will search the Docker Hub index and display results, including details such as the number of times each repository was submitted, an indicator indicating that a particular repository is official (the OFFICIAL column), and indicating whether the repository is what they call a trusted image (the TRUST column). The Docker Hub site allows registered users to create repositories similar to other community development sites such as GitHub. The number of stars in the repository can serve as a proxy metric to represent the quality and popularity of the image or the user's trust.

The Docker Hub also offers a suite of official repositories managed by Docker Inc. or current software maintainers. They are often called libraries.

An image author can publish his / her images in two ways at Docker Hub:

▪ Use the command prompt to import images that you have created independently and on your system. Some find the images pushed this way less reliable because it is unclear how they were built.

▪ Make the Docker file public and use the Docker Hub Continuous Compilation System. Dockerfiles are scripts for building images. Images created from these automatically linked versions are preferred because the Docker file is available for preview before installing the image. Images posted this way will be marked as trusted.

Working with private Docker Hub records or inserting them into records you manage in the Docker Hub requires authentication. In such a case, you can use the Docker login command to connect to the Docker Hub. Once logged in, you can extract private repositories, move to repositories that you control, and tag images in your repositories.

Running docker login will provoke you for your Docker Hub certifications. When you've given them, your command-line customer will be verified, and you'll have the option to get to your private archives. At the point when you've got done with working with your record, you can log out with the docker logout command.

If you need to discover programming to introduce, you'll have to realize where to start your inquiry. The following model exhibits how to look for stores utilizing the docker search command. This command may take a couple of moments. However, it has a break inherent, so it will in the end return. At the point when you run this command, it will just look through the file; nothing will be introduced.

Assume Bob, a product designer, chose that the task he was chipping away at required a database. He had found out about a well known program named Postgres. He thought about whether it was accessible on Docker Hub, so he ran the accompanying command:

docker search postgres

Following a few moments, a few results were returned. At the highest priority on the rundown, he distinguished a common repository with many stars. He additionally preferred that it was an official repository, which implied that the Docker Hub maintainers had painstakingly chosen the proprietors of the repository. He utilized docker dismantle to introduce the picture and proceeded onward with his undertaking.

This is a straightforward case of how to look for archives utilizing the docker command line. The command will scan Docker Hub for any archives with the term postgres. Since Docker Hub is a free open assistance, clients will, in general, develop heaps of open, however close to home duplicates. Docker Hub gives clients a chance to star a repository, like a Facebook Like. This is a sensible intermediary marker for picture quality, however you ought to be mindful so as not to utilize it as a pointer of dependable code.

Suppose somebody develops a repository with a few hundred stars by giving some excellent open source programming. One day a vindictive programmer oversees their repository and distributes a picture to the repository that contains an infection. In spite of the fact that containers may be viable for containing malevolent code, that thought doesn't remain constant for pernicious pictures. On the off chance that an aggressor controls how a picture is fabricated or has focused on an assault explicitly to break out of a debilitated picture, a picture can cause genuine mischief. Consequently, pictures that are constructed utilizing openly accessible contents are viewed as substantially more reliable. In the indexed lists from running docker search, you can tell that a picture was worked from an open content by searching for an [OK] in the section mark AUTOMATED.

Presently you've perceived how to discover programming on Docker Hub without leaving your terminal. Even though you can accomplish most things from the terminal, there are a few things that you can do just through the site.

Docker Hub from the site

If you presently can't seem to unearth it while perusing docker.com, you should pause for a minute to look at *https://hub.docker.com*. Docker Hub gives you a chance to look for vaults, associations, or explicit clients. Client and association profile pages list the storehouses that the record keeps up, ongoing action on the record, and the archives that the record has featured. On repository pages you can see the accompanying:

- General data about the picture gave by the picture distributer

- A rundown of the tags accessible in the repository
- The date the repository was made
- How many times it has been downloaded
- Any comment from enrolled clients

To utilize the projects in these pictures, you'll have to join your terminal to the containers with the goal that the information and yield of your terminal are associated straightforwardly to the running container. The accompanying command exhibits how to do that and run a container that will be evacuated consequently when halted:

docker run - it - rm dockerinaction/ch3_ex2_hunt

At the point when you run this command, the forager chase program will incite you for the password. On the off chance that you know the appropriate response as of now, feel free to enter it now. If not, enter anything, and it will give you an indication. Now, you ought to have every one of the apparatuses you have to complete the action.

At the point when you find the solution, pat yourself on the back and evacuate the pictures utilising the docker rmi command. Solidly, the codes you run will look something like these:

docker rmi dockerinaction/ch3_ex2_hunt

docker rmi <mystery repository>

On the off chance that you were following the models and utilizing the - rm choice on your docker run commands, you ought to have no containers to tidy up. You've taken in a great deal in this model. You've discovered another picture on Docker Hub and utilized the docker run command in another manner. There's a great deal to think about running intelligent containers. The following segment covers that in more noteworthy detail.

Docker Hub is in no way, shape or forms the primary hotspot for programming. Contingent upon the objectives and viewpoint of programming distributers, Docker Hub may not be a fitting circulation point. Shut source or exclusive ventures might not have any desire to chance to distribute their product through an outsider. There are three different approaches to introduce the product:

- You can utilize elective repository vaults or run your very own library.
- You can physically stack pictures from a document.
- You can download a venture from some other source and fabricate a picture utilizing a gave Dockerfile.

Every one of the three of these choices is reasonable for private ventures or corporate framework.

The following hardly any subsections spread how to introduce programming from every elective source.

Using alternative registries

As referenced before, Docker makes the library programming accessible for anybody to run. Facilitating organizations have incorporated it into their contributions, and organizations have started running their very own inner libraries. I'm not going to cover running a vault, yet it's significant that you figure out how to utilize them early.

Utilizing an elective vault is straightforward. It requires no extra design. All you need is the location of the library. The accompanying command will download another "Welcome World" type model from an elective library:

docker pull quay.io/dockerinaction/ch4_hello_registry:latest

The library address is a piece of the full repository detail

The full example is as per the following:

[REGISTRYHOST/][USERNAME/]NAME[: TAG]

Docker realizes how to converse with Docker libraries, so the main contrast is that you indicate the vault have. Now and again, working with libraries will require a confirmation step. At the point when you're done with the welcome library picture you introduced, expel it with the accompanying command:

docker rmi quay.io/dockerinaction/ch4_hello_registry

Libraries are incredible. They empower a client to give up control of picture stockpiling and transportation. In any case, running your very own vault can be convoluted and may make a potential single purpose of a disappointment for your arrangement framework. In the event that running a custom library sounds somewhat confused for your utilization case, and outsider appropriation apparatuses are impossible, you should think about stacking pictures straightforwardly from a document.

Pictures as records

Docker gives a command to stack pictures into Docker from a document. With this apparatus, you can stack pictures that you gained through different channels. Perhaps your organization has decided to convey pictures through a focal record server or some form control framework. Possibly the picture is little enough that your companion sent it to you over email or shared it by means of glimmer drive. Anyway, you happened upon the document, and you can stack it into Docker with the docker load command.

You'll require a picture record to stack before I can show you the docker load command. Since it's far-fetched that you have a picture document lying around, I'll tell you the best way to spare one from a stacked picture. For the reasons for this model, you'll pull busybox: latest. That picture is little and simple to work with. To spare that picture to a document, utilize the docker spare command.

I utilized the .tar filename postfix in this model because the docker spare command makes TAR file documents. You can utilize any filename you need. On the off chance that you miss the – o banner, the subsequent record will be gushed to the terminal.

Layer relationships

Images maintain parent/child connections. In these connections, they work from their folks and structure layers. The documents accessible to a container are the association of the entirety of the layers in the lineage of the picture the container was created from. Images can have associations with some other picture, including images in different repositories with different proprietors.

The layers are an example of the java:6 picture at the hour of this writing. A picture is named when its creator labels and distributes it. A client can create pseudonyms, as you did prior using the docker label command. Until a picture is labeled, the best way to allude to it is to utilize its remarkable identifier (UID) that was produced when the picture was constructed. The guardians of the regular Java 6 picture are marked using the initial 12 digits of their UID. These layers contain basic libraries and conditions of the Java 6 programming. Docker truncates the UID from 65 (base 16) digits to 12 to serve its human clients. Internally and through API get to, Docker utilizes the full 65. It's essential to know about this when you've installed images alongside comparable anonymous images. I wouldn't need you to think something terrible occurred or some vindictive programming had made it into your PC when you see these images included when you utilize the docker images command.

The Java images are sizable. At the hour of this writing, the openjdk-6 picture is 348 MB, and the openjdk-7 picture is 590 MB. You get some space savings when you utilize the runtime-just images, yet even openjre-6 is 200 MB. Again, Java was picked here in light of the fact that its images are especially enormous for a typical reliance.

Container file system abstraction and isolation

Projects that run in containers don't think about the layers of the image. Inside the container, the file system functions as if it were not working on the container or image. From a tank standpoint, it contains restrictive copies of the files the image contains. This becomes conceivable with what is called the join file system. Docker uses a variety of file systems to join and will choose the one that best suits your system. The complexities of how a file association system works have overcome what you need to know to use Docker successfully.

An association file system is an element of a set of basic instruments that combine to create a powerful separation of file systems. Different devices are DTM namespaces and chroot system call.

The file system is used to create mount points in your host file system that conceptualize the use of layers. The layers created are what is packed into the Docker image layers. Similarly, when a Docker image is installed, its layers are downloaded and properly organized for use by the file system provider selected for your system.

The Linux part gives the DTM system a namespace. When Docker creates a container, this new container will have its own MNT namespace, and a second mount point will be created for the container in the image.

In conclusion, chroot is used to make the database of the image file system the root of the unique circumstances of the container. This prevents any item contained in the container from referencing another item in the host file system.

Using chroot and DTM namespaces is necessary to improve the container. When adding a file system to join a formula, Docker containers have some advantages.

Advantages of this toolset and file system structure

The first and perhaps most important advantage of this methodology is that it is basic

The layers must be installed once. If you install an unlimited number of images and they all depend on the standard layer, that base layer and all its main layers must be downloaded or installed once. This implies that you can install some of the program specializations without storing excess files on your computer or downloading repetitive layers. Most advances in virtual machines, on the other hand, store files that are indistinguishable, usually when you have repetitive virtual machines on your computer.

Second, diapers provide a rude way of handling conditions and difficulties separately. This is especially useful for software developers. From a customer standpoint, this benefit will help you quickly sort out the software you use when examining the images and layers you use.

Finally, it is very difficult to create software specializations when small changes can be made to the basic image. Giving specific images helps customers get exactly what they need from the software with minimal customization. This is probably the best motivation to use Docker.

Shortcomings of union file systems

Docker will pick the best file system for the system it's running on. However, no imple-mentation is ideal for each remaining task at hand. Truth be told, there are some particular use situations when you should delay and consider utilizing another Docker highlight.

Different file systems have different properties depending on the properties, size, filenames and characters. Union file systems find themselves often having to interpret the principles of different file systems. At best, they are prepared to provide adequate interpretations. In most pessimistic scenarios, forces are ignored. For example, neither btrfs nor OverlayFS help with the global properties that make SELinux work.

Union file systems use an example called duplicate on-compose, and that makes actualize ing memory-mapped files (the mmap() system call) troublesome. Some union file systems

give usage that works under the correct conditions, yet it might be a superior plan to stay away from memory-mapping files from a picture.

The support file system is another pluggable element of Docker. You can figure out which file system your establishment is utilizing with the information subcommand. In case you need to explicitly reveal to Docker the file system you will use, do so as such with the capacity manager of your choice, or - with when you launch the Docker daemon. You can solve most problems related to maintaining a syndicated file system without changing the capacity provider. This can be understood by volumes

Summary

The errand of introducing and overseeing software on a PC shows a one of a kind arrangement of difficulties. This part clarifies how you can utilize Docker to address them. The center thoughts and highlights secured by this part are as per the following:

- Human Docker clients use vault names to impart which software they might want Docker to introduce.
- Docker Hub is the default Docker library. You can discover software on Docker Hub through either the site or the docker command-line program.
- The docker command-line program makes it easy to introduce software that is conveyed through elective libraries or in different structures.
- The picture archive particular incorporates a vault have field.
- The docker burden and docker spare commands can be utilized to load and spare images from TAR documents.

▪Distributing a Dockerfile with a task improves picture expands on client machines.

▪Images are typically identified with different images in parent/youngster connections. These connections structure layers. At the point when we state that we have introduced a picture, we are stating that we have introduced an objective picture and each picture layer in its genealogy.

Organizing images with layers empowers layer reuse and spares bandwidth during dispersion and extra room on your PC.

Did you see it? Unless your network connection is far better than mine, or you had already installed Java 6 as a dependency of some other image, the download for dockerinaction/ch3_myapp should have been much slower than dockerinaction/ ch3_myotherapp.

When you installed ch3_myapp, Docker determined that it needed to install the openjdk-6 image because it's the direct dependency (parent layer) of the requested image. When Docker went to install that dependency, it discovered the dependencies of that layer and downloaded those first. Once all the dependencies of a layer are installed, that layer is installed. Finally, openjdk-6 was installed, and then the tiny ch3_myapp layer was installed.

When you issued the command to install ch3_myotherapp, Docker identified that openjdk-6 was already installed and immediately installed the image for ch3_myotherapp. This was simpler, and because less than one megabyte of data was transferred, it was faster. But again, to the user, it was an identical process.

From the user perspective, this ability is nice to have, but you wouldn't want to have to try to optimize for it. Just take the benefits where they happen to work out. From the perspective of a software or image author, this ability should play a major factor in your image design.

If you run docker images now, you'll see the following repositories listed:

- dockerinaction/ch3_myapp
- dockerinaction/ch3_myotherapp
- java:6

By default, the docker images command will only show you repositories. Similar to other commands, if you specify the -a flag, the list will include every installed interme-diate image or layer. Running docker images -a will show a list that includes several repositories listed as <none>. The only way to refer to these is to use the value in the IMAGE ID column.

In this example, you installed two images directly, but a third parent repository was installed as well. You'll need to clean up all three. You can do so more easily if you use the condensed docker rmi syntax:

docker rmi \

dockerinaction/ch3_myapp \

dockerinaction/ch3_myotherapp \

java:6

The docker rmi command allows you to specify a space-separated list of images to be removed. This comes in handy when you need to remove a small set of images after an example. I'll be using this when appropriate throughout the rest of the examples in this book.

Persistent storage and shared state with volumes

At this point in the book, you've installed and run a few programs. You've seen some examples of toys, but haven't seen anything that resembles the real world. This chapter presents the quantities of Docker Volume and the strategies you will use to manage your container data.

Think about what it would be like to run a database program in a container. You can also package software with an image at the beginning of the container,

You can initialize an empty database. When programs connect to a database and enter data, where are they stored? Is it in a file inside the container? What happens to this information when you stop the tank or delete it? How would you move your data if you wanted to update a database program?

Imagine another situation where you run different web applications in different containers. Where would you write the log files to survive the tank? How would you access these records to resolve the issue? How can other programs, such as the registration summary tool, access these files? The answer to all these questions involves the use of volumes.

Presentation of volumes.

A set of mount points creates a directory tree of the host or container that describes how to assemble one or more file systems. Volume is the mount point for the container tree where part of the computer directory tree is mounted. Most people know very little about file systems and mount points and rarely adjust them. People have more difficulty with volumes than with any other Docker topic. The lack of knowledge of editing points contributes to the factor.

Without volume, container users are limited to working with a union file system that provides image images. The first file is written to the root file system. The operating system sends changes from the root file system to the top layer of the mounted Union file system. The second file is written to the volume that is embedded in the u / data container directory tree. This change is made directly to the host file system via volume.

Although a union file system works to create and share images, it is far from ideal for working with permanent or shared data. Quantities meet these use cases and play a vital role in container design.

The quantities allow the container data to be managed independently

Semantically, volume is a segmentation and data sharing tool with scope or lifecycle independent of a single container. This is why volumes are an important part of any designed system container that shares or writes files. The following are examples of data whose range or access is different from the container:

- Database and database software.
- Web application versus registration information
- Data processing application with respect to input and output data
- Web server versus static content
- Products versus support tools

Quantities help to separate problems and create modularity in architectural components. This modularity helps you to understand, create, support and reuse more important parts of the system more easily.

Think of it this way: images are suitable for packing and distributing relatively static files, such as programs; The volumes contain dynamic data or specializations. This difference makes it possible to share reusable images and easy data. This separation of relatively static and dynamic file space allows application or image authors to implement advanced models as polymorphic and composting tools.

A polymorphic instrument is one that keeps up a predictable interface yet may have a few executions that accomplish various things. Consider an application, for example, a general application server. Apache Tomcat, for instance, is an application that gives a HTTP interface on a system and dispatches any solicitations it gets to pluggable projects. Tomcat has polymorphic conduct. Utilizing volumes, you can infuse conduct into containers without altering a picture. Then again, consider a database ace gram like MongoDB or MySQL. The estimation of a database is characterized by the information it contains. A database program consistently shows a similar interface yet takes on an entirely extraordinary worth relying upon the information that can be infused with a volume. The polymorphic container design is the subject of area.

All the more generally, volumes empower the division of utilization and host concerns. Sooner or later a picture will be stacked onto a host and a container made from it. Docker thinks minimal about the host where it's running and can just make statements about what documents ought to be accessible to a container. That implies Docker alone has no real way to exploit have explicit offices like mounted system stockpiling or blended turning and strong state hard drives. Yet, a client with information on the host can utilize volumes to delineate in a container to fitting stockpiling on that host.

Presently that you're comfortable with what volumes are and for what reason they're significant, you can begin with them in a true model.

Utilizing volumes with a NoSQL database

The Apache Cassandra venture gives a section database worked in grouping, possible consistency, and direct compose adaptability. It's a mainstream decision in present day framework structures, and an official picture is accessible on Docker Hub. Cassandra resembles different databases in that it stores its information in records on plate. In this area you'll utilize the official Cassandra picture to make a solitary hub Cassandra group, make a keyspace, erase the container, and afterward recuperate that keyspace on another hub in another container.

Begin by making a solitary container that characterizes a volume. This is known as a volume container. Volume containers are one of the propelled examples talked about later in this part:

docker run -d \

- volume/var/lib/cassandra/information \

- Name cass-shared \

Alpine echo Data Container

The volume container will quickly stop. That is suitable for this model. Try not to expel it yet. You're going to utilize the volume it made when you make another container running Cassandra:

docker run -d \

- Volumes-from cass-shared \

- name cass1 \

Cassandra: 2.2

After Docker pulls the cassandra:2.2 picture from Docker Hub, it makes another container and duplicates the volume definitions from the volume container. From that point onward, the two containers have a volume mounted at/var/lib/cassandra/information that focuses to a similar area on the host's catalog tree. Next, start a container from the cassandra:2.2 picture, however run a Cassandra customer device and associate with your running server:

docker run – it - rm \

- interface cass1:cass \

cassandra:2.2 cqlsh cass

Presently you can review or change your Cassandra database from the CQLSH command line. To begin with, search for a keyspace named docker_hello_world:

select *

From system.schema_keyspaces

Where keyspace_name = 'docker_hello_world';

Cassandra should restore an unfilled rundown. This implies the database hasn't been changed by the model. Next, make that keyspace with the accompanying command:

make keyspace docker_hello_world

with replication = {

'class' : 'SimpleStrategy',

'replication_factor': 1

};

Since you've altered the database, you ought to have the option to give a similar question again to see the outcomes and check that your progressions were acknowledged. The accompanying command is equivalent to the one you ran before:

select *

from system.schema_keyspaces

where keyspace_name = 'docker_hello_world';

This time Cassandra should restore a solitary section with the properties you determined when you made the keyspace. In case you're fulfilled that you've associated with and modified your Cassandra hub, quit the CQLSH program to stop the customer container:

Leave and stop the present container quit

The customer container was made with the - rm banner and was consequently expelled when the command halted. Keep tidying up the initial segment of this model by halting and evacuating the Cassandra hub you made:

docker stop cass1

docker rm - vf cass1

The client and Cassandra server you created will be deleted after executing these commands. If the changes you make persist, the only place I can stay is the volume container. If true, the scope of this data has expanded to two containers, and its life cycle has extended beyond the container in which the data was created.

You can try this by repeating these steps. Create a new Cassandra node, connect the client, and find the key space.

The following three commands will test your data recovery:

docker run -d \

—volumes-from cass-shared \

—name cass2 \

cassandra:2.2

docker run –it—rm \

—link cass2:cass \

cassandra:2.2 \

cqlsh cass

select *

from system.schema_keyspaces

where keyspace_name = 'docker_hello_world';

The last direction in this set returns a solitary passage, and it coordinates the keyspace you made in the past holder. This affirms the past cases and exhibits how volumes may be utilized to make tough frameworks. Before proceeding onward, quit the CQLSH program and tidy up your workspace. Try to evacuate that volume holder too:

quit

docker rm - vf cass2 cass-shared

This model shows one approach to utilize volumes without going into how they work, the examples being used, or how to oversee volume life cycle. The rest of this chap-ter jumps further into every feature of volumes, beginning with the various types accessible.

Volume types

There are two types of volume. Each volume is a mount point on the holder registry tree to an area on the host catalog tree, yet the types vary in where that area is on the host. The main sort of volume is a bind mount. Bind mount volumes utilize any client determined catalog or record on the host working framework. The subsequent sort is an overseen volume. Overseen volumes use areas that are made by the Docker daemon in space constrained by the daemon, called Docker oversaw space.

Each sort of volume has preferences and inconveniences. Contingent upon your particular use case, you may need to utilize one or be not able utilize the other. This area investigates each type top to bottom.

Bind mount volumes

A bind mount volume is a volume that focuses to a client indicated area on the host document framework. Bind mount volumes are valuable when the host gives some record or index that should be mounted into the holder registry tree at a particular point

Bind mount volumes are helpful in the event that you need to impart information to different procedures running outside a compartment, for example, parts of the host framework itself. They likewise work on the off chance that you need to share information that lives on your host at some known area with a particular ace gram that runs in a holder.

For instance, assume you're taking a shot at an archive or website page on your neighborhood PC and need to impart your work to a companion. One approach to do so is to use Docker to dispatch a web server and serve content that you've duplicated into the web server picture. In spite of the fact that that would work and may even be a best practice for produc-tion situations, it's bulky to remake the picture each time you need to share a refreshed form of the archive.

Rather, you could utilize Docker to dispatch the web server and bind mount the loca-tion of your record into the new holder at the web server's report root. You can attempt this for yourself. Make another catalog in your home index called test ple-docs. Presently make a record named index.html in that catalog. Include a decent message for your companion to the record. The accompanying order will begin an Apache HTTP server where your new index is bind mounted to the server's archive root:

docker run - d - name bmweb \

- v ~/model docs:/usr/nearby/apache2/htdocs \

- p 80:80 \

httpd:latest

With this compartment running, you ought to have the option to point your internet browser at the IP address where your Docker motor is running and see the document you made.

In this model you utilized the - v choice and an area guide to make the bind mount volume. The guide is delimited with a colon (as is basic with Linux-style order line instruments). The guide key (the way before the colon) is the supreme way of an area on the host record framework, and the worth (the way after the colon) is where it ought to be mounted inside the compartment. You should determine areas with outright ways.

This model addresses a significant quality or highlight of volumes. At the point when you mount a volume on a holder record framework, it replaces the substance that the picture professional vides at that area. In this model, the httpd:latest picture gives some default HTML content at/usr/neighborhood/apache2/htdocs/, yet when you mounted a volume at that area, the substance gave by the picture was superseded by the substance on the host. This conduct is the reason for the polymorphic holder design examined later in the part.

Developing this utilization case, assume you need to ensure that the Apache HTTP web server can't change the substance of this volume. Indeed, even the most believed programming can contain vulnerabilities, and it's ideal to limit the effect of an assault on your site. Luckily, Docker gives an instrument to mount volumes as read-in particular. You can do this by annexing :ro to the volume map detail. In the model, you should change the run command to something like the accompanying:

docker rm - vf bmweb

docker run - name bmweb_ro \

- volume ~/model docs:/usr/neighborhood/apache2/htdocs/:ro \

- p 80:80 \

httpd:latest

By mounting the volume as read-no one but, you can avoid any procedure inside the con-tainer from adjusting the substance of the volume. You can see this in real life by running a speedy test:

docker run - rm \

- v ~/model docs:/testspace:ro \

high \

/canister/sh - c 'reverberation test >/testspace/test'

This command begins a holder with a comparative read-just bind mounts as the web server. It runs a command that attempts to add the word test to a document named test in the volume. The command comes up short because the volume is mounted as read-as it was.

At last, note that if you indicate a host registry that doesn't exist, Docker will make it for you. Even though this can prove to be useful, depending on this usefulness isn't the best idea. It's better to have more control over the ownership and permissions set on a directory.

ls ~/example-docs/absent

```
docker run—rm -v ~/example-docs/absent:/absent alpine:latest \

/bin/sh -c 'mount | grep absent'

ls ~/example-docs/absent
```

Bind mount volumes aren't restricted to indexes, however that is the way they're every now and again utilized. You can utilize bind mount volumes to mount singular records. This gives the adaptability to make or connection assets at a level that maintains a strategic distance from strife with different assets. Think about when you need to mount a particular record into an index that contains different documents. Solidly, assume you just needed to serve a solitary extra document close by the web content that dispatched with some pictures. In the event that you utilize a bind mount of an entire registry over that area, different documents will be lost. By utilizing a particular record as a volume, you can abrogate or infuse singular documents.

The significant thing to note for this situation is that the record must exist on the host before you make the compartment. Something else, Docker will accept that you needed to utilize an index, make it on the host, and mount it at the ideal area (regardless of whether that area is involved by a record).

The primary issue with bind mount volumes is that they tie generally compact compartment depictions to the document arrangement of a particular host. In the event that a holder portrayal relies upon content at a particular area on the host document framework, at that point that depiction isn't convenient to have where the substance is inaccessible or accessible in some other area.

The following enormous issue is that they make an open door to struggle with different holders. It would be an ill-conceived notion to begin numerous occasions of Cassandra that all utilization a similar host area as a volume. Every one of the cases would vie for a similar arrangement of records. Without different devices, for example, record bolts, that would almost certainly bring about the defilement of the database.

Bind mount volumes are suitable apparatuses for workstations or machines with specific concerns. It's smarter to maintain a strategic distance from these sorts of explicit bindings in summed up stages or equipment pools. You can exploit volumes in a host-freethinker and compact path with Docker-oversaw volumes.

Docker-managed volumes

Overseen volumes are unique in relation to binding mount volumes because the Docker daemon makes oversaw volumes in a segment of the host's record framework that is possessed by Docker. Utilizing oversaw volumes is a technique for decoupling volumes from specific areas on the document framework.

Overseen volumes are made when you utilize the - v alternative (or - volume) on docker run yet determine the mount point in the compartment catalog tree.

You made an oversaw volume in the Cassandra The compartment named cass-shared indicated a volume at/var/lib/cassandra/information:

docker

run

-d \

-v

/var/lib/cassandra/data \

—name

cass-shared \

alpine

echo Data Container

When you created this container, the Docker daemon created directories to store the contents of the three volumes somewhere in the part of the host file system that it controls. To find out exactly where this folder is, you can use the filtered command to check the docked window for the Volumes key. The important thing to remove from this result is that Docker created each of the volumes in the directory managed by the host Docker daemon:

docker view -f "{{json .Volumes}}" cass-shared

The inspection subcommand will generate a list of mount points for the container and the corresponding path in the computer directory tree. The output will look like this:

{"/ var / lib / cassandra / data": "/ mnt / sda1 / var / lib / docker / vfs / dir / 632fa59c ..."}

The volume key indicates a value that is the map itself. In this folder, each key is a mount point in the container, and the value is the location of the directory in the host file system. Here we are reviewing the volume container. The card is sorted according to the lexicographic order of their keys and is independent of the order given when creating the container.

Users of the VirtualBox

TIP (Docker Machine or Boot2Docker) should keep in mind that the host path is specified in each value relative to the root file system of their virtual machine, not the host root. Managed volumes are created on a machine running the Docker daemon, but VirtualBox will create link mounting volumes that refer to directories or files on the host computer.

The quantities that manage Docker may seem difficult to use if you manually assemble or connect tools on your desktop, but on larger systems where a particular data location is less important, managed volumes are a much more efficient way of organizing data. , Its use separates all other potential problems with the system. With volumes managed by Docker, it simply says, "I need a place to store some of the data I work with." The point is that Docker can charge all the machines on which Docker is installed. Also, when you finish the volume and ask Docker to clean up all the stuff for you, Docker can confidently delete any directory or file that the container no longer uses. Using volume this way helps to control congestion. As middleware or Docker add-ons develop, users of managed volumes will be able to adopt more advanced features, such as portable volumes.

Sharing access to data is a key feature of volume. If you have partitioned known bundles of files in the file system, you should know how to split a volume between containers without exposing the exact location of the managed containers. The following section describes two ways to share data between containers using volume.

Sharing volumes

Suppose you have a web server running in the container that records all requests you receive in / logs / access. If you want to move these records from your web server to more permanent storage, you can do so with a script in a different container. The amounts of exchange between the tanks are areas where their value becomes more apparent. Just as there are two types of volume, there are two ways of dividing volume between containers.

Sharing depends on the host

You've already read about the tools needed to implement host-dependent sharing. It is said that two or more containers use a host-dependent share when each has a link mount volume for one known location in the host file system. This is the most obvious way of dividing disk space between containers.

In this example, you created two containers: one is called a plath that writes rows to a file and another that shows the top of a file. These containers share the total connection embedding volume. Outside of any container, you can see changes by adding the contents of the directory you created or by viewing a new file.

Explore how containers can be interconnected in this way. The following example starts with four containers: two registers and two units:

docker run—name woolf -d \

—volume ~/web-logs-example:/data \

dockerinaction/ch4_writer_a

docker run—name alcott -d \

-v ~/web-logs-example:/data \

dockerinaction/ch4_writer_b

docker run—rm—entrypoint head \

-v ~/web-logs-example:/towatch:ro \

alpine:latest \

/towatch/logA

docker run—rm \

-v ~/web-logs-example:/toread:ro \

alpine:latest \

head /toread/logB

In this example, he created four containers, each of which contained the same directory as the volume. The first two containers are written to different files in this volume. The third and fourth tanks raise the volume to second and read only. This example is a toy, but it clearly demonstrates a feature that could be useful given the variety of ways people build images and software.

Host-dependent sharing requires the use of link mount volumes, but for related reasons, host-dependent sharing can cause problems or be too expensive to manage if you work with a large number of hosts. machines. The following section provides a shortcut to share managed volumes and link assembly volumes to a set of containers.

General sharing and bookmarking

The run docker command provides an indicator that copies the volumes of one or more containers to a new container. The—volumes-from flag can be configured several times to specify multiple source containers.

Using this metric, he copied the managed volume defined by the volume container into each container running Cassandra. The example is realistic but does not allow to illustrate some specific container behaviors - volumes - from and managed container:

docker run - fowler name \

-v ~ / copies: library / PoEAA \

-v / library / DSL \

Alpine: last \

echo "Fowler Collection created".

docker run - name knuth \

-v /library/TAoCP.vol1 \

-v /library/TAoCP.vol2 \

-v /library/TAoCP.vol3 \

-v /library/TAoCP.vol4.a \

Alpine: last \

echo "Knuth Collection Created"

—volumes-from fowler \

—volumes-from knuth \

alpine:latest ls -l /library/

docker inspect—format "{{json .Volumes}}" reader

In this example, you created two containers that define volumes managed by Docker as well as the volume of connection mounting. Share them with a third container with no label - of volume, you need to inspect previously created containers and and then associate mounting links to host directories managed by Docker. Docker knows all in his name when he uses the flag - notebooks-of. Copy any volume present in the original container specified in the new container. In this case a tainer called drive copied all volumes defined by fowler and knuth.

You can copy quantities directly or transiently. This means that if you copy. volumes from another container will also copy volumes copied from specific files.

Other containers The use of tanks created in the last example generates the following:

docker run - name aggregator \ - volumes-from fowler \ - volumes-from knuth \ alpine:latest \

reverberation "Assortment Created."

docker run - rm \

- volumes-from aggregator \

alpine:latest \

ls - l/library/

Replicated volumes consistently have a similar mount point. That implies that you can't utilize - volumes-from in three circumstances.

In the principal circumstance, you can't utilize - volumes-from if the holder you're fabricate ing needs a mutual volume mounted to an alternate area. It offers no tooling for remapping mount focuses. It will just duplicate and association the mount focuses determined by the predetermined holders. For instance, if the understudy in the last model needed to mount the library to an area like/school/library, they wouldn't have the option to do as such.

The subsequent circumstance happens when the volume sources strife with one another or another volume particular. Sources make an oversaw volume with a similar mount point, at that point a customer of both will get just one of the volume definitions:

docker run - name chomsky - volume/library/ss \ alpine:latest reverberation "Chomsky assortment made."

docker run - name lamport - volume/library/ss \ alpine:latest reverberation "Lamport assortment made."

docker run - name understudy \

- volumes-from chomsky - volumes-from lamport \ alpine:latest ls - l/library/

docker investigate - f "" understudy

Now when you run the model, the yield of docker investigate will show that the last con-tainer has just a solitary volume recorded at/library/ss and its worth is equivalent to one of the other two. Each source holder characterises a similar mount point, and you make a race condition by replicating both to the new compartment. Just one of the two duplicate drama tions can succeed.

A true model where this would restrain is on the off chance that you were replicating the volumes of a few web servers into a solitary holder for review. On the off chance that those servers are on the whole running similar programming or offer basic arrangement (which is almost certainly in a containerised framework), at that point every one of those servers may utilize a similar mount focuses. All things considered, the mount focuses would strife, and you'd have the option to get to just a subset of the necessary information.

The third circumstance where you can't utilize - volumes-from is in the event that you have to change the compose authorization of a volume. This is on the grounds that - volumes-from duplicates the definition of the full volume. For instance, if your source has a volume mounted with read/compose access, and you need to impart that to a compartment that ought to have just understood access, utilizing - volumes-from won't work.

Imparting volumes to the - volumes-from banner is a significant apparatus for building convenient application designs, yet it introduces a few constraints. Utilizing Docker-oversaw volumes decouples holders from the information and document framework struc-ture of the host machine, and that is basic for most creation conditions. The records and catalogs that Docker makes for oversaw volumes still should be represented and kept up. To see how Docker functions with these documents and how to keep your Docker condition clean, you have to comprehend the overseen volume life cycle.

The oversaw volume life cycle

By this point in the section you ought to have quite a couple of holders and volumes to tidy up. I've precluded cleanup guidelines so far so you have an abundance of mate-rial to use in this segment. Overseen volumes have life cycles that are free of any compartment, yet as of this keeping in touch with you can just reference them by the holders that utilization them.

Volume possession

Overseen volumes are inferior elements. You have no real way to share or erase a particular oversaw volume since you have no real way to distinguish an oversaw volume.

Overseen volumes are possibly made when you preclude a bind mount source, and they're just recognizable by the holders that utilization them.

The most noteworthy devotion approach to distinguish volumes is to characterize a solitary compartment for each oversaw volume. In doing as such, you can be quite certain about which volumes you con-sume. All the more significantly, doing so encourages you to erase explicit volumes. Except if you resort to inspecting volume mappings on a compartment and physically tidying up the Docker-oversaw space, evacuating volumes requires a referencing holder, and that makes it imperative to comprehend which compartments claim each oversaw volume.

A holder possesses all oversaw volumes mounted to its record framework, and numerous compartments can claim a volume like in the fowler, knuth, and peruser model. Docker tracks these references on oversaw volumes to guarantee that no as of now referenced volume is erased.

Tidying up volumes

Tidying up oversaw volumes is a manual undertaking. This default usefulness forestalls unplanned pulverisation of possibly significant information. Docker can't erase bind mount volumes because the source exists outside the Docker scope. Doing so could bring about all way of contentions, shakiness, and inadvertent information misfortune.

Docker can erase oversaw volumes while erasing holders. Running the docker rm command with the - v alternative will endeavor to erase any oversaw volumes referenced by the objective compartment. Any oversaw volumes that are referenced by different compartments will be skipped; however, the inward counters will be decremented. This is a protected default, yet it can prompt the dangerous situation

On the off chance that you erase each compartment that references an oversaw volume yet neglect to utilize the - v banner, you'll make that volume a vagrant. Expelling stranded volumes requires untidy manual advances, however relying upon the size of the volumes it might merit the exertion. Then again, there are vagrant volume cleanup contents that you should seriously mull over utilizing. You ought to deliberately check those before running them. You'll have to run those contents as an advantaged client, and in the event that they contain malware, you could be giving over full control of your framework.

It's a superior plan to keep away from the circumstance by getting into the propensity for utilizing the - v choice and utilizing the volume compartment

Docker makes volumes in another manner that we haven't talked about. Picture metadata can give volume determinations In these cases, you may not know about the volumes made for new holders. This is simply the essential motivation to prepare to utilize the - v choice.

Vagrant volumes render plate space unusable until you've tidied them up. You can limit this issue by making sure to tidy them up and utilizing a volume compartment design.

CLEANUP Before perusing further, take a couple of seconds to tidy up the con-tainers that you've made. Use docker ps - a to get a rundown of those holders and make sure to utilize the - v banner on docker rm to forestall vagrant volumes.

Coming up next is a solid case of expelling a compartment from one of the previous models:

docker rm - v understudy

Then again, in case you're utilizing a POSIX-agreeable shell, you can expel every halted holder and their volumes with the accompanying command:

docker rm - v $(docker ps - aq)

Anyway, you achieve the assignment, tidying up volumes is a significant piece of asset the board. Since you have a firm handle on the volume life cycle, sharing mechanisms, and use cases, you ought to be prepared to find out about cutting edge volume designs.

Propelled container designs with volumes

In reality, volumes are used to achieve a wide scope of record framework cus-tomizations and container collaborations. This segment centers around two or three progressed yet regular examples that you may experience or have the motivation to utilize in your very own frameworks.

Volume container design

I utilized an example called a volume container, which is a container that does minimal more than giving a handle to volumes. This is valuable on the off chance that you run over a case for offering a lot of volumes to numerous containers, or on the off chance that you can order a lot of volumes that fit a typical use case;

A volume container shouldn't run in light of the fact that halted containers keep up their volume references. A few of the models you've perused so far utilized the volume container design. The model containers cassshared, fowler, knuth, chomsky, and lamport all ran a straightforward reverberation direction to print something to the terminal and afterward left. At that point you utilized the halted containers as hotspots for the - volumes-from banner when making shopper containers.

Volume containers are significant for keeping an idea about data even in situations where a solitary container should have selective access to certain data. These handles cause it conceivable to effortlessly back up, to reestablish, and move data.

Assume you needed to refresh your database programming (utilize another picture). On the off chance that your database container composes its state to a volume and that volume was characterized by a vol-ume container, the relocation would be as basic as closing down the first data-base container and beginning the enhanced one with the volume container as a volume source. Reinforcement and reestablish tasks could be dealt with correspondingly. This, obviously, expect the new database programming can peruse the capacity organization of the old programming, and it searches for the data at a similar area.

TIP Using a container name prefix, for example, vc_ would be an incredible clue for people or contents not to utilize the - v choice when erasing a container. The particular prefix isn't as significant as setting up some show that peo-ple in your group and the instruments you assemble can depend on.

Volume containers are most valuable when you control and can institutionalize on mount point naming shows. This is on the grounds that each container that duplicates volumes from a volume container acquires its mount point definitions. For instance, a volume container that characterizes a volume mounted at/logs may be helpful to other contain-ers that hope to have the option to get to a volume mounted at/logs. Along these lines, a volume and its mount point become a kind of agreement between containers. Hence, pictures that have explicit volume necessities ought to impart those in their documentation or figure out how to do so automatically.

A model where two containers differ may be the place a volume container contributes a volume mounted at/logs, however, the container that utilizations - volumes-from is hoping to discover logs at/var/logs. For this situation, the devouring container would be not able to access the material it needs, and the framework would come up short.

Consider another model with a volume container named vc_data that contrib-utes two volumes:/data and/ application. A container that has a reliance on the/data volume gave by vc_data yet utilizes/application for something different would break if both vol-umes were replicated along these lines. These two containers are contrary. However Docker has no chance to get of deciding purpose. The blunder wouldn't be found until after the new container was made and bombed somehow or another.

The volume container design is more about effortlessness and show than everything else. It's a basic device for working with data in Docker and can be stretched out in a couple of intriguing ways.

Data-stuffed volume containers

You can expand the volume container example and worth included by pressing containers with data, Once you've adjusted your containers to utilize volumes, you'll discover a wide range of events to share volumes. Volume containers are in a novel situation to seed volumes with data. The data-pressed volume container augmentation formalizes that thought. It depicts how pictures can be utilized to appropriate static assets like design or code for use in containers made with different pictures.

A data-stuffed volume container is worked from a picture that duplicates static content from its picture to volumes it characterizes. In doing as such, these containers can be utilized to appropriate basic engineering data like setup, key material, and code.

You can construct these by hand in the event that you have a picture that has the data you'd like to make accessible by running and characterizing the volume and running a cp direction at container-creation time:

docker run—name dpvc \

-v/config \

dockerinaction/ch4_packed /bin/sh -c 'cp /packed/* /config/'

docker run—rm—volumes-from dpvc \

alpine:latest ls /config

docker run—rm—volumes-from dpvc \

alpine:latest cat /config/packedData

docker rm -v dpvc

The commands in this code share files distributed by a single image. You created three containers: one data-packed volume container and two that copied its volume and inspected the contents of the volume. Again, this is a toy example, but it demon-strates the way that you might consider distributing configuration in your own situa-tions. Using data-packed volume containers to inject material into a new container is the basis for the polymorphic container pattern discussed in the next section.

Polymorphic container pattern

As I stated earlier in the chapter, a polymorphic tool is one that you interact with in a consistent way but might have several implementations that do different things. Using volumes, you can inject different behavior into containers without modifying an image. A polymorphic container is one that provides some functionality that's easily substituted using volumes. For example, you may have an image that contains the binaries for Node.JS and by default executes a command that runs the Node.JS pro-gram located at /app/app.js. The image might contain some default implementation that simply prints "This is a Node.JS application" to the terminal.

You can change the behavior of containers created from this image by injecting your own app.js implementation using a volume mounted at /app/app.js. It might make more sense to layer that new functionality in a new image, but there are some cases when this is the best solution. The first is during development when you might not want to build a new image each time you iterate. The second is during operational events.

Consider a situation where an operational issue has occurred. In order to triage the issue, you might need tools available in an image that you had not anticipated when the image was built. But if you mount a volume where you make additional tools available, you can use the docker exec command to run additional processes in a container:

docker run—name tools dockerinaction/ch4_tools

docker run—rm \

—volumes-from tools \

alpine:latest \

ls /operations/*

docker run -d—name important_application \

—volumes-from tools \

dockerinaction/ch4_ia

docker exec important_application /operations/tools/someTool

docker rm -vf important_application

docker rm -v tools

You can infuse documents into generally static containers to change a wide range of conduct. Most ordinarily, you'll use polymorphic containers to infuse application design. Consider a multi-state arrangement pipeline where an application's setup would change contingent upon where you convey it. You may utilize data-pressed volume containers to contribute condition explicit arrangement at each stage, and afterward your application would search for its setup at some known area:

docker run—name devConfig \

-v /config \

dockerinaction/ch4_packed_config:latest \

/bin/sh -c 'cp /development/* /config/'

docker run—name prodConfig \

```
-v /config \
dockerinaction/ch4_packed_config:latest \
/bin/sh -c 'cp /production/* /config/'
docker run—name devApp \
—volumes-from devConfig \
dockerinaction/ch4_polyapp
docker run—name prodApp \
—volumes-from prodConfig \
dockerinaction/ch4_polyapp
```

You can infuse records into generally static containers to change a wide range of conduct. Most ordinarily, you'll use polymorphic containers to infuse application arrangement. Consider a multi-state arrangement pipeline where an application's setup would change contingent upon where you convey it. You may utilize data-pressed volume containers to contribute condition explicit arrangement at each stage, and afterward your application would search for its setup at some known area:

In this model, you start a similar application twice yet with an alternate design document infused. Utilizing this example you can assemble a straightforward variant controlled design conveyance framework.

Summary

One of the primary significant obstacles in figuring out how to utilize Docker is getting volumes and the document framework. This section covers volumes top to bottom, including the accompanying:

- Volumes enable containers to impart documents to the host or different containers.
- Volumes are portions of the host record framework that Docker mounts into containers at indicated areas.
- There are two kinds of volumes: Docker-oversaw volumes that are situated in the Docker part of the host document framework and tie mount volumes that are found anyplace on the host record framework.
- Volumes have life cycles that are autonomous of a particular container, yet a client can just reference Docker-oversaw volumes with a container handle.
- The vagrant volume issue can make plate space hard to recoup. Utilize the - v alternative on docker rm to dodge the issue.
- The volume container design is helpful for keeping your volumes sorted out and evading the vagrant volume issue.
- The data-pressed volume container design is valuable for disseminating static substance for different containers.
- The polymorphic container design is an approach to form insignificant practical segments and augment reuse.

Network exposure

In the past part you read about how to utilize volumes and work with documents in a compartment. This section manages another regular type of info and yield: network get to.

On the off chance that you have to run a site, database, email server, or any product that relies upon networking, similar to an internet browser inside a Docker compartment, at that point you have to understand how to connect that holder to the network. In the wake of perusing this part you'll have the option to make compartments with network presentation fitting for the application you're running, use network programming in one holder from another, and understand how compartments cooperate with the host and the host's network.

Networking foundation

A brisk diagram of pertinent networking ideas will be useful for understanding the points in this section. This area incorporates just elevated level detail; so in case you're a specialist, don't hesitate to skirt ahead.

Networking is tied in with imparting between forms that could conceivably have a similar nearby assets. To know the material in this section you just need to consider a couple of essential network reflections that are generally utilized by forms. The better understanding you have of networking, the more you'll find out about the mechanics at work. Be that as it may, a profound understanding isn't required to utilize the instruments gave by Docker. On the off chance that anything, the material contained in this should provoke you to freely look into chosen ridiculously up. Those essential deliberations utilized by forms incorporate protocols, network interfaces, and ports.

Basics: protocols, interfaces, and ports

A convention concerning correspondence and networking is a kind of language. Two parties that concur on a convention can understand what each other is conveying. This is vital to successful correspondence. Hypertext Transfer Protocol (HTTP) is one famous network convention that numerous individuals have known about. The convention professional vides the World Wide Web. Countless network protocols and a few layers of correspondence are made by those protocols. For the present, it's just significant that you comprehend what a convention is so you can understand network interfaces and ports.

A network interface has a location and speaks to an area. You can consider between faces as undifferentiated from true areas with addresses. A network interface resembles a letter drop. Messages are conveyed to a letter drop for beneficiaries at that address, and mes-sages are taken from a post box to be conveyed somewhere else.

While a letter box has a postal location, a network interface has an IP address, which is characterized by the Internet Protocol. The subtleties of IP are intriguing however outside of the extent of this book. The significant thing to think about IP addresses is that they are one of a kind in their network and contain data about their area on their network.

It's normal for PCs to have two sorts of interfaces: an Ethernet interface and a loopback interface. An Ethernet interface is what you're likely generally acquainted with. It's utilized to connect to different interfaces and procedures. A loopback interface isn't connected to some other interface. From the outset this may appear to be futile, however it's frequently valuable to have the option to utilize network protocols to speak with different projects on a similar PC. In those cases a loopback is an extraordinary arrangement.

With regards to the post box allegory, a port resembles a beneficiary or a sender. There may be a few people who get messages at a solitary location. For instance, a solitary location may get messages for Wendy Webserver, Deborah

As a general rule, ports are simply numbers and characterized as a major aspect of the Transmission Control Protocol (TCP). Again the subtleties of the convention are past the extent of this book, however I urge you to find out about it some time. Individuals who made standards for star tocols, or organizations that claim a specific item, choose what port number ought to be utilized for explicit purposes. For instance, web servers give HTTP on port 80 as a matter of course. MySQL, a database item, serves its convention on port 3306 of course. Memcached, a quick reserve innovation, gives its convention on port 11211. Ports are composed on TCP messages simply like names are composed on envelopes.

Interfaces, protocols, and ports are on the whole quick worries for programming and clients. By finding out about these things, you build up a superior gratefulness for the manner in which genius grams impart and how your PC fits into the master plan.

Greater picture: networks, NAT, and port sending

Interfaces are single focuses in bigger networks. Networks are characterized in the manner that interfaces are connected together, and that linkage decides an interface's IP address.

Here and there a message has a beneficiary that an interface isn't legitimately connected to, so all things considered it's conveyed to a middle person that realizes how to course the message for conveyance. Returning to the mail illustration, this is like how certifiable mail vehicle riers work.

At the point when you place a message in your outbox, a mail transporter lifts it up and conveys it to a nearby steering office. That office is itself an interface. It will take the message and send it along to the following stop on the course to a goal. A neighborhood steering office for a mail bearer may advance a message to a local office, and then to a nearby office for the goal, and at last to the beneficiary. It's normal for network courses to pursue a comparable example.

This section is worried about interfaces that exist on a solitary PC, so the networks and courses we consider won't be anyplace close to that muddled. Actually, this section is around two explicit networks and the manner in which compartments are appended to them. The main network is the one that your PC is connected to. The second one is a virtual network that Docker makes to connect the entirety of the running compartments to the network that the PC is connected to. That subsequent network is known as a scaffold.

Similarly as the name suggests, an extension is an interface that connects numerous networks with the goal that they can work as a solitary network, Bridges work by specifically sending traffic between the connected networks dependent on another kind of network address. To know the material in this section, you just should be OK with this unique thought.

This has been an extremely harsh prologue to some nuanced subjects. I've extremely just started to expose what's underneath so as to assist you with understanding how to utilize Docker and the networking offices that it rearranges.

Docker container networking

Docker is worried about two kinds of networking: single-have virtual networks and multi-have networks. Neighborhood virtual networks are utilized to give container separation. Multi-have virtual networks give an overlay where any container on a taking an interest host can have its very own routable IP address from some other container in the network.

This part covers single-have virtual networks inside and out. Understanding how Docker separates containers on the network is basic for the security-disapproved. Individuals building networked applications need to know how containerization will affect their arrangement necessities.

Multi-have networking is still in beta at the hour of this composition. Executing it requires a more extensive understanding of other biological system instruments notwithstanding understand-ing the material covering single-have networking. Until multi-have networking settles, it's ideal to begin by understanding how Docker assembles neighborhood virtual networks.

The neighborhood Docker network topology

Docker utilizes highlights of the hidden working framework to manufacture a particular and adaptable virtual network topology. The virtual network is neighborhood to the machine where Docker is introduced and is comprised of courses between taking an interest containers and the more extensive network where the host is connected. You can change the conduct of that network structure and now and again change the structure itself by utilizing command-line alternatives for beginning the Docker daemon and every container.

Containers have their private interface and a different Ethernet interface connected to another virtual interface in the host's namespace. These two connected interfaces structure a connection between the host's network stack and the stack made for every container. Much the same as common home networks, every container is appointed a remarkable private IP address that is not straightforwardly reachable from the outer network. Connections are directed through the Docker connect interface called docker0. You can think about the docker0 interface like your home switch. Every one of the virtual interfaces made for containers is connected to docker0, and together they structure a network. This scaffold between face is connected to the network where the host is appended.

Utilizing the docker command-line apparatus, you can redo the IP tends to utilized, the host interface that docker0 is connected to, and the manner in which containers speak with one another. The connections between interfaces depict how uncovered or separated a particular network container is from the remainder of the network. Docker utilizes bit namespaces to make those private virtual interfaces, yet the namespace itself doesn't give the network disengagement. Network introduction or seclusion is given by the host's firewall governs (each advanced Linux appropriation runs a firewall). With the choices gave, there are four models for network containers.

Four network container prime examples

All Docker containers tail one of four prime examples. These prime examples characterize how a container communicates with other neighborhood containers and the host's network. Every fill an alternate need, and you can think about each as having an alternate level of disengagement. At the point when you use Docker to make a container, it's imperative to deliberately think about what you need to achieve and utilize the most grounded conceivable container without trading off that objective.

The four are prime examples are these:

▪Closed containers

▪Joined containers

▪Bridged containers

▪Open containers

Throughout the following four subsections I present every model. Not many perusers will have an event to utilize every one of the four. In finding out about how to fabricate them and when to utilize them, you'll have the option to make that differentiation yourself.

Shut containers

The most grounded sort of network container is one that doesn't permit any network traffic. These are called shut containers. Procedures running in such a container will approach just to a loopback interface. In the event that they have to discuss just with themselves or one another, this will be reasonable. In any case, any program that expects access to the network or the web won't work accurately in such a container. For instance, if the product needs to download refreshes, it won't have the option to in light of the fact that it can't utilize the network.

Most perusers will originate from a server programming or web application back-ground, and in that setting it very well may be hard to envision a down to earth use for a con-tainer that has no network get to. There are many number of approaches to utilize Docker that it's anything but difficult to disregard volume containers, reinforcement employments, disconnected cluster preparing, or diagnos-tic apparatuses. The test you face isn't advocating Docker for each element yet realizing which highlights best fit the utilization cases that you may be underestimating.

Docker fabricates this sort of container by just avoiding the progression where an exter-nally available network interface is made, the shut prime example has no connection to the Docker connect interface. Projects in these con-tainers can talk just to themselves.

All Docker containers, including shut containers, approach a private interface. You may have experiences with loopback interfaces as of now. It's regular for individuals with moderate understanding to have utilized localhost or 127.0.0.1 as a location in a URL. In these cases you were advising a program to tie to or contact a help bound to your PC's loopback network interface.

By making private loopback interfaces for every container, Docker empowers star grams run inside a container to impart through the network however without that correspondence leaving the container.

You can advise Docker to make a shut container by determining none with the - net banner as a contention to the docker run command:

docker run—rm \

—net none \

alpine:latest \

ip addr

By running this example, you can see that the only available network interface is the return interface, linked to 127.0.0.1. This configuration means three things:

- Any program running in the container can connect to or wait for connections on this interface.
- Nothing outside the container can be associated with this interface.
- No programs running inside this container can reach anything outside the container.

This last point is important and easily demonstrable. If you are connected to the Internet, try to communicate with a popular service that should always be available. In this case, try communicating with Google's public DNS service:

docker run—rm \

—net no \

Alpine: last \

ping -w 2 8.8.8.8

In this example, create a closed container and try to test the speed between your container and the public DNS server provided by Google. This attempt should succeed with a message such as "ping: send to: network unavailable". This makes sense because we know that the container does not have a path to a larger network.

When to use sealed containers

Closed containers shall be used when there is a need for network isolation or the program does not require network access. For example, running a text editor on a terminal does not require network access. Running a random password generation program must be done inside a container without network access to prevent this number from being stolen.

There are not many ways to customize the network configuration for a closed container. Although this species may seem too restrictive, it is the safest of the four options and can be expanded to make it more comfortable. These are not the default values for Docker containers, but it is recommended that you try to justify the use of any weaker element before doing so. Docker creates default containers for the bridge.

Bridged containers

Bridge containers facilitate network isolation and therefore make it easier to start. This archetype is the most adaptable and should be strengthened as a recommended practice. Bridge containers have a private loopback interface and another private interface connected to the rest of the computer via a network bridge.

This section is the longest in this chapter. Bridge containers are the most common archetype of network containers. This chapter introduces several new options that you can use with other archetypes.

All interfaces associated with docker0 are part of the same virtual subnet. This means that they can talk to each other and communicate with a larger network through the docker0 interface.

Reach out

The most common reason for choosing a bridged container is because the process must have access to the network. You can skip—net to create a bridge container the ability to execute a command from a fixed menu or you can set its value in the bridge. I use each shape in the following examples:

docker run—rm \

- network bridge \

Alpine: last \

ip address

Like the first example for closed containers, this command will create a new container from the last Alpine image and list the available network interfaces. This time, two interfaces will be displayed: Ethernet interface and local loop. The output will include details such as IP address and subnet mask of each interface, maximum packet size (MTU), and various interface metrics.

Now that you have confirmed that your mailbox has a different interface with an IP address, try accessing the network again. This time skip the—net flag to see that the bridge is the default Docker network container type:

docker run—rm \

Alpine: last \

ping -w 2 8.8.8.8

Pinging a public DNS server from Google from this bridge container works and no additional features are needed. After executing this command, your container will ping for two seconds and generate a report of the network statistics collected.

You now know that if you have software that needs to access the Internet or another PC on a private network, you can also use a bridged container.

CNR

Domain Name System is a protocol for assigning host names to IP addresses. This task allows clients to group dependencies on a specific host IP address and depend on a host specified by a known name. The most basic way to change outbound communication is to create a name for the IP addresses.

Containers in bridge networks and other computers in your network usually have IP addresses that cannot be routed publicly. This means that if you do not use your own DNS server, you cannot name it. Docker offers several options for customizing the DNS settings of a new container.

First, the docker start command has a—hostime flag that you can use to set the hostname of the new container. This indicator adds an entry to the DNS replacement system inside the container. The entry assigns the host name given to the IP address of the tank bridge:

docker run—rm \

- Hostname \

Alpine: last \

Nslookup bark

This example creates a new container named barker host and runs a program to find the IP address of the same name. Running this example will generate an output similar to this:

Server: 10.0.2.3

Address 1: 10.0.2.3

Name: bark

Address 1: 172.17.0.22 Barker

The IP address in the last line is the bridge IP address for the new container. The IP address listed on the line named Server is the address of the server that gave the task.

The container hostname definition is useful when programs running inside the container need to search for their own IP address or just identify themselves. As other containers do not know this computer name, their use is limited. If you use an external DNS, you can share these host names.

Another option for customizing the DNS configuration of the mailbox is the ability to specify one or more DNS servers to use. To illustrate this, the following example creates a new mailbox and configures a DNS server for this mailbox in Google's public DNS service:

docker run—rm \

—dns 8.8.8.8 \

Alpine: last \

nslookup docker.com

Using a specific DNS can provide consistency if you use Docker on a laptop, and it often moves between ISPs. It is a key tool for people creating services and networks. Here are some important notes about setting up your own DNS:

- The value must be an IP. If you think about that, the reason is obvious. The container would need a DNS server to look up the name.

:: 1 localhost ip6-localhost ip6-loopback

fe00 :: 0 ip6-localnet

ff00 :: 0 ip6-mcastprefix

ff02 :: 1 ip6-allnodes

ff02 :: 2 ip6-allrouters

Test 10.10.10.2

127.0.0.1 docker.com

DNS is a powerful behavior change system. The name map / IP address provides a simple interface that users and programs can use to separate them from specific network addresses. If DNS is the best tool for changing outbound traffic behavior, a firewall and network topology are your best tools for controlling inbound traffic.

Opening inbound communication

Bridged containers aren't open from the host organize of course. Containers are ensured by your host's firewall framework. The default arrange topology gives no course from the host's outer interface to a container interface. That implies there's simply no real way to get to a container from outside the host.

Containers wouldn't be extremely valuable if there were no real way to get to them through the system. Fortunately, that is not the situation. The docker run order gives a banner, - p=[] or - publish=[], that you can use to make a mapping between a port on the host's system stack and the new container's interface. You've utilized this a couple of times prior in this book, however it merits referencing once more. The arrangement of the mapping can have four structures:

- <containerPort>

This structure ties the container port to a powerful port on the entirety of the host's between faces:

docker run - p 3333 ...

- <hostPort>:<containerPort>

This structure ties the predefined container port to the predetermined port on every one of the host's interfaces:

docker run - p 3333:3333 ...

- <ip>::<containerPort>

This structure ties the container port to a unique port on the interface with the predefined IP address:

docker run - p 192.168.0.32::2222 ...

- <ip>:<hostPort>:<containerPort>

This structure ties the container port to the predetermined port on the interface with the predefined IP address:

docker run - p 192.168.0.32:1111:1111 ...

These models expect that your host's IP address is 192.168.0.32. This is self-assertive however valuable to exhibit the component. Every one of the direction sections will make a course from a port on a host interface to a particular port on the container's interface. The various structures offer a scope of granularity and control. This banner is another that can be rehashed the same number of times as you have to give the ideal arrangement of mappings.

The docker run direction gives a substitute method to achieve opening channels. In the event that you can acknowledge a dynamic or vaporous port task on the host, you can utilize the - P, or - distribute all, banner. This banner advises the Docker daemon to make mappings, similar to the primary type of the - p choice for all ports that a picture reports, to expose. Pictures convey a rundown of ports that are exposed for straightforwardness and as an insight to clients where contained administrations are tuning in. For instance, on the chance that you realize that a picture like dockerinaction/ch5_expose exposes ports 5000, 6000, and 7000, every one of the accompanying directions accomplish something very similar:

docker run - d - name dawson \

- p 5000 \

- p 6000 \

- p 7000 \

dockerinaction/ch5_expose

docker run - d - name woolery \

- P \

dockerinaction/ch5_expose

It's anything but difficult to perceive how this can spare a client some composing, yet it asks two inquiries. To begin with, how is this utilized if the picture doesn't expose the port you need to utilize? Second, how would you find which dynamic ports were doled out?

The docker run order gives another banner, - expose, that takes a port number that the container should expose. This banner can be set on different occasions, once for each port:

docker run - d - name philbin \

- expose 8000 \

- P \

dockerinaction/ch5_expose

Utilizing - expose along these lines will add port 8000 to the rundown of ports that ought to be bound to dynamic ports utilizing the - P banner. In the wake of running the model, you can perceive what these ports were mapped to by utilizing docker ps, docker investigate, or another direction, docker port. The port sub-command takes either the

admonition with this alternative is that the range determined must be a subnet of the system doled out to the bridge (in case you're confounded, there's bunches of extraordinary documentation and tooling on the internet to help):

docker - d - fixed-cidr "192.168.0.192/26"

I'm not going to spend an excessive amount of exertion on the last setting. System interfaces have a breaking point to the greatest size of a bundle (a parcel is a nuclear unit of correspondence). By convention, Ethernet interfaces have a most extreme bundle size of 1500 bytes. This is the arranged default. In some particular instances, you'll have to change the MTU on the Docker bridge. At the point when you experience such a situation, you can utilize the - mtu banner to set the size in bytes:

docker - d – mtu 1200

Clients who are increasingly OK with Linux networking natives may jump at the chance to realize that they can give their very own custom bridge interface instead of using the default bridge. To do as such, design your bridge interface and then advise the Docker daemon to utilize it instead of docker0 when you start the daemon. The banner to utilize is - b or - bridge.

On the off chance that you've arranged a bridge named mybridge, you'd start Docker with a command like the following:

docker - d - b mybridge ...

docker - d - bridge mybridge ...

Building custom bridges requires a more profound understanding of Linux portion instruments than is important for this book. However, you should realize that this capacity is accessible on the off chance that you do the examination required.

Joined containers

The following less separated system container model is known as a joined container. These containers share a typical system stack. In this manner, there's no confinement between joined containers. This implies decreased control and security. In spite of the fact that this isn't the least secure paradigm, it's where the dividers of prison have been torn down.

Docker fabricates this sort of a container by providing access to the interfaces created for a particular container to another new container. Interfaces are in this manner shared like oversaw volumes.

The simplest method to see joined containers in activity is to utilize an uncommon case and join it with another container. The main command begins a server that tunes in on the loopback interface. The subsequent command records all the open ports. The subsequent command records the open port created by the main command in light of the fact that the two containers share a similar system interface:

docker run - d - name brady \

- net none alpine: latest \

nc - l 127.0.0.1:3333

docker run - it \

- net container:brady \

alpine: latest netstat – al

By running these commands you can create two containers that offer a similar net-work interface. Since the main container is created as a shut container, the two will just share that single loopback interface. The container estimation of the - net banner gives you a chance to indicate the container that the new container ought to be joined with. Either the container name or its crude ID recognizes the container that the new container ought to reuse.

Containers joined in this manner will maintain different types of detachment. They will keep different file systems, different memory, and so on. Be that as it may, they will have precisely the same system parts. That may sound concerning, however this sort of container can be helpful.

In the last model, you joined two containers on a system interface that has no entrance to the bigger system. In doing in this way, you expanded the handiness of a shut container. You may utilize this example when two different projects with access to two different bits of information need to communicate yet shouldn't share direct access to different's information. Then again, you may utilize this example when you have arranged administrations that need to communicate yet organise access or administration disclosure systems like DNS are inaccessible.

Setting aside security concerns, using joined containers reintroduces port clash issues. A client ought to know about this at whatever point they're joining two containers. It's feasible on the off chance that they're joining containers that run comparable administrations that they will create conflicts. Under those conditions, the conflicts should be settled using progressively conventional techniques like changing application design. These conflicts can happen on any common interfaces. At the point when projects are run outside a container, they share access to the host's interfaces with each other program running on the PC, so this particular degree increase is as yet an enhancement for the present business as usual.

At the point when two containers are joined, all interfaces are shared, and conflicts may hap-pen on any of them. From the outset, it may appear to be senseless to join two containers that need bridge get to. All things considered, they would already be able to communicate over the Docker bridge subnet. Be that as it may, consider circumstances where one procedure needs to screen the other through generally ensured channels. Correspondence between containers is dependent upon firewall rules. In the event that one procedure needs to communicate with another on an unexposed port, the best thing to do might be to join the containers.

Use associated containers when you want to use a single communication interface to communicate between programs in different containers.

Use the provided containers if the program in the container must modify the associated network string and another program uses that modified network.

Use associated mailboxes when you need to monitor network traffic from one application to another mailbox.

Before you start talking about Docker insecurity, since it allows any new container to join the current container, please note that privileged access is required to issue Docker commands. Privileged attackers can do whatever they want, including directly attacking code or data that is executed in any container. In this context, this type of network beam manipulation is not serious.

The big problem is in contexts where people build multi-tenant systems. If you create or plan to use this service, first set up a few accounts and try to access each other. If you can, think twice before using the service for something important. Joining another user's network bundle or mounting a volume is a wonderful problem.

The enclosed containers are a bit weaker, but they are not the weakest type of network containers. This title belongs to open containers.

Open containers

Open containers are dangerous. They do not have a network container and have full access to the host network. This includes access to host critical services. Open containers contain absolutely no insulation and should only be considered when you have no other options. The only useful quality is that non-privileged containers still cannot reconfigure the network string.

This type of container occurs when you specify a host as the value of the—net option in the fixed menu runtime command:

docker run—rm \

—host \

alpine: last ip address

Performing this command will create a container from the last Alpine image and no prison network. When you run ip addr in this container, you can view all the network interfaces of the host. You should see several interfaces in the list, including the docker0 call. As you noticed, this example creates a container that performs a discrete task and then deletes it immediately.

With this configuration, processes can be connected to secure network ports whose number is less than 1024.

Dependencies between Inter- containers

Now that you've learned the type of network containers you can create with Docker and how these containers interact with the network, you need to learn how to use network software in one container from another. You've seen containers use a gateway network to communicate, and you may have started thinking about how to fill a small system. If you consider that the bridge network assigns IP addresses to mailboxes dynamically at creation time, discovering local services can seem complicated.

One solution to the problem is to use a local DNS server and registration point when starting the mailbox. Another solution would be to write in your programs to search the local area network for IP addresses for listening on known ports. Both approaches manage a dynamic environment but require a non-trivial load and additional tools. These approaches will fail if arbitrary communication in the container is disabled. You can force all traffic back and forth through the host interface into known published ports. However, sometimes you may need privileged access to the network port. Docker provides another tool you have already seen dealing with this use case.

Introducing local service discovery links

When you create a container, you can associate it with another container. This destination container must be started when a new container is created. The reason

It's simple. Containers keep their IP address only while they are running. If arrested, they lose their rent.

Adding a link to a new container has three effects:

- Environment variables will be created that describes the destination of the destination container.

- The nickname of the connection will be added to the DNS replacement list of the new mailbox with the destination mailbox IP address.

- More interestingly, if mailbox-mail communication is disabled, Docker will add special firewall rules to allow communication between connected mailboxes.

The first two connection features are great for discovering basic services, but the third allows users to strengthen their local container networks without sacrificing container-to-container communication.

Ports open to communication are those that are exposed in the destination container. Therefore, the -expose flag provides direct access to a specific type of port port mapping container when ICC is enabled. When ICC is disabled,—expose becomes a tool for defining firewall rules and explicitly declaring a container interface on a network. In the same context, connections become a more static dependency statement for the local enforcement service. Here's a simple example. These images do not really exist:

docker run -d—name importantData \

—expose 3306 \

dockerinaction/mysql_noauth \

service mysql_noauth start

docker run -d—name importantWebapp \

—link imporantData:db \

dockerinaction/ch5_web startapp.sh -db tcp://db:3306

docker run -d—name buggyProgram \

dockerinaction/ch5_buggy

Reading through this model, you can see that I've begun some stupidly designed MySQL server (a prevalent database server). The name suggests that the server has disabled any verification necessities and any individual who can associate with the server can get to the information. I at that point began a significant web application that necessities access to the information in the importantData container. I included a link from the importantWebapp con-tainer to the importantData container. Docker will add information to that new container that will portray how to interface with importantData. This way, when the web application opens a database association with tcp://db:3306, it will interface with the database. Ultimately, I began another container that is known to contain carriage code. It's running as a nonprivileged customer, yet an assailant might be able to inspect the bridge organize if the program is undermined.

In case I'm running with inter-container correspondence empowered, assailants could without much of a stretch take the information from the database in the importantData container. They would have the option to do a basic system output to distinguish the open port and then gain access by basically opening an association. Indeed, even an easygoing traffic onlooker may think this association suitable in light of the fact that no container conditions have been emphatically displayed.

On the off chance that I was running this model with inter-container correspondence crippled, an assailant would be not able to arrive at some other containers from the container running the undermined software.

This is a genuinely senseless model. Kindly don't think that basically disabling inter-container correspondence will ensure assets if those assets don't secure themselves. With suitably arranged software, solid system administers, and pronounced help conditions, you can construct systems that accomplish great resistance inside and out.

Link aliases

Links are single direction arrange conditions created when one container is created and indicates a link to another. As referenced already, the - link banner utilized for this pur-present takes a single contention. That contention is a guide from a container name or ID to a moniker. The assumed name can be anything as long as it's extraordinary in the extent of the container is created. Thus, if three containers named a, b, and c as of now exist and are running, at that point I could run the following:

docker run - link a:alias-a - link b:alias-b - link c:alias-c ...

In any case, in the event that I committed an error and relegated a few or all containers to a similar pseudonym, at that point that assumed a name would just contain association information for one of the different containers. For this situation, the firewall rules would even now be created however would be about pointless with-out that association information.

Link aliases create a more elevated level issue. Software running inside a container has to know the assumed name of the container or host it's connecting to so it can play out the query. Like host names, link aliases become an image that numerous gatherings must concur on for a system to work accurately. Link aliases work as an agreement.

An engineer may assemble their application to expect that a database will have an assumed name of "database" and consistently search for it at tcp://database:3306 on the grounds that a DNS supersede with that host name would exist. This normal host name approach would function as long as the individual or procedure building the container either create a link associated with a database or utilizations - add-host to create the host name. On the other hand, the application could generally search for association information from a domain variable named DATABASE_PORT. The earth variable methodology will work just when a link is created with that moniker.

The issue is that there are no reliance announcements or runtime reliance checks. It's simple for the individual building the container to do as such without providing the necessary linkage. Docker clients should either depend on documentation to communicate these conditions or include custom reliance checking and fizzle quick conduct on The ports that are opened for correspondence are those that have been uncovered by the objective container. So the - uncover banner gives an alternate way to only one particu-lar kind of container to have port mapping when ICC is empowered. At the point when ICC is crippled, - uncover turns into a device for defining firewall rules and straightforward presentation of a con-tainer's interface on the system. In a similar setting, links become an increasingly static declaration of nearby runtime administration conditions. Here's a basic model; these images don't exist:

Container startup. I suggest building the reliance checking code first. For instance, the following content is included in dockerinaction/ch5_ff to approve that a link named "database" has been set at startup:

#!/bin/sh

in the event that [- z ${DATABASE_PORT+x}]

at that point

reverberation, "Link assumed name 'database' was not set!"

exit

else

executive "$@"

fi

You can see this content at work by running the following:

docker run -d - name mydb - uncover 3306 \

alpine:latest nc - l 0.0.0.0:3306

docker run -it - rm \

dockerinaction/ch5_ff reverberation This "shouldn't" work.

docker run -it - rm \

- link mydb:wrongalias \

dockerinaction/ch5_ff reverberation Wrong.

docker run -it - rm \

- link mydb:database \

dockerinaction/ch5_ff reverberation It worked.

docker stop mydb && docker rm mydb

This model content depends on the environment modifications made by Docker when links are created. You'll find these extremely valuable when you start building your own images

Environment modifications

I've referenced that creating a link will add association information to another container. This association information is injected in the new container by adding environment factors and a host name mapping in the DNS abrogate system. We should begin with a guide to inspect the link modifications:

docker run -d - name mydb \

- uncover 2222 - expose 3333 - uncover 4444/udp \

alpine:latest nc - l 0.0.0.0:2222

docker run -it - rm \

- link mydb:database \

dockerinaction/ch5_ff env

docker stop mydb && docker rm mydb

This should yield a square of lines that include the following:

DATABASE_PORT=tcp://172.17.0.23:3333

DATABASE_PORT_3333_TCP=tcp://172.17.0.23:3333

DATABASE_PORT_2222_TCP=tcp://172.17.0.23:2222

DATABASE_PORT_4444_UDP=udp://172.17.0.23:4444

DATABASE_PORT_2222_TCP_PORT=2222

DATABASE_PORT_3333_TCP_PORT=3333

DATABASE_PORT_4444_UDP_PORT=4444

DATABASE_PORT_3333_TCP_ADDR=172.17.0.23

DATABASE_PORT_2222_TCP_ADDR=172.17.0.23

DATABASE_PORT_4444_UDP_ADDR=172.17.0.23

DATABASE_PORT_2222_TCP_PROTO=tcp

DATABASE_PORT_3333_TCP_PROTO=tcp

DATABASE_PORT_4444_UDP_PROTO=udp

DATABASE_NAME=/furious_lalande/database

These are an example of environment factors created for a link. Every one of the factors relating to a particular link will utilize the link moniker as a prefix. There will consistently be a single variable with the _NAME addition that includes the name of the present container, a cut, and the link assumed name. For each port uncovered by the linked container, there will be four individual environment factors with the uncovered port in the variable name. The pat-terns are as per the following:

- <ALIAS>_PORT_<PORT NUMBER>_<PROTOCOL TCP or UDP>_PORT

This variable will essentially contain the port number. That is interested on the grounds that the worth will be contained in the variable name. This could be helpful in case you're filtering the rundown of environment factors for those containing the string TCP_PORT. Doing so would render the rundown of ports.

- <ALIAS>_PORT_<PORT NUMBER>_<PROTOCOL TCP or UDP>_ADDR

The estimations of factors with this example will be the IP address of the container serving the association. In the event that the false name is the equivalent, these should all have a similar worth.

- <ALIAS>_PORT_<PORT NUMBER>_<PROTOCOL TCP or UDP>_PROTO

Like factors with the _PORT postfix, the estimations of these factors are really contained within the variable name. It's significant not to expect that the convention will consistently be TCP. UDP is likewise bolstered.

- <ALIAS>_PORT_<PORT NUMBER>_<PROTOCOL TCP or UDP>

Factors of this structure contain all the past information encoded in URL structure.

One extra environment variable of the structure <ALIAS>_<PORT> will be created and will contain association information for one of the uncovered ports in the URL structure.

These environment factors are accessible for any need application designers may have in connecting to linked containers. In any case, on the off chance that designers have the port and convention predetermined, at that point all they truly need is have name goals and they can depend on DNS for that reason.

Link nature and shortcomings

The nature of links is with the end goal that conditions are directional, static, and nontransitive. Nontransitive implies that linked containers won't inherit links. All the more unequivocally, on the off chance that I link container B to container An, and then link container C to container B, there will be no link from container C to container A.

Links work by determining the system information of a container (IP address and uncovered ports) and then injecting that into another container. Since this is done at container creation time, and Docker can't realize what a container's IP address will be before that container is running, links must be worked from new containers to existing containers. This isn't to say that correspondence is one way but instead that disclosure is one way. This additionally implies if a reliance stops for reasons unknown, the link will be broken. Keep in mind that containers maintain IP address rents just when they're running. So if a container is halted or restarted, it will lose its IP rent and any linked containers will have stale information.

This property has made some censure the estimation of links. The issue is that the more profound a reliance falls flat, the more prominent the domino impact of required container restarts. This may be an issue for a few. However, you should think about the particular effect.

In the event that a basic help like a database falls flat, an accessibility occasion has just happened. The picked administration disclosure technique impacts the recuperation routine. Inaccessible assistance may recoup on the equivalent or different IP address. Links will break just if the IP address changes and will require restarts. This leads some to hop to progressively powerful query systems like DNS.

Yet, even DNS systems have the opportunity to-live (TTL) values that may slow the proliferation of IP address changes. On the off chance that an IP address changes during recuperation, it may feel simpler to utilize DNS, however, recuperation would possibly happen all the more rapidly if associations with the database can fall flat, reconnect endeavors can break, and the DNS TTL lapses in less time than it takes to restart a container. In abandoning container linking, you'll be compelled to empower inter-container correspondence.

On the off chance that your applications are delayed to begin and you have to handle IP address changes on administration recuperation, you might need to consider DNS. Something else, consider the static reliance chain that has been displayed using container links. Building a system that restarts proper containers on a reliance disappointment would be a feasible exercise.

This part centered around single-have Docker networking, and in that degree links are incredibly helpful apparatuses. Most environments length more than one PC. Administration versatility is the possibility that assistance could be running on any machine, in any container in a more significant environment. The thought a system where any procedure may run anyplace is more strong than systems with severe territory constraints. I think this is valid; however, it's essential to show how Docker can be utilized in either circumstance.

Summary

Networking is a broad subject that would take a few books to cover appropriately. This section should assist perusers with an essential understanding of system basics to receive the single-have networking offices given by Docker. In reading this material, you took in the following:

- Docker gives four system container models: shut containers, bridged containers, joined containers, and open containers.

- Docker creates a bridge organize that binds participating containers to one another and to the system that the host is joined to.

- The bridge interface created by Docker can be supplanted or modified using docker command-line alternatives when the Docker daemon is begun.

- Options on the docker run command can be utilized to uncover ports on a container's interface, bind ports uncovered by a container to the host's system interface, and link containers to one another.

- Disabling self-assertive inter-container correspondence is straightforward and manufactures a system with protection top to bottom.

- Using links gives a low-overhead neighborhood administration revelation instrument and maps specific container conditions.

Limiting risk with isolation

Containers provide an isolated process context. They do not complete system virtualization. The semantic distinction may appear to be inconspicuous; however the effect is extreme. This section will give information on how to improve security on your system.

The features discussed in this chapter focus on managing or mitigating the risk of running software. You will learn how to grant resource permissions to containers, open access to shared memory, run programs as specific users, control what changes the container can make to your computer, and how to integrate with other Linux isolation tools. Some of these topics include Linux features that are beyond the scope of this book. In these cases, I try to give you an idea of its purpose and some basic use cases. You can integrate them into Docker.

Another final reminder, Docker and the technology it uses are developing projects. After finding the learning tools presented in this chapter, be sure to check out developments, improvements, and new best practices when creating something of value.

Resource Allocation

Physical system resources, such as memory and processor time, are scarce. If the consumption of process resources on a computer exceeds the available physical resources, the processes will have performance problems and may stop running. Creating a system that creates strong isolation means allocating resources to individual containers.

If you want to make sure the program does not overwhelm others on your computer, it is easiest to limit the resources you can use. Docker provides three fixed menu execution indicators, and docker creates commands to process three different types of resource allocation that you can place in the container. These three are memory, processor and peripherals.

Memory limitations

Memory constraints are the most basic constraint you can place on a container. They limit the amount of memory that processes in the container can use. Memory constraints are useful to ensure that the container cannot overwrite others in one system. You can set a limit using the -m or - indicator in Docker Run or Docker creates commands. The flag has value and unity. The carpet is as follows:

<number><optional unit>where unit = b, k, m or g

With regards to these commands, b alludes to bytes, k to kilobytes, m to megabytes, and g to gigabytes. Put this new information to utilize and fire up a database application that you'll use in different models:

docker run -d—name ch6_mariadb \

—memory 256m \

—cpu-shares 1024

—user nobody \

—cap-drop all \

dockerfile/mariadb

With this command, you install database software called MariaDB and start a container with a memory farthest point of 256 megabytes. You may have seen a couple of additional flags on this command. This section covers each of those, yet you may as of now have the option to think about what they do. Something else to note is that you don't uncover any ports or bind any ports to the host's interfaces. It will be least demanding to interface with this database by linking to it from another container. Before we get to that, I need to ensure you have a full understanding of what occurs here and how to utilize memory limits.

The most significant thing to understand about memory limits is that they're not reservations. They don't ensure that the predetermined measure of memory will be profit capable. They're just assurance from overconsumption.

Before you set up a memory remittance, you ought to think about two things. In the first place, can the software you're running work under the proposed memory stipend? Second, can the system you're running on help the recompense?

The primary inquiry is often hard to reply. Rarely to see minimum necessities distributed with open source software nowadays. Regardless of whether it was, however, you'd need to understand how the memory necessities of the software scale dependent on the size of the information you're asking it to handle. Regardless, individuals will in general, overestimate and modify dependent on experimentation. For the situation of memory-touchy apparatuses like databases, gifted professionals, for example, database administrators can improve instructed assessments and suggestions. And still, afterwards, the inquiry is often replied by another: what amount of memory do you have? And that prompts the subsequent inquiry.

Could the system you're running on help the remittance? It's conceivable to set a memory recompense that is greater than the measure of accessible memory on the system. On has that have swap space (virtual memory that expands onto circle), a container may understand the recompense. It's constantly conceivable to force a recompense that is more prominent than any physical memory asset. In those cases the restrictions of the system will consistently top the container.

Finally, understand that there are a few different ways that software can come up short in the event that it depletes the accessible memory. A few programs may come up short with a memory get to blame, while others may begin writing out-of-memory blunders to their logging. Docker neither distinguishes this issue nor endeavors to moderate the issue. All the better it can do is apply the restart rationale you may have determined using the - restart flag portrayed.

CPU

Processing time is similarly as rare as memory; however, the impact of starvation is execution corruption instead of disappointment. A stopped procedure that is waiting for time on the CPU is as yet working accurately. Be that as it may, a moderate procedure might be more awful than a failing one if it's running some significant information processing program, an income-generating web application, or a back-end administration for your application. Docker gives you a chance to restrict a container's CPU assets in two different ways.

To begin with, you can indicate the general load of a container. Linux utilizes this to deflect mine the level of CPU time the container should utilize comparative with other running containers. That rate is for the aggregate of the computing cycles of all processors accessible to the container.

To set the CPU portions of a container and build up its relative weight, both docker run and docker create offer a - CPU-shares flag. The worth ought to be an integer (which implies you shouldn't cite it). Start another container to perceive how CPU shares work:

docker run -d -P—name ch6_wordpress \

—memory 512m \

—cpu-shares 512 \

—user nobody \

—cap-drop net_raw \

—link ch6_mariadb \

wordpress:4.1

This command will download and run WordPress. It is written in PHP and is a great example of software that is challenging to adapt to security risks. Here we begin with some additional precautions. If you want to see it on your computer, use the ch6_wordpress gateway to obtain the port number (port name <port>) on which the service is running and open http: // localhost: <port>. your web browser Remember that if you are using Boot2Docker, you must use boot2docker ip to determine the IP address of the virtual machine on which Docker is running. When available, replace this value with localhost in the previous URL.

When you run the MariaDB container, set its relative weight (CPU units) to 1024 and WordPress to 512. These configurations create a system where the MariaDB container receives two CPU cycles for each WordPress cycle. If you run the third container and set its value - CPU shares in 2048, you will get half of the processing cycle and MariaDB and WordPress will split the other half in the same proportions as before.

CPU stocks differ from memory constraints in that they only apply if there is a time conflict in the CPU. If other processes and tanks are inactive, the container may explode well beyond its limits. This is desirable because it ensures that processor time is not wasted and that limited processes will occur if the processor needs another process. The purpose of this tool is to prevent a process or set of processes from overloading your computer, not to prevent these processes from executing. The default values will not limit the container, and the container can use 100% of the processor.

Another feature that Docker exhibits is the ability to assign a container to a specific set of processors. Most modern hardware uses multi-core processors. The processor can process as many instructions as hearts simultaneously. This is especially useful when running multiple processes on the same computer.

Changing the context is the task of moving from one process to another. Changing context is expensive and can have a significant impact on the performance of your system. In some cases, it may be appropriate to try to minimize the change from text to text by ensuring that critical processes are never performed in the same set of processor cores. You can use the—cpuset-cpus flag when launching a fixed menu or creating a fixed menu to limit the execution of a container in a specific set of processor cores.

You can see the limitations set by the CPU by working on one of the cores of your computer and reviewing its workload:

Start a container limited to a single CPU and run a load generator docker run -d \

—cpuset-cpus 0 \—name ch6_stresser dockerinaction/ch6_stresser

Start a container to watch the load on the CPU under load docker run -it—rm dockerinaction/ch6_htop

After executing the second command, htop displays the current processes and workload of the available processors. The ch6_stresser tank closes after 30 seconds. Therefore, it is important not to delay the execution of this experiment.

When done with the htop, press Q to exit. Before proceeding, close and remove the container called ch6_stresser:

docker rm -vf ch6_stresser

I thought it was exciting when I first used it. To get the best possible score, repeat this experiment several times using different values for the—cpuset-cpus indicator. If this happens, the procedure will be assigned to different hearts or different sets of hearts. The value can be in the form of a list or range:

- 0,1,2: A list that includes the first three CPU cores
- 0-2: range that includes the first three CPU cores

Access to devices

Devices are the last type of resource. This control is different from the memory constraints and the processor in that access to devices is not a limit. It's more like checking the permission of a resource.

Linux systems have all kinds of peripherals, including hard drives, optical drives, USB drives, a mouse, keyboard, audio devices, and webcams. Containers have access to some of these default devices, and Docker creates others for each container (such as virtual terminals).

Occasionally, it may be important to share other devices between the host and the specified container. Imagine a situation where you run computer vision software that requires webcam access. In this case, you must grant access to the container that runs your software to the webcam device connected to the system. You can use the—digit flag to specify a set of devices to install in a new container. The following example assigns your webcam located in / dev / video0 the same location in a new container. Running this example will only work if you have a webcam in / dev / video0:

docker -it—rm \

—device / dev / video0: / dev / video0 \

ubuntu: last ls -al / dev

The specified value must be a map between the device file in the host operating system and the location in the new container. The device indicator can be set several times to allow access to different devices.

People with custom hardware or their own drivers will find this type of access useful for devices. It's better to modify your home operating system.

Shared memory

Linux provides some tools for sharing memory between processes running on the same computer. This form of inter-process communication (IPC) operates at memory speed. It is often used when a delay associated with a network or pipe based on CPI results in software performance of less than the requirement. Best examples of sharing

Memory-based CPIs are used in scientific computing and some popular database technologies, such as PostgreSQL.

Docker creates a default unique IPC space for each container. Linux IPC partition names share primitive memories, such as shared memory blocks with names and semaphores, as well as message queues. It doesn't matter if you are not sure what they are. Note that these are the tools that Linux programs use to coordinate processing. The IPC namespace prevents processes in the container from accessing memory on the host or other containers.

Divide IPC primitives between containers

I created an image called dockerinactionch6_ipc that contains both the manufacturer and the consumer. They communicate using shared memory. The following will help you understand the problem of running in separate containers:

docker -d -u person - name ch6_ipc_producer \

dockerinaction / ch6_ipc -producer

docker -d -u person - name ch6_ipc_consumer \

dockerinaction / ch6_ipc - Consumer

These commands start two containers. The first creates a message line and begins broadcasting messages on it. The second should pull from the message line and compose the messages to the logs. You can perceive what each is doing by using the following commands to inspect the logs of each:

docker logs ch6_ipc_producer

docker logs ch6_ipc_consumer

Notice that something isn't right with the containers you began. The purchaser never observes any messages on the line. Each procedure utilized a similar key to recognize the mutual memory asset, however they alluded to different memory. The explanation is that every container has its very own common memory namespace.

On the off chance that you have to run programs that communicate with shared memory in different containers, at that point you'll have to join their IPC namespaces with the - ipc banner. The - ipc banner has a container mode that will create another container in the equivalent IPC namespace as another objective container.

Utilize the following commands to test joined IPC namespaces for yourself:

docker rm - v ch6_ipc_consumer

docker - d - name ch6_ipc_consumer \

- ipc container:ch6_ipc_producer \

dockerinaction/ch6_ipc - buyer

These commands revamp the buyer container and reuse the IPC namespace of the ch6_ipc_producer container. This time the shopper ought to have the option to get to the same memory area where the server is writing. You can see that it works by using the following commands to view each other's records:

docker log ch6_ipc_producer

docker log ch6_ipc_consumer

Make sure to tidy up your running containers before moving on:

- The v choice will tidy up volumes.
- The f choice will slaughter the container on the off chance that it is running.
- The rm command takes a rundown of containers.

docker rm - vf ch6_ipc_producer ch6_ipc_consumer

There are clear security ramifications to reusing the common memory namespaces of containers. In any case, this alternative is available in case you need it. Sharing memory between containers is a more secure option than sharing a memory with the host.

Using an open memory container

Memory disengagement is an attractive quality. If you experience a circumstance where you have to work in the equivalent namespace as the remainder of the host, you can do so using an open memory container:

docker - d - name ch6_ipc_producer \

- ipc have \

dockerinaction/ch6_ipc – maker

docker - d - name ch6_ipc_consumer \- - ipc have \dockerinaction/ch6_ipc - customer

These containers will have the option to communicate with one another and some other procedures running on the host PC right away. As should be obvious in this model, you empower this element by specifying host on the - ipc banner. You may utilize this in situations when you have to communicate with a procedure that must sudden spike in demand for the host, yet as a rule you should attempt to keep away from this if conceivable.

Feel free to check the source code for this model. It's a revolting yet straightforward C program. You can find it by checking out the source storehouse linked to from the picture's page on Docker Hub.

You can tidy up the containers you created in this segment using a similar cleanup command

docker rm - vf ch6_ipc_producer ch6_ipc_consumer

Open memory containers are a hazard, yet it's a much better plan to utilize them than to run those procedures outside a container.

Understanding users

Docker begins containers as the root client inside that container as a matter of course. The root client has practically full special access to the condition of the container. Any procedures running as that client inherit those authorizations. It pursues that if there's a bug in one of those procedures, they may harm the container. There are approaches to constrain the harm, however the best method to counteract these kinds of issues isn't to utilize the root client.

There are sensible special cases when using the root client is the best if not just accessible alternative. You utilize the root client for building images and at runtime when there's no other alternative. There are other comparative circumstances when you need to run system administration software inside a container. In those cases, the procedure needs advantaged access not exclusively to the container yet additionally to the host operating system. This area covers the scope of answers for these issues.

Introduction to the Linux client namespace

Linux as of late discharged another client (USR) namespace that permits users in one namespace to be mapped to users in another. The new namespace works like the procedure identifier (PID) namespace.

Docker is not yet integrated into the US namespace. This implies that the container that works with the client ID (number, not name) equivalent to the client on the host device has permissions of the host file similar to that of the client. This isn't an issue. The file system accessible inside a container has been mounted so that changes that are made inside that container will remain inside that container's file system. Be that as it may, this impacts volumes.

At the point when Docker embraces the USR namespace, you'll have the option to outline IDs on the host to client IDs in a container namespace. In this way, I could delineate 1000 on my host to client 2 in the container. This is especially valuable for resolving file authorizations issues in cases like reading and writing to volumes.

Working with the run-as client

Before you create a container, it is decent to have the option to determine what username (and client ID) will be utilized as a matter of course. The picture indicates the default. There's right now no real way to examine a picture to find traits like the default client. This information isn't included on Docker Hub. And there's no command to examine picture metadata.

The nearest include accessible is the docker inspect command. If you missed before, the inspect subcommand shows the metadata of a particular container. Container metadata includes the metadata of the picture it was created from. When you've created a container—how about we call it sway—you can get the username that the container is using with the following commands:

docker create - name weave busybox: latest ping localhost

docker inspect weave

docker inspect - - group "{{.Config.User}}" bounce

On the off chance that the outcome is clear, the container will default to running as the root client. In the event that it isn't clear, either the picture creator explicitly named a default run-as client or you set a particular run-as client when you created the container. The - position or - f alternative utilized in the subsequent command enables you to determine a format to render the yield. For this situation, you've chosen the User field of the Config property of the archive. The worth can be any legitimate GoLang format, so in case you're feeling ready, you can get inventive with the outcomes.

There are issues with this methodology. To start with, the run-as client may be changed by whatever content the picture uses to fire up. These are now and again alluded to as boot or init contents. The metadata returned by docker inspect includes just the setup that the container was begun with. So if the client transforms, it won't be reflected there. Second, you need to create a container from a picture in request to get the information. That can be risky.

Right now, the best way to fix the two issues is look inside the picture. You could expand the picture files after you download them and examine the metadata and init contents by hand, however doing so is tedious and simple to get off-base. For the present, it might be smarter to run a straightforward examination to determine the default client. This will tackle the primary issue however not the second:

docker run - - rm - - entrypoint "" busybox:latest whoami

docker run - - rm - - entrypoint "" busybox:latest id

This exhibits two commands that you may use to determine the default client of a picture (for this situation, busybox:latest). Both the whoami and id commands are com-mon among Linux conveyances, and so they're probably going to be accessible in some random picture. The subsequent command is prevalent because it shows both the name and ID subtleties for the run-as client. Both these commands are mindful to unset the entrypoint of the container. This will ensure that the command indicated after the picture name is the command that is executed by the container. These are poor substitutes for a top of the line picture metadata apparatus, yet they take care of business.

You can completely maintain a strategic distance from the default client issue if you change the run-as client when you create the container. The idiosyncrasy with using this is the username must exist on the picture you're using. Different Linux circulations send with different users predefined, and some picture creators diminish or increase that set. You can get a rundown of accessible users in a picture with the following command:

docker run - rm busybox:latest awk - F: '$0=$1'/and so forth/passwd

I won't broadly expound here; however the Linux client database is put away in a file situated at/and so on/passwd. This command will peruse that file and draw a rundown of the usernames. When you've recognized the client you need to utilize, you can create another container with a particular run-as client. Docker gives the - client or - u banner on docker run and docker create for setting the client. This will set the client to "no one":

docker run - - rm \

- user nobody \

busybox:latest id

This command utilized the "no one" client. That client is normal and intended for use in confined benefits situations like running applications. That was only one model. You can utilize any username defined by the picture here, including root. This solitary starts to expose what you can do with the - u or - client banner. The worth can acknowledge any client or gathering pair. It can likewise acknowledge client and gathering names or IDs. At the point when you use IDs instead of names, the choices begin to open up:

Users and volumes

Now that you've learned how users inside containers share the same user ID space as the users on your host system, you need to learn how those two might interact. The main reason for that interaction is the file permissions on files in volumes. For example, if you're running a Linux terminal, you should be able to use these commands directly; otherwise, you'll need to use the boot2docker ssh command to get a shell in your Boot2Docker virtual machine:

echo "e=mc^2" > garbage

chmod 600 garbage

sudo chown root:root garbage

docker run—rm -v "$(pwd)"/garbage:/test/garbage \

-u nobody \

ubuntu:latest cat /test/garbage

docker run—rm -v "$(pwd)"/garbage:/test/garbage \

-u root ubuntu:latest cat /test/garbage

Outputs: "e=mc^2"

#cleanup that garbage sudo rm -f garbage

The second-to-last docker command should fail with an error message like "Permission denied." But the last docker command should succeed and show you the con-tents of the file you created in the first command. This means that file permissions on files in volumes are respected inside the container. But this also reflects that the user ID space is shared. Both root on the host and root in the container have user ID 0. So, although the container's nobody user with ID 65534 can't access a file owned by root on the host, the container's root user can.

Unless you want a file to be accessible to a container, don't mount it into that con-tainer with a volume.

The good news about this example is that you've seen how file permissions are respected and can solve some more mundane—but practical—operational issues. For example, how do you handle a log file written to a volume?

The preferred way is with volume containers. But even then you need to consider file ownership and permission issues. If logs are written to a volume by a process running as user 1001 and another container tries to access that file as user 1002, then file permissions might prevent the operation.

One way to overcome this obstacle would be to specifically manage the user ID of the running user. You can either edit the image ahead of time by setting the user ID of the user you're going to run the container with, or you can use the desired user and group ID:

```
mkdir logFiles

sudo chown 2000:2000 logFiles

docker run—rm -v "$(pwd)"/logFiles:/logFiles \

-u 2000:2000 ubuntu:latest \

/bin/bash -c "echo This is important info > /logFiles/important.log"

docker run—rm -v "$(pwd)"/logFiles:/logFiles \

-u 2000:2000 ubuntu:latest \ /bin/bash -c "echo More info >> /logFiles/important.log"

sudo rm –r logFiles
```

After running this example, you'll see that the file could be written to the directory that's owned by user 2000. Not only that, but any container that uses a user or group with write access to the directory could write a file in that directory or to the same file if the permissions allow. This trick works for reading, writing, and executing files.

Adjusting OS feature access with capabilities

Docker can adjust the feature authorization of processes within containers. In Linux these feature authorizations are called capabilities, but as native support expands to other operating systems, other back-end implementations would need to be provided. Whenever a process attempts to make a gated system call, the capabilities of that process are checked for the required capability. The call will succeed if the process has the required capability and fail otherwise.

When you create a new container, Docker drops a specific set of capabilities by default. This is done to further isolate the running process from the administrative functions of the operating system. In reading this list of dropped capabilities, you might be able to guess at the reason for their removal. At the time of this writing, this set includes the following:

- SETPCAP—Modify process capabilities
- SYS_MODULE—Insert/remove kernel modules
- SYS_RAWIO—Modify kernel memory
- SYS_PACCT—Configure process accounting
- SYS_NICE—Modify priority of processes
- SYS_RESOURCE—Override resource limits
- SYS_TIME—Modify the system clock
- SYS_TTY_CONFIG—Configure TTY devices
- AUDIT_WRITE—Write the audit log

- AUDIT_CONTROL—Configure audit subsystem
- MAC_OVERRIDE—Ignore kernel MAC policy
- MAC_ADMIN—Configure MAC configuration
- SYSLOG—Modify kernel print behavior
- NET_ADMIN—Configure the network
- SYS_ADMIN—Catchall for administrative functions

The default set of capabilities provided to Docker containers provides a reasonable feature reduction, but there will be times when you need to add or reduce this set fur-ther. For example, the capability NET_RAW can be dangerous. If you wanted to be a bit more careful than the default configuration, you could drop NET_RAW from the list of capabilities. You can drop capabilities from a container using the—cap-drop flag on docker create or docker run.

docker run—rm -u nobody \

ubuntu:latest \

/bin/bash -b"capsh—print | grep net_raw"

docker run—rm -u nobody \

—cap-drop net_raw \

ubuntu:latest \

/bin/bash -b "capsh—print | grep net_raw"

In Linux documentation you'll often see capabilities named in all uppercase and prefixed with CAP_, but that prefix won't work if provided to the capability-management options. Use unprefixed and lowercase names for the best results.

Similar to the—cap-drop flag, the—cap-add flag will add capabilities. If you needed to add the SYS_ADMIN capability for some reason, you'd use a command like the following:

docker run—rm -u nobody \

ubuntu:latest \

/bin/bash –b "capsh—print | grep sys_admin"

docker run—rm -u nobody \

—cap-add sys_admin \

ubuntu:latest \

/bin/bash –b "capsh—print | grep sys_admin"

Like other container-creation options, both—cap-add and—cap-drop can be specified multiple times to add or drop multiple capabilities. These flags can be used to build containers that will let a process perform exactly and only what is required for proper operation.

Running a container with full privileges

In those cases when you need to run a system administration task inside a container, you can grant that container privileged access to your computer. Privileged containers maintain their file system and network isolation but have full access to shared memory and devices and possess full system capabilities. You can perform several interesting tasks, like running Docker inside a container, with privileged containers.

The bulk of the uses for privileged containers is administrative. Take, for example, an environment where the root file system is read-only, or installing software outside a container has been disallowed, or you have no direct access to a shell on the host. If you wanted to run a program to tune the operating system (for something like load balancing) and you had access to run a container on that host, then you could simply run that program in a privileged container.

If you find a situation that can be solved only with the reduced isolation of a privileged container, use the—privileged flag on docker create or docker run to enable this mode:

```
docker run—rm \

—privileged \

ubuntu:latest id

docker run—rm \

—privileged \

ubuntu:latest capsh –print

docker run—rm \

—privileged \

ubuntu:latest ls /dev

docker run—rm \

—privileged \

ubuntu:latest ifconfig
```

Privileged containers are still partially isolated. For example, the network namespace will still be in effect. If you need to tear down that namespace, you'll need to combine this with—net host as well.

Stronger containers with enhanced tools

Docker uses reasonable defaults and a "batteries included" toolset to ease adoption and promote best practices. But you can enhance the containers it builds if you bring additional tools. Tools you can use to harden your containers include AppArmor and SELinux. If you use the LXC container provider, you can also provide custom LXC con-figuration and get into fine-tuning containers. If you're using LXC, you can even use a Linux feature called seccomp-bpf (secure computing with system call filtering).

They bring their own nuances, benefits, and required skillsets. Their use is—without question—worth the effort. Support for each varies by Linux distribution, so you may be in for a bit of work. But once you've adjusted your host configuration, the Docker integration is simpler.

Specifying additional security options

Docker provides a single flag for specifying options for Linux Security Modules (LSM) at container creation or runtime. LSM is a framework that Linux adapted to act as an interface layer between the operating system and security providers.

AppArmor and SELinux are both LSM providers. They both provide mandatory access control (MAC—the system defines access rules) and replace the standard Linux discretionary access control (file owners define access rules).

The flag available on docker run and Docker create—security-opt. This flag can be set multiple times to pass multiple values. The values can currently be one of six formats:

- To set a SELinux user label, use the form label:user:<USERNAME> where <USERNAME> is the name of the user you want to use for the label.

- To set a SELinux role label, use the form label:role:<ROLE> where <ROLE> is the name of the role you want to apply to processes in the container.

- To set a SELinux type label, use the form label:type:<TYPE> where <TYPE> is the type name of the processes in the container.

- To set a SELinux level label, use the form label:level:<LEVEL> where <LEVEL> is the level where processes in the container should run. Levels are specified as low-high pairs. Where abbreviated to the low level only, SELinux will interpret the range as single level.

- To disable SELinux label confinement for a container, use the form label:disable.

- To apply an AppArmor profile on the container, use the form label:apparmor: <PROFILE> where <PROFILE> is the name of the AppArmor profile to use.

As you can guess from these options, SELinux is a labeling system. A set of labels, called a *context*, is applied to every file and system object. A similar set of labels is applied to every user and process. At runtime when a process attempts to interact with a file or system resource, the sets of labels are evaluated against a set of allowed rules. The result of that evaluation determines whether the interaction is allowed or blocked.

The last option will set an AppArmor profile. AppArmor is frequently substituted for SELinux because it works with file paths instead of labels and has a training mode that you can use to passively build profiles based on observed application behavior. These differences are often cited as reasons why AppArmor is easier to adopt and maintain.

Fine-tuning with LXC

Docker was originally built to use a software called Linux Containers (LXC). LXC is a container runtime provider—a tool that actually works with Linux to create namespaces and all the components that go into building a container.

As Docker matured and portability became a concern, a new container runtime called libcontainer was built, replacing LXC. Docker ships with libcontainer by default, but Docker uses an interface layer so that users can change the container exe-cution provider. LXC is a more mature library than libcontainer and provides many additional features that diverge from the goals of Docker. If you're running a system where you can and want to use LXC, you can change the container provider and take advantage of those additional features. Before investing too heavily, know that some of those additional features will greatly reduce the portability of your containers.

To use LXC, you need to install it and make sure the Docker daemon was started with the LXC driver enabled. Use the—exec-driver=lxc option when you start the Docker daemon. The daemon is usually configured to start as one of your system's ser-vices. Check the installation instructions on www.docker.com to find details for your distribution.

Once Docker is configured for LXC, you can use the—lxc-conf flag on docker run or Docker create to set the LXC configuration for a container:

```
docker

run

-d \

—lxc-conf="lxc.cgroup.cpuset.cpus=0,1" \

—name

ch6_stresser dockerinaction/ch6_stresser

docker

run

-it—rm dockerinaction/ch6_htop

docker rm -vf ch6_stresser
```

As when you ran a similar example earlier in this chapter, when you've finished with htop, press Q to quit.

If you decide to use the LXC provider and specify LXC-specific options for your containers, Docker won't be aware of that configuration. Certain configurations can be provided that conflict with the standard container changes made for every Docker container. For this reason, you should always carefully validate the configuration against the actual impact of a container.

Build tanks customized for use in cases

Containers are the most important issues. Reasons and ways for people to use them more than I could list. Therefore, it is important when you use Docker to create a container for your use that you take the time to do so appropriately for the software you are running.

The surest tactic to do this would be to start with the most insulated tank you can build and justify the reasons why these restrictions are weakened. In reality, people tend to be a little more reactive than proactive. Which is why I think Docker finds a good compromise with the default container build. Provide reasonable default values without compromising user productivity.

Docker containers are not the most disengaged of course. Docker does not require you to improve these defaults. This will allow you to do production nonsense if you wish. Because of this, Docker looks a lot more like a tool than a burden and is something that people mostly want to use instead of feeling compelled to do so. For those who do not want to do the nonsense of manufacturing, Docker offers a simple interface to improve tank insulation.

Applications

Applicaions are the reason we use computers. Most applications are programs written by other people and use potentially malicious data. Think about your web browser.

A web browser is an example of a program installed on almost all computers. Communicate with web sites, images, scripts, embedded videos, Flash documents, Java applications and more. You certainly didn't create all this content, and most people didn't contribute to web browser projects. How can you trust your web browser to manage all this content properly?

Well, if an attacker takes control of your web browser (or any other application), you will benefit from all the features of this application and the permission of the user running it. They can destroy your computer, delete your files, install other malware, or even launch attacks on other computers from your computer. Therefore, it is not good to ignore it. The question remains: how do you protect yourself when it comes to the risk you should take?

The best approach is to isolate risk. First, make sure the app works as a restricted user. As a result, files on your computer cannot be modified in the event of a problem. Second, limit the capabilities of your browser system. This ensures that your system configuration is more secure. Third, configure the amount of CPU and memory the application can use. Restrictions can reserve resources so that the system can continue to respond. Lastly, it's a good idea to mark the devices you can access specifically. This will save snipers from your webcam, USB, etc.

High-level system services

High-level system services are slightly different from applications. They are not part of the operating system, but your computer makes sure they are up and running. These tools often come with applications outside the operating system but often require privileged access to the operating system to function properly. They provide important functionality to users and other software in the system. Examples include cron, syslogd, dbus, sshd, and docker.

If you do not know these tools (hopefully not all), then everything is fine. They do things like keep system logs, execute scheduled commands, and provide a way to get a secure shell on the system from the network while Docker manages the containers.

Although the provision of services as a root user is common, some require full privileged access. Use functions to customize your access to the specific functions you need.

Low-level system services

Low-level services control things like a device or a bundle of network power. They require privileged access to the delivered system components (for example, firewall software requires administrative access to a network set).

It's weird to see them running in containers. Tasks such as file system administration, device administration, and network administration are the central concerns of the host. Most software that runs in containers must be portable. Because of this, specific machine tasks like these are not generally for use with tanks.

The best exceptions are short-lived configuration containers. For example, in an environment where all implementations take place with images and Docker containers, you do not want to apply changes to the network stack in the same way as with software. In this case, you can pass the configuration image to the host and make changes with the privileged container. In this case, the risk is reduced because you created the insertion configuration, the container does not run for a long time and changes like these are easily audited.

Summary

This chapter introduces the isolation features provided by Linux and explains how Docker uses them to create configurable containers. Thanks to this knowledge, you can customize the container insulation and use Docker in all use cases. This chapter deals with the following points:

- Docker uses control groups that allow the user to set memory limits, processor weights, and major processor limitations, as well as restrict access to specific devices.

- Each Docker container has its own IPC namespace that can be shared with other containers or with the host to facilitate shared memory communication.

Build automation and advanced image considerations

A Dockerfile is a Doc that contains instructions for building an image. The instructions are followed by the Docker image builder from top to bottom and can be used to change anything about an image. Building images from Dockerfiles makes tasks like adding files to a container from your computer simple one-line instructions. This part covers the basics of working with Dockerfile builds and the best reasons to use them, a lean overview of the instructions, and how to add future build behavior. We'll get started with a familiar example.

Packaging Git with a Dockerfile

Let's start by revisiting the Git on Ubuntu example. Having previously built a similar image by hand, you should recognize many of the details and advantages of working with a Dockerfile.

First, create a new directory and from that directory create a new file with your favorite text editor. Name the new file Dockerfile. Write the following five lines and then save the file:

An example Dockerfile for installing Git on Ubuntu FROM ubuntu:latest

MAINTAINER "dockerinaction@allingeek.com" RUN apt-get install -y git

ENTRYPOINT ["git"]

Before dissecting this example, build a new image from it with the docker build command from the same directory containing the Dockerfile. Tag the new image with auto:

docker build—tag ubuntu-git:auto .

Outputs several lines about steps and output from apt-get and will finally display a message like this:

Successfully built 0bca8436849b

Running this command starts the build process. When it's completed, you should have a brand-new image that you can test. View the list of all your ubuntu-git images and test the newest one with this command:

docker images

The new build tagged "auto" should now appear in the list:

REPOSITORY

TAG

IMAGE ID

CREATED

VIRTUAL SIZE

ubuntu-git

auto

0bca8436849b

10

seconds ago

225.9

MB

ubuntu-git

latest

826c66145a59

10

minutes ago

226.6

MB

ubuntu-git

removed

826c66145a59

10

minutes ago

226.6

MB

ubuntu-git

1.9

3e356394c14e

41

hours ago

226 MB

...

Now you can run a Git command using the new image:

docker run—rm ubuntu-git:auto

These commands demonstrate that the image you built with the Dockerfile works and is functionally equivalent to the one you built by hand. Examine what you did to accomplish this:

First, you created a Dockerfile with four instructions:

- FROM ubuntu:latest—Tells Docker to start from the latest Ubuntu image just as you did when creating the image manually.

- MAINTAINER—Sets the maintainer name and email for the image. Providing this information helps people know who to contact if there's a problem with the image. This was accomplished earlier when you invoked commit.

- RUN apt-get install –y git—Tells the builder to run the provided com-mand to install Git.

- ENTRYPOINT ["git"]—Sets the entrypoint for the image to git.

Dockerfiles, like most scripts, can include comments. The builder will ignore any line beginning with a #. Dockerfiles of any complexity needs to be well documented. In addition to improving Dockerfile maintainability, comments help people audit images that they're considering for adoption and spread best practices.

The only special rule about Dockerfiles is that the first instruction must be FROM. If you're starting from an empty image and your software has no dependencies, or you'll provide all the dependencies, then you can start from a special empty repository named scratch.

After you saved the Dockerfile, you started the build process by invoking the docker build command. The command had one flag set and one argument. The—tag flag (or -t for short) specifies the full repository designation that you want to use for the resulting image. In this case, you used ubuntu-git: auto. The argument that you included at the end was a single period. That argument told the builder the location of the Dockerfile. The period told it to look for the file in the current directory.

The docker build command has another flag,—file (or -f for short), that lets you set the name of the Dockerfile. Dockerfile is the default, but with this flag you could tell the builder to look for a file named BuildScript. This flag sets only the name of the file, not the location of the file. That must always be specified in the location argument.

The builder works by automating the same tasks that you'd use to create images by hand. Each instruction triggers the creation of a new container with the specified modification. After the modification has been made, the builder commits the layer and moves on to the next instruction and container created from the fresh layer.

The builder validated that the image specified by the FROM instruction was installed as the first step of the build. If it were not, Docker would have automatically tried to pull the image. Take a look at the output from the build command that you ran:

Sending build context to Docker daemon 2.058 kB

Sending build context to Docker daemon

Step 0 : FROM ubuntu:latest

—-> b39b81afc8ca

You can see that for this situation the base picture indicated by the FROM guidance is ubuntu:latest, which ought to have just been introduced on your machine. The abridged picture ID of the base picture is remembered for the yield.

The next instruction sets the maintainer information on the image. This creates a new container and then commits the resulting layer. You can see the result of this operation in the output for step 1:

Step 1: MAINTAINER "dockerinaction@allingeek.com."

—-> Running in 938ff06bf8f4

—-> 80a695671201

Removing intermediate container 938ff06bf8f4

The output includes the ID of the container that was created and the ID of the com-mitted layer. That layer will be used as the top of the image for the next instruction, RUN. The output for the RUN instruction was clouded with all the output for the com-mand apt-get install -y git. If you're not interested in this output, you can invoke the docker build command with the—quiet or -q flag. Running in quiet mode will suppress output from the intermediate containers. Without the container output, the RUN step produces output that looks like this:

Step 2: RUN apt-get install -y git

—-> Running in 4438c3b2c049

—-> 1c20f8970532

Removing intermediate container 4438c3b2c049

Although this step usually takes much longer to complete, you can see the instruction and input as well as the ID of the container where the command was run and the ID of the resulting layer. Finally, the ENTRYPOINT instruction performs all the same steps, and the output is similarly unsurprising:

Step 3: ENTRYPOINT git

—-> Running in c9b24b0f035c

—-> 89d726cf3514

Removing intermediate container c9b24b0f035c

A new layer is being added to the resulting image after each step in the build. Although this means you could potentially branch on any of these steps, the more important implication is that the builder can aggressively cache the results of each step. If a problem with the build script occurs after several other steps, the builder can restart from the same position after the problem has been fixed. You can see this in action by breaking your Dockerfile.

Add this line to the end of your Dockerfile:

RUN This will not work

Then rerun the build:

docker build—tag ubuntu-git:auto.

The output will show which steps the builder was able to skip in favor of cached results:

Sending build context to Docker daemon 2.058 kB Sending build context to Docker daemon

Step 0 : FROM ubuntu:latest

—-> b39b81afc8ca

Step 1 : MAINTAINER "dockerinaction@allingeek.com"

—-> Using cache

—-> 80a695671201

Step 2: RUN apt-get install -y git

Note use of cache

—-> Using cache

—-> 1c20f8970532

Step 3: ENTRYPOINT git

—-> Using cache

—-> 89d726cf3514

Step 4: RUN This will not work

—-> Running in f68f0e0418b5

/bin/sh: 1: This: not found

INFO[0001] The command [/bin/sh -c This will not work] returned a non-zero code: 127

Steps 1 through 3 were skipped because they were already built during your last build. Step 4 failed because there's no program with the name This in the container. The container output was valuable in this case because the error message informs you about the specific problem with the Dockerfile. If you fix the problem, the same steps will be skipped again, and the build will succeed, resulting in output like Successfully built d7a8ee0cebd4.

The use of caching during the build can save time if the build includes download-ing material, compiling programs, or anything else that is time-intense. If you need a full rebuild, you can use the—no-cache flag on docker build to disable the use of the cache. But make sure you're disabling the cache only when absolutely required.

This short example uses 4 of the 14 Dockerfile instructions. The example was lim-ited in that all the files that were added to the image were downloaded from the network; it modified the environment in a very limited way and provided a very gen-eral tool. The next example with a more specific purpose and local code will provide a more complete Dockerfile primer.

A Dockerfile primer

Dockerfiles are expressive and easy to understand due to their terse syntax that allows for comments. You can keep track of changes to Dockerfiles with any version-control system. Maintaining multiple versions of an image is as simple as keeping dockerfiles multiple. The Dockerfile build process itself uses extensive caching to aid rapid development and iteration. The builds are traceable and reproducible. They integrate easily with existing build systems and many continuous build and integration tools. With all these reasons to prefer Dockerfile builds to hand-made images, it's important to learn how to write them.

The examples in this section cover each of the Dockerfile instructions except for one. The ONBUILD instruction has a specific use case and is covered in the next section. Every instruction is covered here at an introductory level. For deep coverage of each instruction, the best reference will always be the Docker documentation. online at https://docs.docker.com/reference/builder/. Docker also provides a best practices section in its documentation: http://docs.docker.com/reference/builder.

Metadata instructions

The first example builds a base image and two other images with distinct versions of the mailer program. The purpose of the program is to listen for messages on a TCP port and then send those messages to their intended recipients. The first version of the mailer will listen for messages but only log those messages. The second will send the message as an HTTP POST to the defined URL.

One of the best reasons to use Dockerfile builds is that they simplify copying files from your computer into an image. But it's not always appropriate for certain files to be copied to images. The first thing to do when starting a new project is to define which files should never be copied into any images. You can do this in a file called

.dockerignore. In this example you'll be creating three Dockerfiles, and none needs to be copied into the resulting images.

Use your favorite text editor to create a new file named .dockerignore and copy in the following lines:

.dockerignore

mailer-base.df

mailer-logging.df

mailer-live.df

Save and close the file when you've finished. This will prevent the .dockerignore file, or files named mailer-base.df, mailer-log.df, or mailer-live.df, from ever being copied into an image during a build. With that bit of accounting finished, you can begin working on the base image.

Building a base image helps create common layers. Each of the different versions of the mailer will be built on top of an image called mailer-base. When you create a Dockerfile, you need to keep in mind that each Dockerfile instruction will result in a new layer being created. Instructions should be combined whenever possible because the builder won't perform any optimization. Putting this in practice, create a new file named mailer-base.df and add the following lines:

FROM debian:wheezy

MAINTAINER Jeff Nickoloff "dia@allingeek.com"

RUN groupadd -r -g 2200 example && \

useradd -rM -g example -u 2200 example

ENV APPROOT="/app" \

APP="mailer.sh" \

VERSION="0.6"

LABEL base.name="Mailer Archetype" \

base.version="${VERSION}"

WORKDIR $APPROOT

This file does

ADD . $APPROOT

not exist yet

ENTRYPOINT ["/app/mailer.sh"]

EXPOSE 33333

Do not set the default user in the base otherwise

implementations will not be able to update the image

USER example:example

Put it all together by running the docker build command from the directory where the mailer-base file is located. The -f flag tells the builder which filename to use as input:

docker build -t dockerinaction/mailer-base:0.6 -f mailer-base.df .

Five new instructions are introduced in this Dockerfile. The first new instruction is ENV. ENV sets environment variables for an image similar to the—env flag on docker run or docker create. In this case, a single ENV instruction is used to set three distinct environment variables. That could have been accomplished with three subsequent ENV instructions, but doing so would result in the creation of three layers. You can keep things looking well structured by using a backslash to escape the newline charac-ter (just like shell scripting):

Step 3 : ENV APPROOT "/app" APP "mailer.sh" VERSION "0.6"

—-> Running in 05cb87a03b1b

—-> 054f1747aa8d

Removing intermediate container 05cb87a03b1b

Environment variables declared in the Dockerfile are made available to the resulting image but can be used in other Dockerfile instructions as substitutions. In this Dock-erfile the environment variable VERSION was used as a substitution in the next new instruction, LABEL:

Step 4 : LABEL base.name "Mailer Archetype" base.version "${VERSION}"

—-> Running in 0473087065c4

—-> ab76b163e1d7

Removing intermediate container 0473087065c4

The LABEL instruction is used to define key/value pairs that are recorded as additional metadata for an image or container. This mirrors the—label flag on docker run and docker create. Like the ENV instruction before it, multiple labels can and should be set with a single instruction. In this case, the value of the VERSION environment vari-able was substituted for the value of the base.version label. By using an environment variable in this way, the value of VERSION will be available to processes running inside a container as well as recorded to an appropriate label. This increases maintainability of the Dockerfile because it's more difficult to make inconsistent changes when the value is set in a single location.

The next two instructions are WORKDIR and EXPOSE. These are similar in operation to their corresponding flags on the docker run and docker create commands. An environment variable was substituted for the argument to the WORKDIR command:

Step 5: WORKDIR $APPROOT

—-> Running in 073583e0d554

—-> 363129ccda97

Removing intermediate container 073583e0d554

The result of the WORKDIR instruction will be an image with the default working direc-tory set to /app. Setting WORKDIR to a location that doesn't exist will create that location just like the command-line option. Last, the EXPOSE command creates a layer that opens TCP port 33333:

Step 7: EXPOSE 33333

—-> Running in a6c4f54b2907

—-> 86e0b43f234a

Removing intermediate container a6c4f54b2907

The parts of this Dockerfile that you should recognize are the FROM, MAINTAINER, and ENTRYPOINT instructions. In brief, the FROM instruction sets the layer stack to start from the debian: wheezy image. Any new layers built will be placed on top of that image. The MAINTAINER instruction sets the Author value in the image metadata. The ENTRYPOINT instruction sets the executable to be run at container startup. Here, it's set-ting the instruction to exec ./mailer.sh and using the shell form of the instruction.

The ENTRYPOINT instruction has two forms: the shell form and an exec form. The shell form looks like a shell command with whitespace-delimited arguments. The exec form is a string array where the first value is the command to execute and the remain-ing values are arguments. A command specified using the shell form would be executed as an argument to the default shell. Specifically, the command used in this Dockerfile will be executed as /bin/sh –c 'exec ./mailer.sh' at runtime. Most importantly, if the shell form is used for ENTRYPOINT, then all other arguments pro-vided by the CMD instruction or at runtime as extra arguments to docker run will be ignored. This makes the shell form of ENTRYPOINT less flexible.

You can see from the build output that the ENV and LABEL instructions each resulted in a single step and layer. But the output doesn't show that the environment variable values were substituted correctly. To verify that, you'll need to inspect the image:

docker inspect dockerinaction/mailer-base:0.6

TIP Remember, the docker inspect command can be used to view the metadata of either a container or an image. In this case, you used it to inspect an image.

The relevant lines are these:

"Env": [

"PATH=/usr/local/sbin:/usr/local/bin:/usr/sbin:/usr/bin:/sbin:/bin",

"APPROOT=/app",

"APP=mailer.sh",

"VERSION=0.6"

```
],
...
"Labels": {
"base.name": "Mailer Archetype",
"base.version": "0.6"
},
...
"WorkingDir": "/app"
```

The metadata makes it clear that the environment variable substitution works. You can use this form of substitution in the ENV, ADD, COPY, WORKDIR, VOLUME, EXPOSE, and USER instructions.

The last commented line is a metadata instruction USER. It sets the user and group for all further build steps and containers created from the image. In this case, setting it in a base image would prevent any downstream Dockerfiles from installing software. That would mean that those Dockerfiles would need to flip the default back and forth for permission. Doing so would create at least two additional layers. The better approach would be to set up the user and group accounts in the base image and let the implementations set the default user when they've finished building.

The most curious thing about this Dockerfile is that the ENTRYPOINT is set to a file that doesn't exist. The entrypoint will fail when you try to run a container from this base image. But now that the entrypoint is set in the base image, that's one less layer that will need to be duplicated for specific implementations of the mailer. The next two Dockerfiles build mailer.sh different implementations.

File system instructions

Images that include custom functionality will need to modify the file system. A Dockerfile defines three instructions that modify the file system: COPY, VOLUME, and ADD. The Dockerfile for the first implementation should be placed in a file named mailer-logging.df:

```
FROM dockerinaction/mailer-base:0.6
COPY ["./log-impl", "${APPROOT}"]
RUN chmod a+x ${APPROOT}/${APP} && \
chown example:example /var/log
USER example:example
VOLUME ["/var/log"]
CMD ["/var/log/mailer.log"]
```

In this Dockerfile you used the image generated from mailer-base as the starting point. The three new instructions are COPY, VOLUME, and CMD. The COPY instruction will copy files from the file system where the image is being built into the build container. The COPY instruction takes at least two arguments. The last argument is the destina-tion, and all other arguments are source files. This instruction has only one unexpected feature: any files copied will be copied with file ownership set to root. This is the case regardless of how the default user is set before the COPY instruction. It's better to delay any RUN instructions to change file ownership until all the files that you need to update have been copied into the image.

The COPY instruction will honor both shell style and exec style arguments, just like ENTRYPOINT and other instructions. But if any of the arguments contains whitespace, then you'll need to use the exec form.

TIP Using the exec (or string array) form wherever possible is the best prac-tice. At a minimum, a Dockerfile should be consistent and avoid mixing styles.

This will make your Dockerfiles more readable and ensure that instructions behave as you'd expect without detailed understanding of their nuances.

The second new instruction is VOLUME. This behaves exactly as you'd expect if you understand what the—volume flag does on a call to docker run or docker create. Each value in the string array argument will be created as a new volume definition in the resulting layer. Defining volumes at image build time is more limiting than at run-time. You have no way to specify a bind-mount volume or read-only volume at image build time. This instruction will only create the defined location in the file system and then add a volume definition to the image metadata.

The last instruction in this Dockerfile is CMD. CMD is closely related to ENTRYPOINT instruction. They both take either shell or exec forms and are both used to start a process within a container. But there are a few important differences.

The CMD command represents an argument list for the entrypoint. The default entrypoint for a container is /bin/sh. If no entrypoint is set for a container, then the val-ues are passed, because the command will be wrapped by the default entrypoint. But if the entrypoint is set and is declared using the exec form, then you use CMD to set default arguments. This base for this Dockerfile defines the ENTRYPOINT as the mailer com-mand. This Dockerfile injects an implementation of mailer.sh and defines a default argument. The argument used is the location that should be used for the log file.

Before building the image, you'll need to create the logging version of the mailer program. Create a directory at ./log-impl. Inside that directory create a file named mailer.sh and copy the following script into the file:

```
#!/bin/sh

printf "Logging Mailer has started.\n"

while true

do

MESSAGE=$(nc -l -p 33333)

printf "[Message]: %s\n" "$MESSAGE" > $1
```

sleep 1

done

The structural specifics of this script are unimportant. All you need to know is that this script will start a mailer daemon on port 33333 and write each message that it receives to the file specified in the first argument to the program. Use the following command to build the mailer-logging image from the directory containing mailer-logging.df:

docker build -t dockerinaction/mailer-logging -f mailer-logging.df .

The results of this image build should be anti-climactic. Go ahead and start up a named container from this new image:

docker run -d—name logging-mailer dockerinaction/mailer-logging

The logging mailer should now be built and running. Containers that link to this implementation will have their messages logged to /var/log/mailer.log. That's not very interesting or useful in a real-world situation, but it might be handy for testing.

An implementation that sends email would be better for operational monitoring.

The next implementation example uses the Simple Email Service provided by Amazon Web Services to send email. Get started with another Dockerfile. Name this file mailer-live.df:

FROM dockerinaction/mailer-base:0.6

ADD ["./live-impl", "${APPROOT}"]

RUN apt-get update && \

apt-get install -y curl python && \

curl "https://bootstrap.pypa.io/get-pip.py" -o "get-pip.py" && \

python get-pip.py && \

pip install awscli && \

rm get-pip.py && \

chmod a+x "${APPROOT}/${APP}"

RUN apt-get install -y netcat

USER example:example

CMD ["mailer@dockerinaction.com", "pager@dockerinaction.com"]

This Dockerfile includes one new instruction, ADD. The ADD instruction operates simi-larly to the COPY instruction with two important differences. The ADD instruction will

▪ Fetch remote source files if a URL is specified

▪ Extract the files of any source determined to be an archive file

The auto-extraction of archive files is the more useful of the two. Using the remote fetch feature of the ADD instruction isn't good practice. The reason is that although the feature is convenient, it provides no mechanism for cleaning up unused files and results in additional layers. Instead, you should use a chained RUN instruction like the third instruction of mailer-live.df.

The other instruction to note in this Dockerfile is the CMD instruction, where two arguments are passed. Here you're specifying the From and To fields on any emails that are sent. This differs from mailer-logging.df, which specifies only one argument.

Next, create a new subdirectory named live-impl under the location containing mailer-live.df. Add the following script to a file in that directory named mailer.sh:

```
#!/bin/sh

printf "Live Mailer has started.\n"

while true

do

MESSAGE=$(nc -l -p 33333)

aws ses send-email—from $1 \

—destination {\"ToAddresses\":[\"$2\"]} \

—message "{\"Subject\":{\"Data\":\"Mailer Alert\"},\ \"Body\":{\"Text\":{\"Data\":\"$MESSAGE}\"}}}"

sleep 1

done
```

The key takeaway from this script is that, like the other mailer implementation, it will wait for connections on port 33333, take action on any received messages, and then sleep for a moment before waiting for another message. This time, though, the script will send an email using the Simple Email Service command-line tool. Build and start a container with these two commands:

```
docker build -t dockerinaction/mailer-live -f mailer-live.df

docker run -d—name live-mailer dockerinaction/mailer-live
```

If you link a watcher to these, you'll find that the logging mailer works as advertised. But the live mailer seems to be having difficulty connecting to the Simple Email Service to send the message. With a bit of investigation, you'll eventually realize that the container is misconfigured. The aws program requires certain environment variables to be set.

You'll need to set AWS_ACCESS_KEY_ID, AWS_SECRET_ACCESS_KEY, and AWS_DEFAULT_REGION in order to get this example working. Discovering execution preconditions this way can be frustrating for users. Section 8.4.1 details an image design pattern that reduces this friction and helps adopters.

Before you get to design patterns, you need to learn about the final Dockerfile instruction. Remember, not all images contain applications. Some are built as plat-forms for downstream images. Those cases specifically benefit from the ability to inject downstream build-time behavior.

Injecting downstream build-time behavior

Only one Dockerfile instruction isn't covered in the primer. That instruction is ONBUILD. The ONBUILD instruction defines instructions to execute if the resulting image is used as a base for another build. For example, you could use ONBUILD instruc-tions to compile a program that's provided by a downstream layer. The upstream Dockerfile copies the contents of the build directory into a known location and then compiles the code at that location. The upstream Dockerfile would use a set of instructions like this:

```
ONBUILD COPY [".", "/var/myapp"]

ONBUILD RUN go build /var/myapp
```

The instructions following ONBUILD instructions aren't executed when their contain-ing Dockerfile is built. Instead, those instructions are recorded in the resulting image's metadata under ContainerConfig.OnBuild. The previous instructions would result in the following metadata inclusions:

```
...

"ContainerConfig": {

...

"OnBuild": [

"COPY [\".\", \"/var/myapp\"]",

"RUN go build /var/myapp"

],

...
```

This metadata is carried forward until the resulting image is used as the base for another Dockerfile build. When a downstream Dockerfile uses the upstream image (the one with the ONBUILD instructions) in a FROM instruction, those ONBUILD instruc-tions are executed after the FROM instruction and before the next instruction in a Dockerfile.

Consider the following example to see exactly when ONBUILD steps are injected into a build. You need to create two Dockerfiles and execute two build commands to get the full experience. First, create an upstream Dockerfile that defines the ONBUILD instructions. Name the file base.df and add the following instructions:

```
FROM busybox:latest
```

WORKDIR /app

RUN touch /app/base-evidence

ONBUILD RUN ls -al /app

You can see that the image resulting from building base.df will add an empty file named base-evidence to the /app directory. The ONBUILD instruction will list the con-tents of the /app directory at build time, so it's important that you not run the build in quiet mode if you want to see exactly when changes are made to the file system.

The next file to create is the downstream Dockerfile. When this is built, you will be able to see exactly when the changes are made to the resulting image. Name the file downstream.df and include the following contents:

FROM dockerinaction/ch8_onbuild

RUN touch downstream-evidence

RUN ls -al .

This Dockerfile will use an image named dockerinaction/ch8_onbuild as a base, so that's the repository name you'll want to use when you build the base. Then you can see that the downstream build will create a second file and then list the contents of /app again.

With these two files in place, you're ready to start building. Run the following to create the upstream image:

docker build -t dockerinaction/ch8_onbuild -f base.df .

The output of the build should look like this:

Sending build context to Docker daemon 3.072 kB

Sending build context to Docker daemon

Step 0 : FROM busybox:latest

—-> e72ac664f4f0

Step 1 : WORKDIR /app

—-> Running in 4e9a3df4cf17

—-> a552ff53eedc

Removing intermediate container 4e9a3df4cf17 Step 2 : RUN touch /app/base-evidence—-> Running in 352819bec296

—-> bf38c3e396b2

Removing intermediate container 352819bec296 Step 3 : ONBUILD run ls -al /app—-> Running in fd70cef7e6ca

—-> 6a53dbe28364

Removing intermediate container fd70cef7e6ca Successfully built 6a53dbe28364

Then build the downstream image with this command:

docker build -t dockerinaction/ch8_onbuild_down -f downstream.df .

The results clearly show when the ONBUILD instruction (from the base image) is executed:

Sending build context to Docker daemon 3.072 kB

Sending build context to Docker daemon

Step 0 : FROM dockerinaction/ch8_onbuild

Executing 1 build triggers Trigger 0, RUN ls -al /app Step 0 : RUN ls -al /app

—-> Running in dd33ddea1fd4 total 8

drwxr-xr-x

2

root

root

4096

Apr 20

23:08 .

drwxr-xr-x

30

root

root

4096

Apr

20

23:08 ..

-rw-r—r—

1

root

root

0

Apr

20

23:08 base-evidence

—-> 92782cc4e1f6

Removing intermediate container dd33ddea1fd4 Step 1 : RUN touch downstream-evidence—-> Running in 076b7e110b6a

—-> 92cc1250b23c

Removing intermediate container 076b7e110b6a

Step 2 : RUN ls -al .

—-> Running in b3fe2daac529

total 8

drwxr-xr-x

2

root

root

4096

Apr 20

23:08 .

drwxr-xr-x

31

root

root

4096

Apr 20

23:08 ..

-rw-r—r—

1

root

root

0

Apr 20

23:08 base-evidence

-rw-r—r—

1

root

root

0

Apr 20

23:08 downstream-evidence

—-> 55202310df7b

Removing intermediate container b3fe2daac529 Successfully built 55202310df7b

You can see the builder registering the ONBUILD instruction with the container meta-data in step 3 of the base build. Later, the output of the downstream image build shows which triggers (ONBUILD instructions) it has inherited from the base image. The builder discovers and processes the trigger immediately after step 0, the FROM instruc-tion. The output then includes the result of the RUN instruction specified by the trigger. The output shows that only evidence of the base build is present. Later, when the builder moves on to instructions from the downstream Dockerfile, it lists the con-tents of the /app directory again. The evidence of both changes is listed.

That example is more illustrative than it is useful. You should consider browsing Docker Hub and looking for images tagged with onbuild suffixes to get an idea about how this is used in the wild. Here are a few of my favorites:

- https://registry.hub.docker.com/_/python/
- https://registry.hub.docker.com/_/golang/
- https://registry.hub.docker.com/_/node/

Using startup scripts and multiprocess containers

Whatever tooling you choose to use, you'll always need to consider a few image design aspects. You'll need to ask yourself whether the software running in your container requires any startup assistance, supervision, monitoring, or coordination with other in-container processes. If so, then you'll need to include a startup script or initialization program with the image and install it as the entrypoint.

Environmental preconditions validation

Failure modes are difficult to communicate and can catch someone off guard if they occur at arbitrary times. If container configuration problems always cause failures at startup time for an image, users can be confident that a started container will keep running.

In software design, failing fast and precondition validation are best practices. It makes sense that the same should hold true for image design. The preconditions that should be evaluated are assumptions about the context.

Docker containers have no control over the environment where they're created. They do, however, have control of their own execution. An image author can solidify the user experience of their image by introducing environment and dependency vali-dation prior to execution of the main task. A container user will be better informed about the requirements of an image if containers built from that image fail fast and display descriptive error messages.

For example, WordPress requires certain environment variables to be set or container links to be defined. Without that context, WordPress would be unable to connect to the database where the blog data is stored. It would make no sense to start WordPress in a container without access to the data it's supposed to serve. WordPress images use a script as the container entrypoint. That script validates that the container context is set in a way that's compatible with the contained version of WordPress. If any required condition is unmet (a link is undefined or a variable is unset), then the script will exit before starting WordPress, and the container will stop unexpectedly.

This type of startup script is generally use-case specific. If you're packaging a specific piece of software in an image, you'll need to write the script yourself. Your script should validate as much of the assumed context as possible. This should include the following:

- Presumed links (and aliases)
- Environment variables
- Network access
- Network port availability
- Root file system mount parameters (read-write or read-only)
- Volumes
- Current user

You can use whatever scripting or programming language you want to accomplish the task. In the spirit of building minimal images, it's a good idea to use a language or scripting tool that's already included with the image. Most base images ship with a shell like /bin/sh or /bin/bash. Shell scripts are the most common for that reason.

Consider the following shell script that might accompany a program that depends on a web server. At container startup, this script enforces that either another container has been linked to the web alias and has exposed port 80 or the WEB_HOST environment variable has been defined:

```
#!/bin/bash

set -e

if [ -n "$WEB_PORT_80_TCP" ]; then

if [ -z "$WEB_HOST" ]; then

WEB_HOST='web'

else

echo >&2 '[WARN]: Linked container, "web" overridden by $WEB_HOST.' echo >&2 "===> Connecting to WEB_HOST ($WEB_HOST)"

fi

fi

if [ -z "$WEB_HOST" ]; then

echo >&2 '[ERROR]: specify a linked container, "web" or WEB_HOST environ-

ment variable'

exit 1

fi

exec "$@" # run the default command
```

If you're unfamiliar with shell scripting, this is an appropriate time to learn it. The topic is approachable, and there are several excellent resources for self-directed learn-ing. This specific script uses a pattern where both an environment variable and a container link are tested. If the environment variable is set, the container link will be ignored. Finally, the default command is executed.

Images that use a startup script to validate configuration should fail fast if someone uses them incorrectly, but those same containers may fail later for other reasons. You can combine startup scripts with container restart policies to make reliable containers. But container restart policies are not perfect solutions. Containers that have failed and are waiting to be restarted aren't running. This means that an operator won't be able to execute another process within a container that's in the middle of a backoff window. The solution to this problem involves making sure the container never stops.

Initialization processes

UNIX-based computers usually start an initialization (init) process first. That init pro-cess is responsible for starting all the other system services, keeping them running, and shutting them down. It's often appropriate to use an init-style system to launch, manage, restart, and shut down container processes with a similar tool.

Init processes typically use a file or set of files to describe the ideal state of the ini-tialized system. These files describe what programs to start when to start them, and what actions to take when they stop. Using an init process is the best way to launch

multiple programs, clean up orphaned processes, monitor processes, and automati-cally restart any failed processes.

If you decide to adopt this pattern, you should use the init process as the entry-point of your application-oriented Docker container. Depending on the init program you use, you may need to prepare the environment beforehand with a startup script.

For example, the runit program doesn't pass environment variables to the pro-grams it launches. If your service uses a startup script to validate the environment, it won't have access to the environment variables it needs. The best way to fix that problem might be to use a startup script for the runit program. That script might write the environment variables to some file so the startup script for your application can access them.

There are several open source init programs. Full-featured Linux distributions ship with heavyweight and full-featured init systems like SysV, Upstart, and systemd. Linux Docker images like Ubuntu, Debian, and CentOS typically have their init programs installed but nonfunctioning out of the box. These can be complex to con-figure and typically have hard dependencies on resources that require root access. For that reason, the community has tended toward the use of lighter-weight init programs.

Popular options include runit, BusyBox init, Supervisord, and DAEMON Tools. These all attempt to solve similar problems, but each has its benefits and costs. Using an init process is a best practice for application containers, but there's no perfect init program for every use case. When evaluating any init program for use in a container, consider these factors:

- Additional dependencies the program will bring into the image
- File sizes
- How the program passes signals to its child processes (or if it does)
- Required user access
- Monitoring and restart functionality (backoff-on-restart features are a bonus)
- Zombie process cleanup features

Whichever init program you decide on, make sure your image uses it to boost adopter confidence in containers created from your image. If the container needs to fail fast to communicate a configuration problem, make sure the init program won't hide that failure.

These are the tools at your disposal to build images that result in durable contain-ers. Durability is not security, and although adopters of your durable images might trust that they will keep running as long as they can, they shouldn't trust your images until they've been hardened.

Building hardened application images

As an image author, it's difficult to anticipate all the scenarios where your work will be used. For that reason, harden the images you produce whenever possible. *Hardening an image* is the process of shaping it in a way that will reduce the attack surface inside any Docker containers based on it.

A general strategy for hardening an application image is to minimize the software included with it. Naturally, including fewer components reduces the number of potential vulnerabilities. Further, building minimal images keeps image download times short and helps adopters deploy and build containers more rapidly.

There are three things that you can do to harden an image beyond that general strategy. First, you can enforce that your images are built from a specific image. Second, you can make sure that regardless of how containers are built from your image, they will have a sensible default user. Last, you should eliminate a common path for root user escalation.

Content addressable image identifiers

The image identifiers discussed so far in this book are all designed to allow an author to update images in a transparent way to adopters. An image author chooses what image their work will be built on top of, but that layer of transparency makes it diffi-cult to trust that the base hasn't changed since it was vetted for security problems. Since Docker 1.6, the image identifier has included an optional digest component.

An image ID that includes the digest component is called a content addressable image identifier (CAIID). This refers to a specific layer containing specific content, instead of simply referring to a particular and potentially changing layer.

Now image authors can enforce a build from a specific and unchanging starting point as long as that image is in a version 2 repository. Append an @ symbol followed by the digest in place of the standard tag position.

Use docker pull and observe the line labeled digest in the output to discover the digest of an image from a remote repository. Once you have the digest, you can use it as the identifier to FROM instructions in a Dockerfile. For example, consider the follow-ing, which uses a specific snapshot of debian:jessie as a base:

```
docker pull debian:jessie

# Output:

# ...

# Digest: sha256:d5e87cfcb730...

# Dockerfile:
```

```
FROM debian@sha256:d5e87cfcb730...

...
```

Regardless of when or how many times the Dockerfile is used to build an image, they will all use the content identified with that CAIID as their base. This is particularly use-ful for incorporating known updates to a base into your images and identifying the exact build of the software running on your computer.

Although this doesn't directly limit the attack surface of your images, using CAIIDs will prevent it from changing without your knowledge. The next two practices do address the attack surface of an image.

User permissions

The known container breakout tactics all rely on having system administrator privi-leges inside the container. This section covers standard practices for establishing reasonable user defaults for images.

First, please understand that a Docker user can always override image defaults when they create a container. For that reason, there's no way for an image to prevent containers from running as the root user. The best things an image author can do are create other non-root users and establish a non-root default user and group.

Dockerfile includes a USER instruction that sets the user and group in the same way you would with the docker run or docker create command. The instruction itself was covered in the Dockerfile primer. This section is about considerations and best practices.

The best practice and general guidance is to drop privileges as soon as possible. You can do this with the USER instruction before any containers are ever created or with a startup script that's run at container boot time. The challenge for an image author is to determine the earliest appropriate time.

If you drop privileges too early, the active user may not have permission to complete the instructions in a Dockerfile. For example, this Dockerfile won't build correctly:

```
FROM busybox:latest

USER 1000:1000

RUN touch /bin/busybox
```

Building that Dockerfile would result in step 2 failing with a message like touch: /bin/busybox: Permission denied. File access is obviously impacted by user changes. In this case UID 1000 doesn't have permission to change the ownership of the file /bin/busybox. That file is currently owned by root. Reversing the second and third lines would fix the build.

The second timing consideration is the permissions and capabilities needed at runtime. If the image starts a process that requires administrative access at runtime, then it would make no sense to drop user access to a non-root user before that point. For example, any process that needs access to the system port range (1–1024) will need to be started by a user with administrative (at the very least CAP_NET_ADMIN) privileges. Consider what happens when you try to bind to port 80 as a non-root user with Netcat. Place the following Dockerfile in a file named UserPermissionDenied.df:

```
FROM busybox:latest

USER 1000:1000

ENTRYPOINT ["nc"]

CMD ["-l", "-p", "80", "0.0.0.0"]
```

Build the Dockerfile and run the resulting image in a container. In this case the user (UID 1000) will lack the required privileges, and the command will fail:

```
docker

build \

-t

dockerinaction/ch8_perm_denied \

-f

UserPermissionDenied.df \

.



docker

run dockerinaction/ch8_perm_denied


# Output:

# nc: bind: Permission denied
```

In cases like these, you may see no benefit in changing the default user. Instead, any startup scripts that you build should take on the responsibility of dropping permis-sions as soon as possible. The last question is which user should be dropped into?

Docker currently lacks support for the Linux USR namespace. This means that UID 1000 in the container is UID 1000 on the host machine. All other aspects apart from the UID and GID are segregated, just as they would be between computers. For exam-ple, UID 1000 on your laptop might be your username, but the username associated with UID 1000 inside a BusyBox container is default.

Ultimately, until Docker adopts the USR namespace, it will be difficult for image authors to know which UID/GID is appropriate to use. The only thing we can be sure of is that it's inappropriate to use common or system-level UID/GIDs where doing so can be avoided. With that in mind, it's still burdensome to use raw UID/GID numbers. Doing so makes scripts and Dockerfiles less readable. For that reason, it's typical for image authors to include RUN instructions that create users and groups used by the image. The following is the second instruction in a Postgres Dockerfile:

```
# add our user and group first to make sure their IDs get assigned

# consistently, regardless of whatever dependencies get added

RUN groupadd -r postgres && useradd -r -g postgres postgres
```

This instruction simply creates a postgres user and group with automatically assigned UID and GID. The instruction is placed early in the Dockerfile so that it will always be cached between rebuilds, and the IDs remain consistent regardless of other users that are added as part of the build. This user and group could then be used in a USER instruction. That would make for a safer default. But Postgres containers require ele-vated privileges during startup. Instead, this particular image uses a su or sudo-like program called gosu to start the Postgres process as the postgres user. Doing so makes sure that the process runs without administrative access in the container.

User permissions are one of the more nuanced aspects of building Docker images. The general rule you should follow is that if the image you're building is designed to run some specific application code, then the default execution should drop user per-missions as soon as possible.

A properly functioning system should be reasonably secure with reasonable defaults in place. Remember, though, an application or arbitrary code is rarely perfect and could be intentionally malicious. For that reason, you should take additional steps to reduce the attack surface of your images.

SUID and SGID permissions

The last hardening action to cover is the mitigation of SUID or SGID permissions. The well-known file system permissions (read, write, execute) are only a portion of the set defined by Linux. In addition to those, two are of particular interest: SUID and SGID.

These two are similar in nature. An executable file with the SUID bit set will always execute as its owner. Consider a program like /usr/bin/passwd, which is owned by the root user and has the SUID permission set. If a non-root user like bob executes passwd, he will execute that program as the root user. You can see this in action by building an image from the following Dockerfile:

FROM ubuntu:latest

Set the SUID bit on whoami RUN chmod u+s /usr/bin/whoami

Create an example user and set it as the default

RUN adduser—system—no-create-home—disabled-password—disabled-login \—shell /bin/sh example

USER example

Set the default to compare the container user and

the effective user for whoami

CMD printf "Container running as: %s\n" $(id -u -n) && \

printf "Effectively running whoami as: %s\n" $(whoami)

Once you've created the Dockerfile, you need to build an image and run the default command in a container:

docker build -t dockerinaction/ch8_whoami .

docker run dockerinaction/ch8_whoami

Doing so prints results like these to the terminal:

Container running as: example

Effectively running whoami as: root

The output of the default command shows that even though you've executed the whoami command as the example user, it's running from the context of the root user. The SGID works similarly. The difference is that the execution will be from the owning group's context, not the owning user.

Running a quick search on your base image will give you an idea of how many and which files have these permissions:

docker run—rm debian:wheezy find / -perm +6000 -type f

It will display a list like this:

/sbin/unix_chkpwd

/bin/ping6

/bin/su

/bin/ping

/bin/umount

/bin/mount

/usr/bin/chage

/usr/bin/passwd

/usr/bin/gpasswd

/usr/bin/chfn

/usr/bin/newgrp

/usr/bin/wall

/usr/bin/expiry

/usr/bin/chsh

/usr/lib/pt_chown

This command will find all of the SGID files:

docker run—rm debian:wheezy find / -perm +2000 -type f

The resulting list is much shorter:

/sbin/unix_chkpwd

/usr/bin/chage

/usr/bin/wall

/usr/bin/expiry

Each of the listed files in this particular image has the SUID or SGID permission, and a bug in any of them could be used to compromise the root account inside a container. The good news is that files that have either of these permissions set are typically useful during image builds but rarely required for application use cases. If your image is going to be running software that's arbitrary or externally sourced, it's a best practice to mitigate this risk of escalation.

Fix this problem and either delete all these files or unset their SUID and SGID per-missions. Taking either action would reduce the image's attack surface. The following Dockerfile instruction will unset the SUID and GUID permissions on all files currently in the image:

RUN for i in $(find / -type f \(-perm +6000 -o -perm +2000 \)); \ do chmod ug-s $i; done

Hardening images will help users build hardened containers. Although it's true that no hardening measures will protect users from intentionally building weak containers, those measures will help the more unsuspecting and most common type of user.

Summary

Most Docker images are built automatically from Dockerfiles. This chapter covers the build automation provided by Docker and Dockerfile best practices. Before moving on, make sure that you've understood these key points:

- Docker provides an automated image builder that reads instructions from Dockerfiles.
- Each Dockerfile instruction results in the creation of a single image layer.
- Merge instructions whenever possible to minimize the size of images and layer count.
- Dockerfiles include instructions to set image metadata like the default user, exposed ports, default command, and entrypoint.
- Other Dockerfile instructions copy files from the local file system or remote location into the produced images.
- Downstream builds inherit build triggers that are set with ONBUILD instructions in an upstream Dockerfile.
- Startup scripts should be used to validate the execution context of a container before launching the primary application.
- A valid execution context should have appropriate environment variables set, network dependencies available, and an appropriate user configuration.
- Init programs can be used to launch multiple processes, monitor those pro-cesses, reap orphaned child processes, and forward signals to child processes.

- Images should be hardened by building from content addressable image identifiers, creating a non-root default user, and disabling or removing any executable with SUID or SGID permissions.

Conclusions

Both Docker Machine and Docker Swarm provide functionality that enhances the applications for the Docker Engine. These and other related technologies will help you apply what you have learned in this book as you grow from using Docker on a single computer into managing fleets of containers distributed across many computers. It is important to have a thorough understanding of these points as you grow into this space:

▪A user can use Docker Machine to create a local virtual machine or machine in the cloud with a single create command.

▪The Docker Machine env and config subcommands can be used to configure Docker clients to work with remote Docker Engines that were provisioned with Docker Machine.

▪Docker Swarm is a protocol that is backward-compatible with the Docker Remote API and provides clustering facilities over a set of member nodes.

▪A Swarm manager program implements the Swarm API and handles container scheduling for the cluster.

▪Docker Machine provides flags for provisioning both Swarm nodes and managers.

▪Docker Swarm provides three different scheduling algorithms that can be tuned through the use of filters.

▪Labels and other default attributes of a Docker Engine can be used as filtering criteria via container scheduling constraints.

▪Container scheduling affinities can be used to place containers on the same host as other containers or images that match a provided pattern or expression.

▪When any Docker client is configured to communicate with a Swarm endpoint, that client will interact with the entire Swarm as if it were a single Docker machine.

▪Docker Swarm will schedule dependent containers on the same node until multi-host networking is released or you provide another service-discovery mechanism and disable the dependency Swarm filter.

▪Multi-host networking will abstract container locality from the concerns of applications within Docker containers. Each container will be a host on the overlay network

Introduction to Kubernetes

In this book, we will assist you with learning to assemble and manage Kubernetes bunches. You will be given a portion of the basic container ideas and the operational setting, at every possible opportunity. All through the book, you'll be given examples that you can apply as you progress through the book. Before the finish of the book, you ought to have a strong foundation and even dabble in a portion of the more advance points, for example, federation and security.

This chapter will give a brief overview of containers and how they fill in as well as why management and orchestration are important to your business and/or venture team. The chapter will also give a brief overview of how Kubernetes orchestration can enhance our container management strategy and how we can get a basic Kubernetes group up, running, and ready for container deployments.

This chapter will incorporate the accompanying points:

- Presenting container operations and management
- Why container management is important?
- The advantages of Kubernetes
- Downloading the latest Kubernetes
- Installing and starting up another Kubernetes bunch
- The segments of a Kubernetes bunch
- A brief overview of containers

In recent years, containers have developed in popularity out of control. You would be hard-squeezed to attend an IT gathering without finding popular sessions on Docker or containers in general.

Docker lies at the heart of the mass adoption and the energy in the container space. As Malcom McLean upset the physical transportation world during the 1950s by creating a standardized dispatching container, which is utilized today for everything from ice shape trays to automobiles (you can allude to more details about this in point 1 in the References area at the finish of the chapter), Linux containers are changing the software advancement world by making application conditions portable and steady across the infrastructure landscape. As an organization, Docker has taken the current container innovation to another level by making it easy to execute and replicate across situations and suppliers.

What is a container?

At the center of the container, innovations are control gatherings (cgroups) and namespaces. Additionally, Docker utilizes association filesystems for added advantages to the container improvement process.

Cgroups work by allowing the host to share and also limit the assets each procedure or container can devour. This is important for both, asset utilization and security, as it counteracts denial-of-administration attacks on the host's hardware assets. Several containers can share CPU and memory while staying inside the predefined constraints.

Namespaces offer another type of isolation for process interaction inside operating frameworks. Namespaces limit the perceivability a procedure has on other procedures, organizing, filesystems, and client ID parts. Container forms are constrained to see just what is in the same namespace. Procedures from containers or the host forms are not straightforwardly accessible from inside this container procedure. Additionally, Docker gives each container its very own systems administration stack that ensures the attachments and interfaces in a similar fashion.

Association filesystems are also a key advantage of utilizing Docker containers. Containers run from an image. Much like an image in the VM or Cloud world, it speaks to state at a particular point in time. Container images snapshot the filesystem, however will in general be a lot smaller than a VM. The container shares the host bit and generally runs an a lot smaller arrangement of procedures, so the filesystem and boot strap period will in general be a lot smaller. Despite the fact that those constraints are not carefully upheld. Second, the association filesystem allows for proficient storage, download, and execution of these images.

The easiest way to understand association filesystems is to consider them like a layer cake with each layer baked freely. The Linux bit is our base layer; then, we may add an OS, for example, Red Hat Linux or Ubuntu. Next, we may add an application, for example, Nginx or Apache. Each change creates another layer. Finally, as you make changes and new layers are added, you'll always have a top layer (think icing) that is a writable layer.

What makes this really effective is that Docker caches the layers the first occasion when we construct them. In this way, suppose that we have an image with Ubuntu and then add Apache and assemble the image. Next, we fabricate MySQL with Ubuntu as the base. The subsequent form will be a lot faster because the Ubuntu layer is already cached. Essentially, our chocolate and vanilla layers, from the previous Layered filesystem figure, are already baked. We just need to bake the pistachio (MySQL) layer, assemble, and add the good to beat all).

For what reason are containers so cool?

Containers all alone are not another innovation and have in fact been around for a long time. What really separates Docker is the tooling and ease of utilization they have brought to the network. Present day improvement practices advance the utilization of Continuous Integration and Continuous Deployment. These procedures, when done right, can have a profound impact on your software item quality.

The advantages of Continuous Integration/Continuous Deployment

ThoughtWorks characterizes Continuous Integration as an improvement practice that expects engineers to integrate code into a shared archive several times each day. By having a continuous procedure of building and sending code, organizations are able to ingrain quality control and testing as part of the everyday work cycle. The outcome is that updates and bug fixes happen a lot faster and the overall quality improves.

Nonetheless, there has always been a challenge in creating advancement conditions that match that of testing and generation. Often irregularities in these conditions make it hard to gain the full advantage of continuous conveyance.

Utilizing Docker, engineers are currently able to have really portable deployments. Containers that are conveyed on an engineer's laptop are easily sent on an in-house staging server. They are then easily transferred to the creation server running in the cloud. This is because Docker develops containers with fabricate documents that indicate parent layers. One advantage of this is that it turns out to be exceptionally easy to guarantee OS, package, and application variants are the same across improvement, staging, and creation situations.

Because all the conditions are packaged into the layer, the same host server can have different containers running a variety of OS or package renditions. Further, we can have various languages and frameworks on the same host server without the typical reliance clashes we would get in a virtual machine (VM) with a solitary operating framework.

Resource utilization

The well-characterized isolation and layer filesystem also make containers ideal for running frameworks with a small impression and domain-explicit purposes. A streamlined deployment and release process means we can send rapidly and often. As such, many companies have diminished their deployment time from weeks or months to days and hours now and again. This improvement life cycle loans itself incredibly well to small, targeted teams dealing with small lumps of a larger application.

Microservices and orchestration

As we break down an application into quite certain domains, we need a uniform way to communicate between all the various pieces and domains. Web administrations have filled this need for a considerable length of time, however the added isolation and granular center that containers bring have paved a way for microservices.

The definition for microservices can be somewhat shapeless, however a definition from Martin Fowler, a regarded author and speaker on software improvement, says this (you can allude to more details about this in point 2 in the References area at the finish of the chapter):

So, the microservice architectural style is an approach to building up a solitary application as a suite of small administrations, each running in its very own procedure and communicating with lightweight mechanisms, often an HTTP resource API. These administrations are worked around business capabilities and autonomously deployable by completely automated deployment machinery. There is a bare least of centralized management of these administrations, which may be written in various programming languages and utilize various data storage advancements.

As the turn to containerization and as microservices advance in an organization, they will before long need a strategy to maintain many containers and microservices. A few organizations will have hundreds or even thousands of containers running in the years ahead.

Future challenges

Life cycle forms alone are an important bit of operations and management. By what means will we automatically recuperate when a container fails? Which upstream administrations are affected by such an outage? By what means will we patch our applications with minimal vacation? In what capacity will we scale up our containers and administrations as our traffic develops?

Systems administration and handling are also important concerns. A few procedures are part of the same help and may profit by the closeness to the system. Databases, for example, may send large amounts of data to a particular microservice for handling. In what manner will we place containers near each other in our cluster? Is there regular data that should be accessed? In what capacity will new administrations be found and made available to other frameworks?

Resource utilization is also a key. The small impression of containers means that we can upgrade our infrastructure for greater utilization. Broadening the savings started in the elastic cloud will take us much further toward limiting wasted hardware. In what manner will we plan workloads most proficiently? In what manner will we guarantee that our important applications always have the correct resources? How might we run less important workloads on spare capacity?

Finally, portability is a key factor in moving many organizations to containerization. Docker makes it exceptionally easy to send a standard container across various operating frameworks, cloud suppliers, and on-premise hardware or even engineer laptops. Notwithstanding, despite everything we need tooling to move containers around. In what capacity will we move containers between various hubs on our cluster? By what method will we turn out updates with minimal disturbance? What procedure do we use to perform blue-green deployments or canary releases?

Whether you are starting to work out individual microservices and separating worries into isolated containers or in the event that you essentially want to take full advantage of the portability and immutability in your application advancement, the requirement for management and orchestration turns out to be clear. This is the place orchestration instruments, for example, Kubernetes offer the greatest value.

The introduction of Kubernetes

Kubernetes (K8s) is an open source venture that was released by Google in June, 2014. Google released the extend as part of a push to share their own infrastructure and innovation advantage with the network at large.

Google launches 2 billion containers seven days in their infrastructure and has been utilizing container innovation for over a decade. Originally, they were building a framework named Borg, presently called Omega, to plan their vast quantities of workloads across their consistently expanding data focus impression. They took many of the exercises they learned throughout the years and revamped their current data focus management apparatus for wide adoption by the remainder of the world. The outcome was the Kubernetes open-source venture (you can allude to more details about this in point 3 in the References area at the finish of the chapter).

Since its initial release in 2014, K8s has experienced rapid improvement with commitments all across the open-source network, including Red Hat, VMware, and Canonical. The 1.0 release of Kubernetes went live in July, 2015. From that point forward, it's been a fast-paced advancement of the undertaking with wide help from one of the largest open-source networks on GitHub today. We'll be covering adaptation 1.5 all through the book. K8s gives organizations a device to deal with a portion of the major operations and management concerns. We will investigate how Kubernetes helps deal with resource utilization, high availability, updates, patching, organizing, administration disclosure, checking, and logging.

Our first cluster

Kubernetes is upheld on a variety of platforms and OSes. For the examples in this book, I utilized a Ubuntu 16.04 Linux VirtualBox for my customer and Google Compute Engine (GCE) with Debian for the cluster itself. We will also take a brief take a gander at a cluster running on Amazon Web Services (AWS) with Ubuntu.

To save some cash, both GCP and AWS offer complementary plans and trial offers for their cloud infrastructure. It merits utilizing these free trials for your Kubernetes learning, if conceivable.

The greater part of the ideas and examples in this book should chip away at any installation of a Kubernetes cluster. To get more information on other platform arrangements, allude to the Kubernetes beginning page on the accompanying GitHub link:

http://kubernetes.io/docs/beginning aides/

To start with, how about we make sure that our condition is appropriately set up before we install Kubernetes.

Start by updating packages:

$ sudo apt-get update

Install Python and twist in the event that they are absent:

$sudo apt-get install python

$sudo apt-get install twist

Install the gcloud SDK:

$ twist https://sdk.cloud.google.com | bash

We should start another shell before gcloud is on our path.

Arrange your Google Cloud Platform (GCP) account information. This should automatically open a program from where we can sign in to our Google Cloud account and authorize the SDK:

$ gcloud auth login

On the off chance that you have issues with login or want to utilize another program, you can optionally utilize the -no-launch-program command. Reorder the URL to the machine and/or program of your decision. Sign in with your Google Cloud credentials and snap Allow on the consents page. Finally, you ought to get an authorization code that you can reorder back into the shell where the brief is waiting.

A default task ought to be set, yet we can confirm this with the accompanying command:

$ gcloud config list venture

We can alter this and set another default venture with this command. Make sure to utilize venture ID and not extend name, as pursues:

$ gcloud config set task <PROJECT ID>

We can discover our undertaking ID in the support at the accompanying URL:

https://console.developers.google.com/venture

Alternatively, we can list active ventures:

$ gcloud alpha undertakings list

Since we have our condition set up, installing the latest Kubernetes variant is done in a solitary advance, as pursues:

$ twist - sS https://get.k8s.io | bash

It may take a moment or two to download Kubernetes relying upon your association speed. Earlier forms would automatically call the kube-up.sh content and start constructing our cluster. In rendition 1.5, we should call the kube-up.sh content ourselves to launch the cluster. As a matter of course, it will utilize the Google Cloud and GCE:

$ kubernetes/cluster/kube-up.sh

After you run the kube-up.sh content, we will see many lines move past. How about we take a gander at them each area in turn:

In the event that your gcloud segments are not cutting-edge, you may be provoked to update them.

The first image, GCE essential check, shows the checks for requirements as well as making sure that all segments are modern. This is explicit to each supplier. On account of GCE, it will confirm that the SDK is installed and that all segments are exceptional. If not, you will see a brief at this point to install or update:

Presently the content is turning up the cluster. Again, this is explicit to the supplier. For GCE, it first checks to make sure that the SDK is arranged for a default extend and zone. In the event that they are set, you'll see those in the yield.

Next, it uploads the server binaries to Google Cloud storage, as found in the Creating gs:...

lines:

It then checks for any bits of a cluster already running. Then, we finally start creating the cluster. In the yield in the previous figure Master creation, we see it creating the master server, IP address, and appropriate firewall configurations for the cluster:

Finally, it creates the flunkies or hubs for our cluster. This is the place our container workloads will actually run. It will continually circle and wait while all the followers start up. As a matter of course, the cluster will have four hubs (cronies), however K8s underpins having more than 1000 (and soon past). We will return to scaling the hubs later on in the book.

Presently that everything is created, the cluster is initialized and started. Assuming that everything goes well, we will get an IP address for the master. Also, note that configuration along with the cluster management credentials are put away in

home/<Username>/.kube/config:

Then, the content will validate the cluster. At this point, we are never again running supplier explicit code. The validation content will question the cluster via the kubectl.sh content. This is the central content for managing our cluster. In this case, it checks the quantity of followers found, enlisted, and in a ready state. It circles through surrendering the cluster to 10 minutes to complete initialization.

After a fruitful startup, a summary of the followers and the cluster segment health is imprinted on the screen:

Finally, a kubectl cluster-information command is run, which yields the URL for the master administrations including DNS, UI, and checking. We should take a gander at a portion of these segments.

Kubernetes UI

Open a program and run the accompanying code:

https://<your master ip>/ui/

The certificate is self-marked as a matter of course, so you'll have to overlook the warnings in your program before continuing. After this, we will see a login dialog. This is the place we utilize the credentials recorded during the K8s installation. We can discover them at any time by essentially utilizing the config command:

$ kubectl config see

The main dashboard takes us to a page with very little display from the beginning. There is a link to send a containerized app that will take you to a GUI for deployment. This GUI can be an extremely easy way to begin conveying apps without agonizing over the YAML syntax for Kubernetes. Be that as it may, as your utilization of containers matures, it's great practice to utilize the YAML definitions that are registered to source control.

On the off chance that you click on the Nodes link on the left-hand side menu, you will see a few measurements on the present cluster hubs:

At the top, we see an aggregate of the CPU and memory usages pursued by a posting of our cluster hubs. Tapping on one of the hubs will take us to a page with detailed information about that hub, its health, and various measurements.

The Kubernetes UI has a lot of other perspectives that will turn out to be increasingly valuable as we start launching real applications and adding configurations to the cluster.

Grafana

Another service installed as a matter of course is Grafana. This instrument will give us a dashboard to see measurements on the cluster nodes. We can access it utilizing the accompanying syntax in a program:

https://<your master

ip>/api/v1/intermediary/namespaces/kube-framework/services/observing grafana

From the main page, click on the Home dropdown and select Cluster. Here, Kubernetes is actually running various services. Heapster is utilized to gather the resource usage on the cases and nodes and stores the information in InfluxDB. The outcomes, for example, CPU and memory usage, are what we find in the Grafana UI. We will investigate this top to bottom in, Monitoring and Logging.

The kubectl content has commands to investigate our cluster and the workloads running on it. You can discover it in the/kubernetes/customer/receptacle organizer. We will utilize this command all through the book, so we should take one moment to set up our condition. We can do as such by putting the binaries envelope on our PATH, in the accompanying manner:

$export PATH=$PATH:/<Path where you downloaded K8s>/kubernetes/customer/canister

$chmod +x/<Path where you downloaded K8s>/kubernetes/customer/canister

You may decide to download the kubernetes organizer outside your home envelope, so alter the first command as appropriate.

It is also a smart thought to make the changes permanent by adding the fare command as far as possible of your .bashrc document in your home index.

Since we have kubectl on our path, we can start working with it. It has many commands. Since we have not spun up any applications yet, a large portion of these commands won't be exceptionally intriguing. Be that as it may, we can investigate with two commands immediately.

In the first place, we have already observed the cluster-data command during initialization, yet we can run it again at any time with the accompanying command:

$ kubectl cluster-data

Another valuable command is get. It tends to be utilized to see as of now running services, cases, replication controllers, and much more. Here are the three examples that are helpful right out of the gate:

List the nodes in our cluster:

$ kubectl get nodes

List cluster occasions:

$ kubectl get occasions

Finally, we can perceive any services that are running in the cluster, as pursues:

$ kubectl get services

To start with, we will just observe one service, named kubernetes. This service is the center API server for the cluster.

Services running on the master

We should delve somewhat more profound into our new cluster and its center services. As a matter of course, machines are named with the kubernetes-prefix. We can adjust this utilizing

$KUBE_GCE_INSTANCE_PREFIX before a cluster is spun up. For the cluster we just started, the master ought to be named kubernetes-master. We can utilize the gcloud command-line utility to SSH into the machine. The accompanying command will start a SSH session with the master hub. Make certain to substitute your venture ID and zone to match your condition.

Also, note that you can launch SSH from the Google Cloud comfort utilizing the accompanying syntax:

$ gcloud figure ssh - zone "<your gce zone>" "kubernetes-master"

On the off chance that you have issue with SSH via the Google Cloud CLI, you can utilize the Console which has a worked in SSH customer. Just go to the VM instances page and you'll consider a To be choice as a segment in the kubernetes-master listing. Alternatively, the VM instance details page has the SSH choice at the top.

When we are signed in, we ought to get a standard shell brief. How about we run the docker command that channels for Image and Status:

$ sudo docker ps - format 'table {{.Image}}t{{.Status}}'

Despite the fact that we have not conveyed any applications on Kubernetes yet, we note that there are several containers already running. Coming up next is a brief depiction of each container:

fluentd-gcp: This container gathers and sends the cluster logs record to the Google Cloud Logging service.

Hub issue finder: This container is a daemon that sudden spikes in demand for each hub and presently identifies issues at the hardware and part layer.

rescheduler: This is another add-on container that makes sure critical parts are always running. In cases of low resources availability, it may even expel less critical cases to make room.

glbc: This is another Kubernetes add-on container that gives Google Cloud Layer 7 load balancing utilizing the new Ingress capability.

kube-addon-manager: This part is center to the expansion of Kubernetes through various add-ons. It also periodically applies any changes to

the/and so on/kubernetes/addons index.

etcd-void dir-cleanup: An utility to cleanup void keys in etcd.

kube-controller-manager: This is a controller manager that controls a variety of cluster capacities, guaranteeing accurate and modern replication is one of its vital jobs. Additionally, it screens, manages, and finds new nodes. Finally, it manages and updates service endpoints.

kube-apiserver: This container runs the API server. As we investigated in the Swagger interface, this RESTful API allows us to create, inquiry, update, and expel various segments of our Kubernetes cluster.

kube-scheduler: This scheduler takes unscheduled units and ties them to nodes based on the present planning algorithm.

etcd: This runs the etcd software worked by CoreOS, and it is an appropriated and steady key-value store. This is the place the Kubernetes cluster state is put away, updated, and recovered by various segments of K8s.

pause: This container is often alluded to as the case infrastructure container and is utilized to set up and hold the systems administration namespace and resource limits for each case.

I precluded the amd64 for many of these names to make this increasingly conventional.

The motivation behind the units remains the same.

To leave the SSH session, basically type exit at the brief.

In the following chapter, we will also show how a couple of these services cooperate in the main image, Kubernetes center architecture.

Services running on the flunkies

We could SSH to one of the flunkies, however since Kubernetes plans workloads across the cluster, we would not see all the containers on a solitary crony. Be that as it may, we can take a gander at the cases running on all the cronies utilizing the kubectl command:

$ kubectl get cases

Since we have not started any applications on the cluster yet, we don't perceive any cases. Notwithstanding, there are actually several framework cases running bits of the Kubernetes infrastructure. We can see these cases by indicating the kube-framework namespace. We will investigate namespaces and their significance later, however for the time being, the - namespace=kube-framework command can be utilized to take a gander at these K8s framework resources, as pursues:

$ kubectl get cases - namespace=kube-framework

We should see something similar to the accompanying:

etcd-void dir-cleanup-kubernetes-master

etcd-server-occasions kubernetes-master

etcd-server-kubernetes-master

fluentd-cloud-logging-kubernetes-master

fluentd-cloud-logging-kubernetes-flunky bunch xxxx

heapster-v1.2.0-xxxx

kube-addon-manager-kubernetes-master

kube-apiserver-kubernetes-master

kube-controller-manager-kubernetes-master

kube-dns-xxxx

kube-dns-autoscaler-xxxx

kube-intermediary kubernetes-follower bunch xxxx

kube-scheduler-kubernetes-master

kubernetes-dashboard-xxxx

l7-default-backend-xxxx

l7-lb-controller-v0.8.0-kubernetes-master checking influxdb-grafana-xxxx hub issue identifier v0.1-xxxx rescheduler-v0.2.1-kubernetes-master

The initial six lines should look familiar. A portion of these are the services we saw running on the master and will see bits of these on the nodes. There are a couple of additional services we have not seen at this point. The kube-dns alternative gives the DNS and service disclosure plumbing, kubernetes-dashboard-xxxx is the UI for Kubernetes, l7-default-backend-xxxx gives the default load balancing backend for the new Layer-7 load balancing capability, and heapster-v1.2.0-xxxx and observing inundation grafana give the Heapster database and UI to screen resource usage across the cluster. Finally, kube-intermediary kubernetes-crony bunch xxxx is the intermediary which guides traffic to the best possible backing services and units running on our cluster.

On the off chance that we did SSH into a random follower, we would see several containers that stumble into a couple of these units. A sample may resemble this image:

Again, we saw a similar range of services with teachers. The services we did not see with the teacher are:

kubedns: This container monitors Kubernetes endpoint services and resources and synchronizes changes in DNS searches.

kube-dnsmasq: This is another container that provides DNS caching.

Dnsmasq-metrics: provides a metrics report for clustered DNS services.

l7-defaultbackend: this is the default system used to manage the GCE L7 and Ingress load balance.

kube-proxy: this is a network and utility proxy for your cluster. This component ensures that service traffic is directed to where your workloads are running in the cluster. We will explore this in more detail later in the book.

Hits: This tank is for monitoring and analysis.

addon-resizer: this cluster tool is used to scale the container.

heapster_grafana: Uses and monitors resources.

heapster_influxdb: this time is the database for Heapster data.

Auto Scale Cluster: This cluster tool is used for scaling

of the container in proportion to the size of the cluster.

exechealthz: performs capsule health checks.

Again, I omitted amd64 for many of these names to make it more general. The purpose of the pods remains the same.

Separate the cluster

Well, this is our first cluster at GCE, but let's explore other providers. To simplify things, we need to eliminate the one we just created at GCE. We can disassemble the cluster with a simple command:

$ kube-down.sh

Work with other vendors

Kubernetes uses the GCE provider for Google Cloud by default. We can override this default by setting the KUBERNETES_PROVIDER environment variable.

Let's try to configure a cluster in AWS. Before you begin, you must install and configure the AWS Command Line Interface (AWS) on our behalf. The installation and configuration documentation for the AWS CLI can be found at the following links:

Installation documentation:

http://docs.aws.amazon.com/cli/latest/userguide/installing.html#instal l-bundle-other-os

Configuration documentation:

http://docs.aws.amazon.com/cli/latest/userguide/cli-chap-getting-start ed.html

So, this is a simple parameter of the environment variable, as follows:

$ export KUBERNETES_PROVIDER = aws

Again, we can use the kube-up.sh command to activate the cluster as follows:

$ kube-up.sh

As with GCE, the installation activity takes a few minutes. It will organize the files in S3 and create the corresponding instances, virtual private cloud (VPC), security groups, etc., in our AWS account. The Kubernetes cluster will then be configured and started. When everything is finished and started, we should see a cluster confirmation at the end of the result:

Note that the region in which the cluster was created is determined by

KUBE_AWS_ZONE environment variable. By default, it is set to west-2a (the region is derived from this availability zone). Even if a region is defined in your AWS CLI, it will use the region defined in KUBE_AWS_ZONE.

Again we go to SSH as a teacher. This time we can use the native SSH client. We will find the key files in / home / <name>> /.ssh:

$ ssh -v -i / home / <username> / ssh / kube_aws_rsa ubuntu @ <Your primary IP address>

We will use sudo docker ps—format 'table {{.Image}} t {{. Status}} 'for research

Containers in operation. We should see the following:

We see some of the same containers as our GCE cluster. However, several are missing. We see the basic components of Kubernetes, but lack the fluentd-gcp service, as well as some of the new tools as a node issue detector, reprogrammer, glbc, cubes-addon-manager and etcd-empty-dir-cleanup. This reflects some subtle differences in the cube-up scenario between different public cloud providers. Finally, this is decided by the efforts of the large open Kubernetes community, but GCP often offers many of the latest features.

Elasticsearch and Kibana are configured for us by AWS providers. We can find Kibana's user interface using a URL with the following syntax:

https: // <your primary IP address> / api / v1 / proxy / namespace / kube-system / services / kibana-logging

As with the user interface, you will be prompted to enter the administrator credentials that you can obtain using the config command, as shown below:

$ Kubectl configuration view

You must configure your index during your first visit. You can leave default values and select @timestamp for the name of the Time field. Then click Create and you will be taken to the index settings page. From there, click the Discover tab at the top to explore the license plates:

Cluster reset

You just tested the cluster in AWS. For the rest of the book, I will base my examples on the GCE group. For a better experience, you can easily return to the GCE cluster.

Simply disassemble the AWS cluster as follows:

$ kube-down.sh

Then create a new GCE cluster using the following elements:

$ export KUBERNETES_PROVIDER = gce

$ kube-up.sh

Edit your Cube-up settings

It is interesting to know the parameters used for the kube-up.sh script. Each provider in kubernetes / cluster / folder has its own folder containing the config-default.sh script.

For example, kubernetes / cluster / aws / config-default.sh has default settings for using kube-up.sh with AWS. At the beginning of this script, you will see many of these defined values, as well as environment variables that can be used to override the default values.

In the following example, the ZONE variable is set for the script and uses an environment variable value called KUBE_AWS_ZONE. If this variable is not defined, it will use the default us-west-2a value:

ZONE = $ {KUBE_AWS_ZONE: -us-west-2a}

Understanding these settings will help you get the most out of your kube-up.sh script.

Kube-up.sh alternatives

The Kube-up.sh script is always a very convenient way to start using Kubernetes on the platform you choose. However, it is not perfect and can sometimes succeed when conditions are not.

Fortunately, since the creation of K8, several alternative methods have emerged for cluster creation. Two of these GitHub projects are KOP and cubes-aws. Although the latter is linked to AWS, both offer an alternative way to easily mount your new cluster:

https://github.com/kubernetes/kops

https://github.com/coreos/kube-aws

In addition, several managed services have been created, including Google Container Engine (GKE) and Microsoft Azure Container Service (ACS), which provide automated installation and some cluster operations. We will review a short demonstration in Chapter 12, Ready for Production.

Out of nowhere

Finally, there is the possibility of starting over. Fortunately, starting with version 1.4, the Kubernetes team focused on simplifying the cluster configuration process. To this end, they introduced kubeadm for Ubuntu 16.04, CentOS 7 and HypriotOS v1.0.1 +.

Let's take a quick look at how to create a cluster in AWS using the kubeadm tool.

Cluster configuration

We will first need to secure our main cluster and nodes. We are currently limited to the above mentioned operating systems and version. Additionally, it is recommended that you have at least 1 GB of RAM and connect all nodes to the network.

For this visit, we will need an instance of t2.medium (primary node) and three instances of size t2.mirco (nodes) in AWS. These examples have an expandable processor and are loaded with at least 1GB of RAM. We will need to create a master node and three working nodes.

We will also need to create cluster security groups. The following ports are required for the teacher:

Once you have these SGs, go ahead and create four instances (one t2.medium and three t2.mircos) using Ubuntu 16.04. If you are new to AWS, see the documentation for creating EC2 instances at the following URL:

http://docs.aws.amazon.com/AWSEC2/latest/UserGuide/LaunchingAndUsingInsances.html

Be sure to identify the instance of t2.medium as the master and join the main security group. List the other three nodes and connect them to the security group.

These steps are adapted to the detailed procedures in the manual. For more information or to use the Ubuntu alternative, see https: // kub

ernetes.io/docs/getting-started-guides/kubeadm/.

Installation of Kubernetes components (kubelet and kubeadm)

Then we will need SSH in all four instances and install Kubernetes components.

As a root, do the accompanying in all four instances:

1. Update packages and install apt-transport-https package so we can download HTTPS from source:

$ apt-get update

$ apt-get install - y apt-transport-https

2. Install the Google Cloud Public Key:

$ twist - s https://packages.cloud.google.com/apt/doc/apt-key.gpg | adding apt key -

3. Then create a source list to download the Kubernetes package with your favorite proofreader:

$ vi/and so on/apt/sources.list.d/kubernetes.list

4. Utilize the accompanying as substance for this document and save it:

deb http://apt.kubernetes.io/kubernetes-xenial main

List 1-1. /and so forth/apt/sources.list.d/kubernetes.list

5. Update your feeds again:

apt-get update

- Install Docker and Kubernetes major segments:

$ apt-get install - y docker.io

$ apt-get the chance to install - y kubelet kubeadm kubectl kubernetes-cni

Set up a teacher

In the case you have recently chosen as a teacher, we will initialize the teacher.

Run the accompanying command again as root:

$ kubeadm init

Note that initialization can just be done once. In the event that you have issues, you will require one reset.

Hub Union

After fruitful initialization, you will get a join command that nodes can utilize.

Duplicate this later for the joining procedure. It should resemble this:

$ kubeadm join - token = <a token> <primary IP address>

The token is utilized to authenticate the cluster nodes. So make certain to keep yourself in a safe place for future reference.

organizing

Our cluster will require a system layer for underground communications. Note that kubeadm requires a CNI-compatible system structure. You can discover a list of at present available add-ons here:

http://kubernetes.io/docs/admin/addons/

For our example, we will utilize calico. We should create calico parts in our cluster utilizing the accompanying yaml. For your benefit, you can download it here:

http://docs.projectcalico.org/v1.6/beginning/kubernetes/installation/have ed/kubeadm/calico.yaml

When you have this document in your master, create the parts with the accompanying command:

$ kubectl apply - f calico.yaml

Allow it a moment to run the installer, then list the solid shape framework nodes to check:

$ kubectl get cases - namespace = kube-framework

You ought to get a list similar to the accompanying with three new shape and finished task not appeared:

Join the gathering

Presently we have to execute the association command we recently duplicated, in each of our hub instances:

$ kubeadm join - token = <a token> <primary IP address>

When done, you ought to have the option to see all nodes of the host utilizing this command:

$ kubectl gets nodes

summary

We briefly survey the operation of containers and their adaptation to new models of microservice architecture. You should now have a superior understanding of how these two powers will require various operations and administrative tasks and how Kubernetes offers amazing features to address these difficulties. We create two unique clusters in GCE and AWS and investigate the startup content as well as some integrated features of Kubernetes. Finally, we take a gander at alternatives to the kube-up content and test the new kubeadm apparatus in AWS utilizing Ubuntu 16.04.

In the following segment, we will investigate the basic idea and abstractions gave by K8 to managing containers and groups of complete applications. We will also audit basic planning, service revelation, and health control.

2

Pods, Services, Replication Controllers, and Labels

This chapter will cover the center Kubernetes develops, namely cases, services, replication controllers, replica sets, and labels. A couple of straightforward application examples will be incorporated to demonstrate each build. The chapter will also cover basic operations for your cluster. Finally, health checks and booking will be presented with a couple of examples.

This chapter will talk about the accompanying points:

Kubernetes overall architecture

Introduction to center Kubernetes develops, namely cases, services, replication controllers, replica sets, and labels

Understanding how labels can ease management of a Kubernetes cluster

Understanding how to screen services and container health

Understanding how to set up booking constraints based on available cluster resources

The architecture

Although, Docker brings a supportive layer of abstraction and tooling around container management, Kubernetes carries similar assistance to orchestrating containers at scale and managing full application stacks.

K8s climbs the stack giving us builds to deal with management at the application or service level. This gives us automation and tooling to guarantee high availability, application stack, and service-wide portability. K8s also allows better control of resource usage, for example, CPU, memory, and circle space across our infrastructure.

Kubernetes gives this more significant level of orchestration management by giving us key develops to join numerous containers, endpoints, and data into full application stacks and services. K8s also gives the tooling to manage the when, where, and what number of the stack and its parts:

we see the center architecture of Kubernetes. Most administrative interactions are done via the kubectl content and/ or RESTful service calls to the API.

Note the ideas of the ideal state and actual state carefully. This is the key to how Kubernetes manages the cluster and its workloads. All the bits of K8s are constantly attempting to screen the current actual state and synchronize it with the ideal state characterized by the administrators via the API server or kubectl content. There will be times when these states don't match up, yet the framework is always attempting to accommodate the two.

Master

Essentially, master is the brain of our cluster. Here, we have the center API server, which maintains RESTful web services for questioning and characterizing our ideal cluster and workload state. It's important to take note of that the control pane just accesses the master to initiate changes and not the nodes legitimately.

Additionally, the master incorporates the scheduler, which works with the API server to plan workloads as units on the actual follower nodes. These cases incorporate the various containers that make up our application stacks. Of course, the basic Kubernetes scheduler spreads cases across the cluster and uses various nodes for matching unit replicas. Kubernetes also allows determining necessary resources for each container, so planning can be altered by these additional factors.

The replication controller/replica set works with the API server to guarantee that the right number of case replicas are running at any given time. This is exemplary of the ideal state idea. On the off chance that our replication controller/ replica set is characterizing three replicas and our actual state is two duplicates of the case running, then the scheduler will be summoned to add a third unit some place on our cluster. The same is valid if there are such a large number of units running in the cluster at any given time. Along these lines, K8s is always pushing toward that ideal state.

Finally, we have etcd running as a dispersed configuration store. The Kubernetes state is put away here and etcd allows values to be watched for changes. Think about this as the brain's shared memory.

Hub (once in the past followers)

In each hub, we have a few parts. The kubelet interacts with the API server to update the state and to start new workloads that have been summoned by the scheduler.

Kube-intermediary gives basic load balancing and coordinates the traffic bound for explicit services to the best possible unit on the backend. Allude to the Services area later in this chapter.

Finally, we have some default cases, which run various infrastructure services for the hub. As we investigated briefly in the past chapter, the units incorporate services for Domain Name System (DNS), logging, and case health checks. The default case will run alongside our planned units on each hub.

In v1.0, flunky was renamed to hub, yet there are still remnants of the term follower in a portion of the machine naming contents and documentation that exists on the Web. For clarity, I've added the term flunky in addition to hub in a couple of places all through the book.

Center builds

Presently, we should jump somewhat more profound and investigate a portion of the center abstractions Kubernetes gives. These abstractions will make it easier to consider our applications and ease the weight of life cycle management, high availability, and planning.

pods

The pods allow you to keep connected containers close to the network and hardware infrastructure. Data can live near the application, so processing can be done without generating long delays due to network travel. Similarly, shared data can be stored in volumes split between multiple containers. The pods basically allow for the logical grouping of containers and parts of our applications.

Although pods can run one or more containers inside, the pad itself can be one of many running on a Kubernetes node (minion). As we will see, darkness gives us a logical group of containers into which we can then copy, plan, and balance service endpoints.

Example under

Let's look at the capsule in action. We will run the Node.js application in the cluster. You will need a GCE cluster for this; If you haven't started yet, check out our first cluster in Chapter 1, Introduction to Kubernetes.

Now, let's create a directory for our definitions. In this example, we will create a folder in the subfolders / sample books of our home directory:

$ mkdir book examples

$ cd book examples

$ mkdir 02_example

$ cd 02_example

Download the sample code

Sample code files can be downloaded from your account at http://www.packtpub.com for any Packt Publishing book you purchased. If you purchased the book elsewhere, visit http://www.packtpub.com/support and register to receive the files directly by email.

Use your favorite editor to create the following file:

apiVersion: v1

like: Under

metadata:

name: node-js-pod

Specifications:

tanks:

- name: node-js-pod

image: bits / apache: back ports:

- containerPort: 80

Listing 2-1: nodejs-pod.yaml

This file is named node-js-pod with the last bitnami / apache container running on port 80. We can confirm this with the following command:

$ kubectl create -f nodejs-pod.yaml

The output is as follows:

under "node-js-pod" created

This gives us the floor that guides the specified tank. We can see more information about the substrate by executing the following command:

$ kubectl describes pods / node-js-pod

You will see a lot of information, such as floor status, IP address, and even relevant log events. You will notice that the floor IP address is a private IP address. We cannot access directly from a local computer. Don't worry, because the kubectl exec command reflects the functionality of Docker execution. Once the floor is started, with this function we can execute the command in the floor:

$ kubectl exec node-js-pod - curl <private IP>

By default, this executes the command on the first container found, but you can select a specific one using the -c arguments.

After the command is executed, you should see the HTML code. We'll have a better view later in this chapter, but for now, we can see that our module is really working as expected.

labels

Labels give us a second level of categorization, which becomes very useful in terms of business and day-to-day management. Like tags, tags can also be used as a basis for service discovery and as a useful grouping tool for daily operations and administrative tasks.

Tags are simple key-value pairs. You will see them in subsystems, replication controllers, replica kits, services and more. The label serves as the selector and tells Kubernetes resources to collaborate on various operations. Think of it as a filtering option.

We will explore labels in more detail in this chapter, but first we will explore the three remaining constructs: services, replication controllers, and replica sets.

The container's afterlife

As Werner Vogels, CTO of AWS, famously said everything fails all the time; containers and cases can and will crash, become ruined, or maybe even simply get accidentally shut off by a cumbersome admin jabbing around on one of the nodes. Solid strategy and security practices like implementing least benefit curtail a portion of these episodes, yet involuntary workload slaughter happens and is essentially a fact of operations.

Fortunately, Kubernetes gives two truly valuable develops to keep this grave affair all cleaned up behind the curtains. Services and replication controllers/replica sets enable us to keep our applications running with little interference and graceful recuperation.

Services

Services allow us to abstract access away from the buyers of our applications. Utilizing a reliable endpoint, clients and other programs can access cases running on your cluster seamlessly.

K8s achieves this by making sure that each hub in the cluster runs an intermediary named kube-intermediary. As the name proposes, the activity of kube-intermediary is to intermediary communication from a service endpoint back to the comparing unit that is running the actual application.

Participation of the service load balancing pool is controlled by the utilization of selectors and labels. Units with matching labels are added to the list of candidates where the service forwards traffic. A virtual IP address and port are utilized as the section focuses for the service, and the traffic is then forwarded to a random unit on a target port characterized by either K8s or your definition document.

Updates to service definitions are observed and coordinated from the K8s cluster master and propagated to the kube-intermediary daemons running on each hub.

Right now, kube-intermediary is running on the hub have itself. There are plans to containerize this and the kubelet as a matter of course later on.

Replication controllers and replica sets

Replication controllers (RCs), as the name recommends, manage the quantity of nodes that a unit and included container images run on. They guarantee that an instance of an image is being run with the particular number of duplicates.

As you start to operationalize your containers and cases, you'll need a way to turn out updates, scale the quantity of duplicates running (both here and there), or basically guarantee that at least one instance of your stack is always running. RCs create a significant level mechanism to make sure that things are operating effectively across the whole application and cluster.

RCs are just charged with guaranteeing that you have the ideal scale for your application. You characterize the quantity of unit replicas you want running and give it a template for how to create new cases. Much the same as services, we will utilize selectors and labels to characterize a case's participation in a replication controller.

Kubernetes doesn't require the exacting behavior of the replication controller, which is ideal for long-running procedures. In fact, work controllers can be utilized for brief workloads which allow occupations to be rushed to a fulfillment state and are appropriate for batch work.

Replica sets, are another sort, as of now in Beta, that speak to an improved variant of replication controllers. Right now, the main distinction comprises of having the option to utilize the new set-based label selectors as we will find in the accompanying examples.

Our first Kubernetes application

Before we proceed onward, we should take a glance at these three ideas in real life. Kubernetes ships with various examples installed, however we will create another example from scratch to illustrate a portion of the ideas.

We already created a case definition record, however as you learned, there are many advantages to running our cases via replication controllers. Again, utilizing the book- examples/02_example envelope we made earlier, we will create some definition records and start a cluster of Node.js servers utilizing a replication controller approach. Additionally, we'll add an open face to it with a load-balanced service.

Utilize your favorite editorial manager to create the accompanying record:

apiVersion: v1

kind: ReplicationController

metadata:

name: hub js

labels:

name: hub js

spec:

replicas: 3

selector:

name: hub js

template:

metadata:

labels:

name: hub js

spec:

containers:

- name: hub js

image: jonbaier/hub express-info:latest ports:

- containerPort: 80

Listing 2-2: nodejs-controller.yaml

This is the main resource definition document for our cluster, so how about we take a more intensive look. You'll take note of that it has four first-level components (kind, apiVersion, metadata, and spec). These are regular among all top-level Kubernetes resource definitions:

Kind: This discloses to K8s the sort of resource we are creating. In this case, the sort is

ReplicationController. The kubectl content uses a solitary create command

for all kinds of resources. The advantage here is that you can easily create various resources of various kinds without the requirement for determining individual parameters for each sort. In any case, it necessitates that the definition documents can recognize what it is they are determining.

apiVersion: This essentially reveals to Kubernetes which rendition of the schema we are utilizing.

Metadata: This is the place we will give the resource a name and also indicate labels that will be utilized to search and choose resources for a given operation. The metadata component also allows you to create annotations, which are for the non-recognizing information that may be helpful for customer apparatuses and libraries.

Finally, we have spec, which will vary based on the sort or kind of resource we are creating. In this case, it's ReplicationController, which guarantees the ideal number of units are running. The replicas component characterizes the ideal number of units, the selector component advises the controller which cases to watch, and finally, the template component characterizes a template to launch another case. The template segment contains the same pieces we saw in our case definition earlier. An important thing to note is that the selector values need to match the labels values indicated in the unit template. Recollect that this matching is utilized to choose the units being managed.

Presently, how about we take a gander at the service definition:

apiVersion: v1

kind: Service

metadata:

name: hub js

labels:

name: hub js

spec:

type: LoadBalancer

ports:

- port: 80 selector:

name: hub js

Listing 2-3: nodejs-rc-service.yaml

The YAML here is similar to ReplicationController. The main contrast is found in the service spec component. Here, we characterize the Service type, listening port, and selector, which tell the Service intermediary which units can answer the service.

Kubernetes bolsters both YAML and JSON formats for definition documents.

Create the Node.js express replication controller:

$ kubectl create - f nodejs-controller.yaml

The yield is as per the following:

replicationcontroller "hub js" created

This gives us a replication controller that guarantees that three duplicates of the container are always running:

$ kubectl create - f nodejs-rc-service.yaml

The yield is as per the following:

service "hub js" created

On GCE, this will create an external load balancer and forwarding rules, however you may need to add additional firewall rules. In my case, the firewall was already open for port 80. Be that as it may, you may need to open this port, especially in the event that you convey a service with ports other than 80 and 443.

Alright, presently we have a running service, which means that we can access the Node.js servers from a reliable URL. We should take a glance at our running services:

$ kubectl get services

In the first image (Services listing), we should take note of that the hub js service is

running, and in the IP(S) segment, we ought to have both a private and an open

(130.211.186.84 in the screen capture) IP address. In the event that you don't see the external IP, you may

need to wait a moment for the IP to be allocated from GCE. How about we check whether we can associate by

opening up people in general address in a program:

You should see something like the figure Container data application . In the event that we visit on numerous occasions, you should take note of that the container name changes. Essentially, the service load balancer is rotating between available units on the backend.

Programs usually cache pages, so to really observe the container name change, you may need to clear your cache or utilize an intermediary like this one:

https://hide.me/en/intermediary

How about we take a stab at playing chaos monkey a piece and murder off a couple of containers to perceive what Kubernetes does. So as to do this, we have to see where the cases are actually running. To start with, how about we list our cases:

$ kubectl get cases

Presently, how about we get some more details on one of the cases running a hub js container. You can do this with the depict command with one of the case names listed in the last command:

$ kubectl depict unit/hub js-sjc03

You should see the first yield. The information we need is the Node: area. How about we utilize the hub name to SSH (short for Secure Shell) into the (follower) hub running this workload:

$gcloud process - venture "<Your venture ID>" ssh - zone "<your gce zone>" "<Node from

case describe>"

Once SSHed into the hub, on the off chance that we run a sudo docker ps command, we should see at least two containers: one running the pause image and one running the actual hub express-data image. You may see more if the K8s booked more than one replica on this hub.

How about we grab the container ID of the jonbaier/hub express-information image (not gcr.io/google_containers/pause) and slaughter it off to perceive what happens. Save this container ID some place for later:

$ sudo docker ps - filter="name=node-js"

$sudo docker stop <node-express container id>

$sudo docker rm <container id>

$sudo docker ps - filter="name=node-js"

Except if you are really fast you'll probably take note of that there is as yet a hub express-data container running, yet look carefully and you'll take note of that the container id is extraordinary and the creation time stamp shows just a couple of moments ago. On the off chance that you return to the service URL, it is working as normal. Feel free to leave the SSH session until further notice.

Here, we are already observing Kubernetes playing the job of on-call operations guaranteeing that our application is always running.

We should check whether we can discover any proof of the outage. Go to the Events page in the Kubernetes UI. You can discover it by navigating to the Nodes page on the main K8s dashboard. Select a hub from the list (the same one that we SSHed into) and look down to Events on the hub details page.

You should see three late occasions. Initially, Kubernetes pulls the image. Second, it creates another container with the pulled image. Finally, it starts that container again. You'll take note of that, from the time stamps, this all happens in under a second. Time taken may vary based on the cluster measure and image pulls, yet the recuperation is exceptionally brisk.

You may notice that if you open your browser in the direction of the load balancer, the load balancer always responds with the page. You can find the IP address of the load management tool using the kubectl get services command.

This happens for several reasons. First, the status check fails not only because / status does not exist, but the page on which the service shows still works normally between restarts. Second, livenessProbe is only responsible for restarting the tank during a state control failure. There is a separate preparation probe that will remove the container from the endpoint group in the answer service under.

Let's change the status control of a page that exists in our container to get proper status control. We will also add an availability check and refer it to a nonexistent status page. Open the nodejs-health-controller.yaml file and edit the specifications section

Match List 2-8 and save it as nodejs-health-controller-2.yaml:

apiVersion: v1

Type: ReplicationController

metadata:

name: node-js

tags:

name: node-js

Specifications:

Replicas: 3

selector:

name: node-js

Model:

metadata:

tags:

name: node-js

Specifications:

tanks:

- name: node-js

image: jonbaier / node-express-info: last

connectors:

- containerPort: 80 living spaces:

HTTP httpGet status check:

way: /

Port: 80 InitialDelaySeconds: 30 timeoutSeconds: 1

readinessProbe:

HTTP httpGet status check:

route: / country /

Port: 80 InitialDelaySeconds: 30 timeoutSeconds: 1

Example 2-8: nodejs-health-controller-2.yaml

This time, we will remove the old RC that kills the pods and create a new RC with our updated YAML file:

$ kubectl remove rc -l name = node-js

$ kubectl create -f nodejs-health-controller-2.yaml

Now, when we describe one of the pods, we only see the creation of pods and tanks. However, you will notice that the IP load balancer no longer works. If we execute the command described in one of the new nodes, we see an error message about the availability check, but the subkey continues to run. If we change the path of the free / busy probe: /, we can respond again to the main requests for service. Open nodejs-health-controller-2.yaml in the editor and make this update immediately. Then delete and recreate the replication driver:

$ kubectl remove rc -l name = node-js

$ kubectl create -f nodejs-health-controller-2.yaml

Now the IP load balancer should work again. Hold these modules as we will reuse them. Networks, load balancers and Ingress.

TCP controls

Kubernetes also supports status checks with simple TCP socket checks and also with custom command line scripts. The following fragments are examples of what two uses in a YAML file look like:

livenessProbe:

executive:

order:

- / usr / bin / health / checkHttpServce.sh

initialDelaySeconds: 90

timeoutSeconds: 1

Listing 2-9: Health Check Using Command Line Script

livenessProbe:

TCPSocket:

port: 80

initialDelaySeconds: 15

timeoutSeconds: 1

Sheets 2-10: Status Checking Using a Simple TCP Socket

Life cycle hook or smart stop

When you encounter problems in real-life scenarios, you may need to take additional action before closing the container or shortly after starting it. Kubernetes actually provides lifecycle hooks for these types of uses.

The following controller definition example defines an action after startup and an action before stopping before Kubernetes moves the container to the next phase of its life cycle.

apiVersion: v1

Type: ReplicationController

metadata:

name: apache hook

tags:

name: apache hook

Specifications:

Replicas: 3

selector:

name: apache hook

Model:

metadata:

tags:

name: apache hook

Specifications:

tanks:

- name: apache-hook

image: bits / apache: back ports:

- containerPort: 80 life cycle:

poststart:

HttpGet:

path: http://my.registration-server.com/register/

port: 80

pre-stop:

executive:

command: ["/ usr / local / bin / apachectl", "- k", "graceful-stop"]

More on labels

As referenced beforehand, labels are simply basic key-value pairs. They are available on cases, replication controllers, replica sets, services, and more. In the event that you recall our service YAML, in Listing 2-3: nodejs-rc-service.yaml, there was a selector attribute. The selector attribute reveals to Kubernetes which labels to use in discovering cases to forward traffic for that service.

K8s allows clients to work with labels straightforwardly on replication controllers, replica sets, and services. How about we alter our replicas and services to incorporate a couple of more labels. Indeed, utilize your favorite editorial manager and create these two records, as pursues:

```
apiVersion: v1
kind: ReplicationController
metadata:
name: hub js-labels
labels:
name: hub js-labels
app: hub js-express
deployment: test
spec:
replicas: 3
selector:
name: hub js-labels
app: hub js-express
deployment: test
template:
metadata:
labels:
name: hub js-labels
app: hub js-express
deployment: test
spec:
```

containers:

- name: hub js-labels

image: jonbaier/hub express-info:latest ports:

- containerPort: 80

Listing 2-4: nodejs-labels-controller.yaml

apiVersion: v1

kind: Service

metadata:

name: hub js-labels

labels:

name: hub js-labels

app: hub js-express

deployment: test

spec:

type: LoadBalancer

ports:

- port: 80 selector:

name: hub js-labels

app: hub js-express

deployment: test

Listing 2-5: nodejs-labels-service.yaml

Create the replication controller and service as pursues:

$ kubectl create - f nodejs-labels-controller.yaml

$ kubectl create - f nodejs-labels-service.yaml

How about we have a go at searching for replicas with test deployments:

$ kubectl get rc - l deployment=test

The accompanying screen capture is the aftereffect of the former command:

You'll see that it just returns the replication controller we just started. What about services with a label named segment? Utilize the accompanying command:

$ kubectl get services - l part

The accompanying screen capture is the aftereffect of the first command:

Here, we see the center Kubernetes service as it were. Finally, allows simply get the hub js servers we started in this chapter. See the accompanying command:

$ kubectl get services - l "name in (hub js,node-js-labels)"

Additionally, we can perform management tasks across various cases and services. For example, we can murder all replication controllers that are part of the demo deployment (in the event that we had any running), as pursues:

$ kubectl erase rc - l deployment=demo

Otherwise, murder all services that are part of a creation or test deployment (again, on the off chance that we had any running), as pursues:

$ kubectl erase service - l "deployment in (test, generation)"

It's important to take note of that, while label choice is very useful in day-to-day management tasks, it requires appropriate deployment cleanliness on our part. We have to make sure that we have a tagging standard and that it is actively followed in the resource definition records for all that we run on Kubernetes.

While we utilized service definition YAML records to create our services so far, you can actually create them utilizing a kubectl command as it were. To give this a shot, first run the get cases command and get one of the hub js case names. Next, utilize the accompanying open command to create a service endpoint for simply that case:

$ kubectl uncover units hub js-gxkix - port=80 - name=testing-celebrity - create-external-load-balancer=true

This will create a service named testing-celebrity and also an open celebrity (load balancer IP) that can be utilized to access this unit over port 80.

There are number of other optional parameters that can be utilized. These can be found with the accompanying command:

kubectl uncover - help

Replica sets

As examined earlier, replica sets are the better than ever form of replication controllers. They take advantage of set-based label choice, yet they are as yet thought to be beta at time of this composition.

This is an example of a ReplicaSet based on and similar to the

ReplicationController in listing 2.4:

apiVersion: augmentations/v1beta1

```
kind: ReplicaSet
metadata:
name: hub js-rs
spec:
replicas: 3
selector:
matchLabels:
app: hub js-express
deployment: test
matchExpressions:
- {key: name, operator: In, values: [node-js-rs]}
template:
metadata:
labels:
name: hub js-rs
app: hub js-express
deployment: test
spec:
containers:
- name: hub js-rs
image: jonbaier/hub express-info:latest ports:
- containerPort: 80
```

Listing 2-6: nodejs-labels-replicaset.yaml

Health checks

Kubernetes gives two layers of health checking. To start with, as HTTP or TCP checks, K8s can attempt to interface with a particular endpoint and give a status of healthy on an effective association. Second, application-explicit health checks can be performed utilizing command-line contents.

How about we take a gander at a couple of health checks in real life. In the first place, we'll create another controller with a health check:

apiVersion: v1

kind: ReplicationController

metadata:

name: hub js

labels:

name: hub js

spec:

replicas: 3

selector:

name: hub js

template:

metadata:

labels:

name: hub js

spec:

containers:

- name: hub js

image: jonbaier/hub express-info:latest ports:

- containerPort: 80

livenessProbe:

An HTTP health check httpGet:

path:/status/

port: 80 initialDelaySeconds: 30 timeoutSeconds: 1

Listing 2-7: nodejs-health-controller.yaml

Note the addition of the livenessprobe component. This is our center health check component. From here, we can indicate httpGet, tcpScoket, or executive. In this example, we use httpGet to play out a straightforward check for a URI on our container. The test will check the path and port determined and restart the unit in the event that it doesn't effectively return.

Status codes somewhere in the range of 200 and 399 are all viewed as healthy by the test.

Finally, initialDelaySeconds gives us the adaptability to delay health checks until the unit has got done with initializing. The timeoutSeconds value is basically the break value for the test.

We should utilize our new health registration controller to replace the old hub js RC. We can do this utilizing the replace command, which will replace the replication controller definition:

$ kubectl replace - f nodejs-health-controller.yaml

Replacing the RC all alone won't replace our containers because despite everything it has three healthy cases from our first run. How about we execute off those units and let the updated ReplicationController replace them with containers that have health checks:

$ kubectl erase cases - l name=node-js

Presently, after waiting a moment or two, we can list the cases in a RC and grab one of the case

IDs to review somewhat more profound with the portray command:

$ kubectl depict rc/hub js

Presently, utilize the accompanying command for one of the cases:

$ kubectl portray units/hub js-7esbp

At the top, we will see the overall unit details. Contingent upon your planning, under State, it will either show Running or Waiting with a CrashLoopBackOff reason and some blunder information. A piece underneath that we can see information on our Liveness test and we will probably observe a failure check above 0. Further down we have the unit occasions. Again, contingent upon your planning, you are probably going to have various occasions for the unit. Inside a moment or two, you'll note a pattern of murdering, started, and created occasions repeating again and again. You ought to also observe a note in the Killing passage that the container is unhealthy. This is our health check failing because we don't have a page reacting at/status.

Listing 2-11: apache-snares controller.yaml

You'll note for the postStart snare, we characterize a httpGet action, yet for the preStop snare, I characterize an executive action. Similarly as with our health checks, the httpGet action attempts to make a HTTP call to the particular endpoint and port combination, while the executive action runs a local command in the container.

The httpGet and executive actions are both upheld for the postStart and preStop snares. On account of preStop, a parameter named reason will be sent to the handler as a parameter. See the accompanying table for valid values:

Note that snare calls are conveyed at least once. Therefore, any rationale in the action ought to gracefully handle different calls. Another important note is that postStart runs before a case enters its ready state. On the off chance that the snare itself fails, the case will be viewed as unhealthy.

Application planning

Since we understand how to run containers in units and even recuperate from failure, it may be helpful to understand how new containers are planned on our cluster nodes.

As referenced earlier, the default behavior for the Kubernetes scheduler is to spread container replicas across the nodes in our cluster. In the absence of all other constraints, the scheduler will place new cases on nodes with the least number of other cases having a place with matching services or replication controllers.

Additionally, the scheduler gives the ability to add constraints based on resources available to the hub. Today, this incorporates least CPU and memory allocations. Regarding Docker, these utilization the CPU-shares and memory limit flags under the spreads.

At the point when additional constraints are characterized, Kubernetes will check a hub for available resources. In the event that a hub doesn't meet all the constraints, it will move to the following. In the event that no nodes can be discovered that meet the criteria, then we will see a booking blunder in the logs.

The Kubernetes roadmap also has plans to help networking and storage. Because planning is such an important bit of overall operations and management for containers, we ought to hope to consider many to be in this area as the undertaking develops.

Booking example

How about we take a glance at a brisk example of setting some resource limits. On the off chance that we take a gander at our K8s dashboard, we can get a brisk snapshot of the present state of resource usage on our cluster

utilizing https://<your master

ip>/api/v1/intermediary/namespaces/kube-framework/services/kubernetes-dashboard and tapping on Nodes on the left-hand side menu.

This view shows the aggregate CPU and memory across the entire cluster, nodes, and master. In this case, we have fairly low CPU utilization, however a not too bad lump of memory being used.

How about we see what happens when I attempt to turn up a couple of more units, yet this time, we will ask for

512Mi for memory and 1500 m for the CPU. We'll utilize 1500 m to determine 1.5 CPUs; since each hub just has 1 CPU, this should bring about failure. Here's an example of RC definition:

apiVersion: v1

kind: ReplicationController

metadata:

name: hub js-constraints

labels:

name: hub js-constraints

spec:

replicas: 3

selector:

name: hub js-constraints

template:

metadata:

labels:

name: hub js-constraints

spec:

containers:

- name: hub js-constraints

image: jonbaier/hub express-info:latest ports:

- containerPort: 80 resources:

limits:

memory: "512Mi"

cpu: "1500m"

Listing 2-12: nodejs-constraints-controller.yaml

To open the first document, utilize the accompanying command:

$ kubectl create - f nodejs-constraints-controller.yaml

The replication controller finishes effectively, however on the off chance that we run a get units command, we'll note the hub js-constraints cases are stuck in a pending state. On the off chance that we look somewhat nearer with the depict cases/<pod-id> command, we'll note a booking blunder (for case id utilize one of the case names from the principal command):

$ kubectl get units

$ kubectl portray cases/<pod-id>

Note, in the base occasions segment, that the WarningFailedScheduling case blunder listed

in Events is accompanied by fit failure on node....Insufficient cpu after the

blunder. As you can see, Kubernetes couldn't locate a fit in the cluster that met all the constraints we characterized.

On the off chance that we currently adjust our CPU constraint down to 500 m, and then recreate our replication controller, we ought to have all three units running inside a couple of seconds.

Summary

We investigated the overall architecture for Kubernetes, as well as the center develops, gave to assemble your services and application stacks. You ought to have a superior understanding of how these abstractions make it easier to manage the existence cycle of your stack and/or services in general and not simply the individual segments. Additionally, we took a direct see how to manage some basic day-to-day tasks utilizing cases, services, and replication controllers. We also saw how to utilize Kubernetes to automatically react to outages via health checks. Finally, we investigated the Kubernetes scheduler and a portion of the constraints clients can determine to impact booking placement.

In the following chapter, we will plunge into the networking layer of Kubernetes. We'll perceive how networking is done and also take a gander at the center Kubernetes intermediary that is utilized for traffic directing. We will also take a gander at service disclosure and the logical namespace groupings.

Networking, Load Balancers, and Ingress

In this section, let us see how the Kubernetes cluster manages the network and how it differs from other approaches. We will describe the three requirements of Kubernetes network solutions and explore why they are necessary for easy operation. In addition, we will examine the problem for Kubernetes proxy services and work on each node. Finally, we will see a brief description of some of the characteristics of higher-level isolation across multiple organizations.

This chapter covers the following points:

Kubernetes Network

Advanced Services Concepts

Discovery service

DNS

Namespace restrictions and quotas

Kubernetes Network

Networking is a vital concern for manufacturing operations. At the service level, we need a reliable way for our application components to be located and communicate with one another. Introducing the container and grouping it into the mix of things make it more complicated, because now we need to consider a few name names. Communication and discovery become an exploit that must go beyond the container IP space, the host network, and sometimes even the network topologies of multiple data centers.

Kubernetes uses its origins in the sorting tools Google has used for the last ten years. Networking is an area where Google has outpaced the competition with one of the largest networks in the world. Previously, Google developed its hardware and software-defined network switches (SDNs) to give them greater control, redundancy, and efficiency in their daily network work (see paragraph 1 for more details). see the section at the end of the chapter for details). Several lessons learned from managing and networking two billion tanks a week were distilled to Kubernetes and served as the basis for the creation of K8 networks.

Networking in Kubernetes requires that each pod has its IP address. Implementation details may vary depending on the underlying infrastructure provider. However, all implementations must follow certain basic rules. First, and then Kubernetes does not allow the use of Network Address Translation (NAT) for container-to-node traffic or container-to-node traffic (minion). In addition, the IP address of the internal container must match the IP address used to communicate with it.

These rules preserve much of the complexity of the network suite and facilitate the design of applications. In addition, they eliminate the need to re-examine network communication in legacy applications migrated from existing infrastructure. Finally, in new applications, they enable larger scale management of hundreds and even thousands of applications and services.

K8s does this IP magic on a scale by using a placeholder. Remember that a paused container is often referred to as an infrastructure container pod, and it is your important task to reserve network resources for our application containers to run later. The pause container contains the network namespace and the IP of the entire basement and can be used by all running containers. The break container joins first and contains a namespace, while the next containers join as they begin.

Networking capabilities

Kubernetes offers a wide range of networking options. Some solutions work with native AWS and GCP layers. There are various overlapping complements, some of which will be addressed in the next section. Finally, the CNI (Container Networking Interface) plugins are compatible. CNI should be a common additional container architecture. It is currently compatible with several orchestration tools such as Kubernetes, Mesos and CloudFoundry. Discover more information about:

https://github.com/containernetworking/cni.

For a complete list of compatible network options, always consult the Kubernetes documentation.

Comparing networks

To better understand the container network, it might be instructive to consider alternative approaches to the container network. This following approaches do not make an exhaustive list, but should provide an overview of the options available.

Docker

The Docker Engine creates three sorts of systems as a matter of course. These are connected, host, and none.

The spanned system is the default decision except if generally determined. In this mode, the holder has its own systems administration namespace and is then crossed over by means of virtual interfaces to the host (or hub on account of K8s) arrange. In the connected system, two holders can utilize a similar IP extend in light of the fact that they are disconnected. Subsequently, administration correspondence requires some extra port mapping through the host side of system interfaces.

Docker likewise underpins a host arrange, which enables the holders to utilize the host organize stack. Execution is extraordinarily profited since it evacuates a degree of system virtualization; nonetheless, you lose the security of having a separated system namespace. Moreover, port use must be overseen all the more cautiously since all compartments share an IP.

At last, Docker underpins a none system, which creates a holder with no outer interface. Just a loopback gadget is appeared in the event that you investigate the system interfaces.

In every one of these situations, we are still on a solitary machine, and outside of a host mode, the holder IP space isn't accessible, outside that machine. Associating holders crosswise over two machines at that point requires NAT and port mapping for correspondence.

Docker client characterized systems

So as to address the cross-machine correspondence issue and permit more prominent adaptability, Docker likewise bolsters client characterized systems through system modules. These systems exist autonomous of the holders themselves. In this manner, compartments can join the equivalent existing systems. Through the new module engineering, different drivers can be accommodated different system use cases.

The first of these is the scaffold driver, which enables making of systems to some degree like the default connect organize.

The second is the overlay driver. So as to facilitate over numerous hosts, they should all concur on the accessible systems and their topologies. The overlay driver utilizes a dispersed key-esteem store to synchronize the system creation over numerous hosts.

Docker likewise underpins a Macvlan driver, which utilizes the interface and sub-interfaces on the host. Macvlan offers an increasingly proficient system virtualization and seclusion as it sidesteps the Linux connect.

The module system will permit a wide scope of systems administration potential outcomes in Docker. Actually, huge numbers of the outsider alternatives, for example, Weave have just created their very own Docker arrange modules.

Weave

Weave gives an overlay system to Docker holders. It tends to be utilized as a module with the new Docker arrange module interface, and it is additionally perfect with Kubernetes through a CNI module. In the same way as other overlay systems, many reprimands the presentation effect of the epitome overhead. Note that they have as of late included a review discharge with Virtual Extensible LAN (VXLAN) exemplification support, which enormously improves execution. For more data, visit

ast-datapath/.

Wool

Wool originates from CoreOS and is an etcd-supported overlay. Wool gives a full subnet to each host/hub empowering a comparable example to the Kubernetes practice of a routable IP for every unit or gathering of holders. Wool remembers a for bit VXLAN epitome mode for better execution and has a test multi-organize mode like the overlay Docker module. For more data, visit https://github.com/coreos/wool.

Undertaking Calico

Undertaking Calico is a layer 3-based systems administration model that uses the implicit steering elements of the Linux bit. Courses are engendered to virtual switches on each host by means of the Border Gateway Protocol (BGP). Calico can be utilized for anything from little scale sends to huge Internet-scale establishments. Since it works at a lower level on the system stack, there is no requirement for extra NAT, burrowing, or overlays. It can associate straightforwardly with the hidden system foundation. Moreover, it has helped to arrange level ACLs to give extra disconnection and security. For more data visit the accompanying URL:

http://www.projectcalico.org/.

Waterway

Waterway blends both Calico for arrange approach and Flannel for overlay into one arrangement. It underpins both Calico and Flannel type overlays and uses the Calico strategy requirement rationale. Clients can look over overlay and non-overlay alternatives with this arrangement as it consolidates the highlights of the former two undertakings. For more data visit the accompanying URL:

https://github.com/tigera/trench

Adjusted plan

It's essential to bring up the parity Kubernetes is attempting to accomplish by putting the IP at the case level. Utilizing special IP addresses at the host level is tricky as the number of compartments develops. Ports must be utilized to uncover benefits on explicit holders and permit outer correspondence. Moreover, the intricacy of running different administrations that could think about one another (and their custom ports) and dealing with the port space turns into a major issue.

Be that as it may, relegating an IP address to every holder can be pointless excess. In instances of sizable scale, overlay systems and NATs are required so as to address every holder. Overlay systems include inactivity, and IP locations would be taken up by backend benefits also since they have to speak with their frontend partners.

Here, we truly observe a preferred position in the deliberations that Kubernetes gives at the application and administration level. In the event that I have a web server and a database, we can keep them on a similar case and utilize a solitary IP address. The web server and database can utilize the nearby interface and standard ports to impart, and no custom arrangement is required. Further, benefits on the backend are not unnecessarily presented to other application stacks running somewhere else in the group (yet potentially on a similar host). Since the case sees a similar IP address that the applications running inside it see, administration disclosure doesn't require any extra interpretation.

On the off chance that you need the adaptability of an overlay arrange, you can at present utilize an overlay at the case level. Weave, Flannel, and Project Calico can be utilized with Kubernetes just as a plenty of different modules and overlays accessible at this point.

This is additionally extremely accommodating with regards to booking the remaining burdens. It is a key to have a basic and standard structure for the scheduler to coordinate requirements and understand where space exists on the group's system at some random time. This is a powerful situation with an assortment of uses and assignments running, so any extra multifaceted nature here will have undulating impacts.

There are additionally suggestions for administration disclosure. New administrations coming on the web must decide and enlist an IP address on which the remainder of the world, or possibly group, can contact them. In the event that NAT is utilized, the administrations will require an extra system to gain proficiency with their remotely confronting IP.

Propelled administrations

How about we investigate the IP technique as it identifies with administrations and correspondence between holders. In the event that you review, in the Services segment, Chapter 2, Pods, Services, Replication Controllers, and Labels, you discovered that Kubernetes is utilizing kube-intermediary to decide the correct unit IP address and port serving each solicitation. In the background, kube-proxy is really utilizing virtual IPs and iptables to make this enchantment work

Kube-proxy currently has two modes—userspace and iptables. Starting at now, 1.2 iptables is the default mode. In the two modes, kube-proxy is running on each host. Its first obligation is to screen the API from the Kubernetes ace. Any updates to administrations will trigger an update to iptables from kube-proxy. For instance, when another help is created, a virtual IP address is picked and a standard in iptables is set, which will guide its traffic to kube-proxy by means of a random port. Accordingly, we currently have an approach to catch administration ordained traffic on this hub. Since kube-proxy is running on all hubs, we have group wide goals for the administration VIP (short for virtual IP). Moreover, DNS records can point to this VIP also.

In the userspace mode, we have a snare created in iptables, yet the proxying of traffic is as yet handled by kube-proxy. The iptables rule is just sending traffic to the administration passage in kube-proxy now. Once kube-proxy gets the traffic for specific assistance, it should then advance it to a case in the administration's pool of candidates. It does this utilizing a random port that was chosen during administration creation.

It is likewise conceivable to constantly advance traffic from a similar client IP to the equivalent backend unit/ compartment utilizing the sessionAffinity component in your administration definition.

In the iptables mode, the units are coded legitimately in the iptable guidelines. This evacuates the reliance on kube-proxy for really proxying the traffic. The solicitation will go directly to iptables and then on to the unit. This is quicker and expels a potential purpose of disappointment.

Outer administrations

In the past section, we saw a couple of administration models. For testing and exhibition purposes, we needed every one of the administrations to be remotely open. This was arranged by the sort: LoadBalancer component in our administration definition. The LoadBalancer type creates an outer burden balancer on the cloud supplier. We should take note of that help for outside burden balancers differs by supplier, as does the usage. For our situation, we are utilizing GCE, so coordination is quite smooth. The main extra arrangement required is to open firewall rules for the outer help ports.

How about we burrow somewhat more profound and do a portray command on one of the administrations from the Pods, Services, Replication Controllers, and Labels:

$ kubectl depict administration/hub js-names

In the yield, in the former figure, you'll note a few key components. Our Namespace: is

set to default, Type: is LoadBalancer, and we have the outer IP recorded under LoadBalancer Ingress:. Further, we see Endpoints:, which shows us the IPs of the units accessible to answer administration demands.

Interior administrations

How about we investigate different sorts of administrations we can convey. To start with, as a matter of course, administrations are just inside confronting. You can determine a kind of clusterIP to accomplish this, be that as it may, if no sort is characterized, clusterIP is the expected sort. How about we investigate a model; note the absence of the sort component:

apiVersion: v1

kind: Service

metadata:

name: hub js-inner

names:

name: hub js-inner

spec:

ports:

- port: 80 selector:

name: hub js

Posting 3-1: nodejs-administration internal.yaml

Utilize this leaning to create the administration definition file. You'll require a solid variant of the hub js RC (Listing 2-7: nodejs-wellbeing controller-2.yaml). As should be obvious, the selector coordinates on the units named hub js that our RC propelled in the anterior part. We will create the administration and then rundown the as of now running administrations with a channel:

$kubectl create - f nodejs-administration internal.yaml

$kubectl get administrations - l name=node-js-inner

As should be obvious, we have another help, however just a single IP. Further, the IP address isn't remotely open. We won't have the option to test the administration from an internet browser this time. Be that as it may, we can utilize the handy kubectl executive command and endeavor to associate from one of the different cases. You will require hub js-case (Listing 2-1: nodejs-pod.yaml) running. At that point, you can execute the accompanying command:

$ kubectl executive hub js-unit - twist <node-js-inside IP>

This enables us to run a docker executive command as though we had a shell in the hub js-case holder. It at that point hits the inward help URL, which advances to any cases with the hub js name.

On the off chance that everything is great, you ought to recover the crude HTML yield. In this way, you effectively created an inner just help. This can be valuable for backend administrations that you need to make accessible to different compartments running in your group, yet not open to the world on the loose.

Custom burden adjusting

The third kind of administration that K8s permits is the NodePort type. This sort enables us to uncover help through the host or hub (crony) on a particular port. In this manner, we can utilize the IP address of any hub (crony) and access our administration on the alloted hub port. Kubernetes will appoint a hub port as a matter of course in the scope of 3000-32767, however you can likewise determine your own custom port. In the model in Listing 3-2: nodejs-administration nodeport.yaml, we pick port 30001, as pursues:

```
apiVersion: v1

kind: Service

metadata:

name: hub js-nodeport

names:

name: hub js-nodeport

spec:

ports:

- port: 80

nodePort: 30001

selector:

name: hub js

type: NodePort
```

Posting 3-2: nodejs-administration nodeport.yaml

By and by, create this YAML definition file and create your administration, as pursues:

```
$ kubectl create - f nodejs-administration nodeport.yaml
```

You'll take note of a message about opening firewall ports. Like the outside burden balancer type, NodePort is uncovering your administration remotely utilizing ports on the hubs. This could be valuable if, for instance, you need to utilize your heap balancer before the hubs. How about we ensure that we open those ports on GCP before we test our new assistance.

From the GCE VM occurrence reassure, click on the subtleties for any of your hubs (followers). At that point click on the system, which typically defaults except if generally indicated during creation. In Firewall rules, we can include a standard by clicking Add firewall rule.

We would now be able to test our new help, by opening a program and utilizing an IP address of any hub (follower) in your bunch. The configuration to test the new assistance is as per the following:

http://<Minoion IP Address>:<NodePort>/

At last, the most recent form has included an ExternalName type, which maps a CNAME to the administration..

Cross-node proxy

Recollect that kube-proxy is running on every one of the nodes, along these lines, regardless of whether the unit isn't running there, the traffic will be given a proxy to the suitable host. Allude to the Cross-node traffic figure for a visual on how the traffic streams. A client makes a solicitation to an outside IP or URL. The solicitation is adjusted by Node for this situation. In any case, the case doesn't occur to run on this node. This isn't an issue in light of the fact that the case IP addresses are routable. Thus, Kube- proxy or iptables just passes traffic onto the unit IP for this administration. The system steering at that point finishes on Node 2, where the mentioned application lives:

Custom ports

Administrations additionally enable you to outline traffic to different ports; at that point the compartments and units uncover themselves. We will create a help that uncovered port 90 and advances traffic to port 80 on the units. We will call the node-js-90 unit to mirror the custom port number. Create the accompanying two definition files:

apiVersion: v1

kind: ReplicationController

metadata:

name: node-js-90

names:

name: node-js-90

spec:

copies: 3

selector:

name: node-js-90

layout:

metadata:

names:

name: node-js-90

spec:

compartments:

- name: node-js-90

picture: jonbaier/node-express-info:latest ports:

- containerPort: 80

Posting 3-3: nodejs-customPort-controller.yaml

apiVersion: v1

kind: Service

metadata:

name: node-js-90

names:

name: node-js-90

spec:

type: LoadBalancer

ports:

- port: 90

targetPort: 80

selector:

name: node-js-90

Posting 3-4: nodejs-customPort-service.yaml

You'll take note of that in the administration definition, we have a targetPort component. This component advises the administration the port to use for cases/holders in the pool. As we saw in past models, on the off chance that you don't determine targetPort, it accept that it's a similar port as the administration. This port is as yet utilized as the administration port, be that as it may, for this situation, we are going to uncover the administration on port 90 while the holders serve content on port 80.

Create this RC and administration and open the fitting firewall rules, as we did in the last model. It might pause for a minute for the outside burden balancer IP to proliferate to the get administration command. When it does, you ought to have the option to open and see our commonplace web application in a program utilizing the accompanying arrangement:

http://<external administration IP>:90/

Different ports

Another custom port use case is that of different ports. Numerous applications uncover various ports, for example, HTTP on port 80 and port 8888 for web servers. The accompanying model shows our application reacting on the two ports. By and by, we'll additionally need to include a firewall rule for this port, as we accomplished for Listing 3-2: nodejs-administration nodeport.yaml already:

```
apiVersion: v1
kind: ReplicationController
metadata:
name: node-js-multi
marks:
name: node-js-multi
spec:
imitations: 3
selector:
name: node-js-multi
format:
metadata:
marks:
name: node-js-multi
spec:
holders:
- name: node-js-multi
picture: jonbaier/node-express-multi:latest ports:
- containerPort: 80
- containerPort: 8888
```

Posting 3-5: nodejs-multi-controller.yaml

```
apiVersion: v1
kind: Service
```

```
metadata:
name: node-js-multi
marks:
name: node-js-multi
spec:
type: LoadBalancer
ports:
- name: http
convention: TCP
port: 80
- name: counterfeit administrator http
convention: TCP
port: 8888
selector:
name: node-js-multi
```

Posting 3-6: nodejs-multi-service.yaml

The application and holder itself must tune in on the two ports for this to work. In this model, port 8888 is utilized to speak to a phony administrator interface.

On the off chance that, for instance, you need to tune in on port 443, you would require a legitimate SSL attachment tuning in on the server.

Entrance

We talked about already how Kubernetes utilizes the administration unique as a way to proxy traffic to support case dispersed all through our bunch. While this is useful in both scaling and unit recuperation, there are further developed steering situations that are not tended to by this structure.

Keeping that in mind, Kubernetes has included an Ingress asset, which takes into account custom proxying and burden adjusting to a back help. Consider it an additional layer or bounce in the steering way before traffic hits our administration. Similarly as an application has a help and support cases, the Ingress asset needs both an Ingress passage point and an Ingress controller that play out the custom rationale. The passage point characterizes the courses and the controller really handles the directing. For our models, we will utilize the default GCE backend.

A few restrictions to know about when utilizing the Ingress API can be found here:

https://github.com/kubernetes/contrib/mass/ace/entrance/cont rollers/gce/BETA_LIMITATIONS.md

As you may review, in Chapter 1, Introduction to Kubernetes, we saw that a GCE group returns with a default which gives Layer 7 burden adjusting capacity. We can see this controller running on the off chance that we take a gander at the kube-system namespace:

$ kubectl get rc - namespace=kube-system

We should see a RC recorded with the l7-default-backend-v1.0 name

This gives the Ingress controller piece that really courses the traffic characterized in our Ingress section focuses. How about we create a few assets for an Ingress.

To begin with, we will create a couple of new replication controllers with my httpwhalesay picture. This is a remix of the first whalesay that was shown in a program. The accompanying posting shows the YAML. Notice the three runs that let us join a few assets into one YAML file:

apiVersion: v1

kind: ReplicationController

metadata:

name: whale-entrance a

spec:

reproductions: 1

format:

metadata:

marks:

application: whale-entrance a

```
spec:
holders:
- name: sayhey
picture: jonbaier/httpwhalesay:0.1
command: ["node", "index.js", "Whale Type A, Here."] ports:
- containerPort: 80
-
apiVersion: v1
kind: ReplicationController
metadata:
name: whale-entrance b
spec:
imitations: 1
format:
metadata:
marks:
application: whale-entrance b
spec:
holders:
- name: sayhey
picture: jonbaier/httpwhalesay:0.1
command: ["node", "index.js", "Hello man, It's Whale B, Just Chillin.'"]
ports:
- containerPort: 80
```

Posting 3-7. whale-rcs.yaml

Notice that we are making cases with a similar holder, yet different beginning up parameters. Observe these parameters for some other time. We will likewise create Service endpoints for every one of these RCs:

```
apiVersion: v1

kind: Service

metadata:

name: whale-svc-a

marks:

application: whale-entrance a

spec:

type: NodePort

ports:

- port: 80

nodePort: 30301

convention: TCP

name: http

selector:

application: whale-entrance a

-

apiVersion: v1

kind: Service

metadata:

name: whale-svc-b

marks:

application: whale-entrance b

spec:

type: NodePort

ports:

- port: 80

nodePort: 30284
```

convention: TCP

name: http

selector:

application: whale-entrance b

-

apiVersion: v1

kind: Service

metadata:

name: whale-svc-default

marks:

application: whale-entrance a

spec:

type: NodePort

ports:

- port: 80

nodePort: 30302

convention: TCP

name: http

selector:

application: whale-entrance a

Posting 3-8. whale-svcs.yaml

Again create these with the kubectl create - f command, as pursues:

$kubectl create - f whale-rcs.yaml

$kubectl create - f whale-svcs.yaml

We should see messages about the RCs and Services fruitful creation. Next, we have to characterize the Ingress section point. We will utilize http://a.whale.hey and http://b.whale.hey as our demo passage focuses:

apiVersion: expansions/v1beta1

kind: Ingress

metadata:

name: whale-entrance

spec:

rules:

- host: a.whale.hey http:

ways:

- path:/backend:

serviceName: whale-svc-a

servicePort: 80

- host: b.whale.hey http:

ways:

- path:/backend:

serviceName: whale-svc-b

servicePort: 80

Posting 3-9. whale-ingress.yaml

Once more, use kubectl create - f to create this Ingress. When this is effectively created, we should sit tight a couple of seconds for GCE to give the Ingress a static IP address. Utilize the accompanying command to watch the Ingress asset:

$ kubectl get entrance

Since this is definitely not an enrolled space name, we should indicate the goals in the twist command, this way:

$ twist - resolve a.whale.hey:80:130.211.24.177 http://a.whale.hey/

We can likewise attempt the subsequent URL and we will get our second RC:

$ twist - resolve b.whale.hey:80:130.211.24.177 http://b.whale.hey/

We see that the images are nearly the equivalent, then again, actually the words from each whale mirror the startup parameters from each RC we began before. In this way our two Ingress indicates are coordinating traffic different backends.

In this model, we utilized the default GCE backend for an Ingress controller. Kubernetes enables us to manufacture our own and Nginx really has a couple of forms accessible too.

Movements, multicluster, and more

As you've seen up until now, Kubernetes offers an elevated level of adaptability and customization to create a help reflection around your compartments running in the group. Be that as it may, there might be times where you need to point to something outside your group.

A case of this would work with heritage systems or even applications running on another bunch. On account of the previous, this is a superbly decent system so as to relocate to Kubernetes and compartments all in all. We can start to deal with the administration endpoints in Kubernetes while sewing the stack together utilizing the K8s organization ideas. Also, we can even begin bringing once again bits of the stack, as the frontend, each in turn as the association refactors applications for microservices and/or containerization.

To enable access to non-case based applications, the administrations build enables you to utilize endpoints that are outside the bunch. Kubernetes is really making an endpoint asset each time you create an assistance that utilizations selectors. The endpoints object monitors the unit IPs in the heap adjusting pool. You can see this by running a get endpoints command, as pursues:

$ kubectl get endpoints

You should see something like this:

NAMEENDPOINTS

http-pd10.244.2.29:80,10.244.2.30:80,10.244.3.16:80

kubernetes10.240.0.2:443

node-js10.244.0.12:80,10.244.2.24:80,10.244.3.13:80

You'll take note of a section for every one of the administrations we as of now have running on our bunch. For most administrations, the endpoints are only the IP of each case running in a RC. As I referenced, Kubernetes does this naturally dependent on the selector. As we scale the reproductions in a controller with coordinating marks, Kubernetes will refresh the endpoints consequently.

On the off chance that we need to create a help for something that isn't a case and along these lines has no marks to choose, we can without much of a stretch do this with both an assistance and endpoint definition, as pursues:

apiVersion: v1

kind: Service

metadata:

name: custom-administration

spec:

type: LoadBalancer

ports:

- name: http

convention: TCP

port: 80

Posting 3-10: nodejs-custom-service.yaml

apiVersion: v1

kind: Endpoints

metadata:

name: custom-administration

subsets:

- addresses:

- ip: <X.X.X.X> ports:

- name: http

port: 80

convention: TCP

Posting 3-11: nodejs-custom-endpoint.yaml

In the previous model, you'll have to supplant <X.X.X.X> with a genuine IP address, where the new help can point to. For my situation, I utilized the general population load balancer IP from the node-js-multi administration we created before in posting 3-6. Feel free to create these assets now.

In the event that we presently run a get endpoints command, we will see this IP address at port 80 related with the custom-administration endpoint. Further, in the event that we take a gander at the administration subtleties, we will see the IP recorded in the Endpoints area:

$ kubectl portray administration/custom-administration

We can try out this new assistance by opening the custom-administration outside IP from a program.

Custom addressing

Another choice to customize administrations is with the clusterIP component. In our models up until now, we've not determined an IP address, which implies that it picks the inward address of the administration for us. In any case, we can include this component and pick the IP address ahead of time with something like clusterip: 10.0.125.105.

There might be times when you would prefer not to stack balance and would prefer to have DNS with A records for each unit. For instance, software that requirements to imitate information uniformly to all nodes may depend on A records to convey information. For this situation, we can utilize a model like the accompanying one and set clusterip to None. Kubernetes won't allot an IP address and rather just dole out A records in DNS for every one of the units. In the event that you are utilizing DNS, the administration ought to be accessible at node-js-none or node-js-none.default.cluster.local from inside the group. We have the accompanying code:

apiVersion: v1

kind: Service

metadata:

name: node-js-none

marks:

name: node-js-none

spec:

clusterIP: None

ports:

- port: 80 selector:

name: node-js

Posting 3-12: nodejs-headless-service.yaml

Test it out after you create this administration with the trusty executive command:

$ kubectl executive node-js-case - twist node-js-none

Administration disclosure

As we examined before, the Kubernetes ace monitors all help definitions and updates. Revelation can happen in one of three different ways. The initial two techniques use Linux condition factors. There is support for the Docker connect style of condition factors, yet Kubernetes additionally has its naming show. Here is a case of what our node-js administration model may look like utilizing K8s condition factors (note IPs will change):

NODE_JS_PORT_80_TCP=tcp://10.0.103.215:80

NODE_JS_PORT=tcp://10.0.103.215:80

NODE_JS_PORT_80_TCP_PROTO=tcp

NODE_JS_PORT_80_TCP_PORT=80

NODE_JS_SERVICE_HOST=10.0.103.215

NODE_JS_PORT_80_TCP_ADDR=10.0.103.215

NODE_JS_SERVICE_PORT=80

Posting 3-13: Service condition factors

Another alternative for disclosure is through DNS. While condition factors can be valuable when DNS isn't accessible, it has downsides. The system creates factors at creation time, so benefits that come online later won't be found or would require some extra tooling to refresh all the system situations.

DNS

DNS comprehends the issues seen with condition factors by enabling us to reference the administrations by their names. As administrations restart, scale out, or show up once more, the DNS sections will refresh and guaranteeing that the administration name consistently indicates the most recent framework. DNS is set up naturally in a large portion of the upheld suppliers.

On the off chance that DNS is bolstered by your supplier, yet not set up, you can arrange the accompanying factors in your default supplier config when you create your Kubernetes group:

ENABLE_CLUSTER_DNS="${KUBE_ENABLE_CLUSTER_DNS:- true}"

DNS_SERVER_IP="10.0.0.10"

DNS_DOMAIN="cluster.local"

DNS_REPLICAS=1

With DNS dynamic, administrations can be gotten to in one of two structures—either the administration name itself, <service-name> or a completely qualified name that incorporates the namespace, <service-

name>.<namespace-name>.cluster.local. In our models, it would appear to be like node-js-90 or node-js-90.default.cluster.local.

Multitenancy

Kubernetes likewise has an extra build for confinement at the group level. By and large, you can run Kubernetes and never stress over namespaces; everything will run in the default namespace if not indicated. In any case, in situations where you run multitenancy networks or need wide scale isolation and detachment of the bunch assets, namespaces can be utilized to this end.

To begin, Kubernetes has two namespaces—default and kube-system. The kube-system namespace is utilized for all the system-level compartments

The UI, logging, DNS, and so on are altogether run in kube-system. Everything else the client creates runs in the default namespace. Be that as it may, our asset definition files can alternatively indicate a custom namespace. For testing, how about we investigate how to construct another namespace.

To start with, we'll have to create a namespace definition file like the one in this posting:

apiVersion: v1

kind: Namespace

metadata:

name: test

Posting 3-14: test-ns.yaml

We can feel free to create this file with our handy create command:

$ kubectl create - f test-ns.yaml

Presently we can create assets that utilization the test namespace. Coming up next is a case of a unit utilizing this new namespace:

apiVersion: v1

kind: Pod

metadata:

name: utility

namespace: test

spec:

holders:

- image: debian:latest command:

- sleep

- "3600"

name: utility

Posting 3-15: ns-pod.yaml

While the case can in any case get to administrations in different namespaces, it should utilize the long DNS

type of <service-name>.<namespace-name>.cluster.local. For instance, if you somehow managed to run a command from inside the holder in Listing 3-15: ns-pod.yaml, you could utilize node-js.default.cluster.local to get to the Node.js

Here is a note about asset use. Eventually in this book, you may come up short on space on your bunch to create new Kubernetes assets. The planning will fluctuate dependent on bunch size, however it's great to remember this and do some tidy up now and again. Utilize the accompanying commands to expel old models:

$ kubectl erase unit <pod name>

$ kubectl erase svc <service name>

$kubectl erase rc <replication controller name>

$kubectl erase rs <replicaset name>

Breaking points

We should examine our new namespace more. Run the depict command as pursues:

$ kubectl depict namespace/test

Kubernetes enables you as far as possible the assets utilized by singular cases or compartments and the assets utilized by the general namespace utilizing portions. You'll take note of that there are no asset points of confinement or shares at present set on the test namespace.

Assume we need to restrain the impression of this new namespace; we can set quantities, for example, the accompanying:

apiVersion: v1

kind: ResourceQuota

metadata:

name: test-shares

namespace: test

spec:

hard:

cases: 3

administrations: 1

replicationcontrollers: 1

Posting 3-16: quota.yaml

As a general rule, namespaces would be for bigger application networks and would most likely never have portions this low. I am utilizing this so as to ease outline of the ability in the model.

Here, we will create a portion of 3 cases, 1 RC, and 1 assistance for the test namespace. As you likely speculated, this is executed by and by our trusty create command:

$ kubectl create - f quota.yaml

Since we have that set up, how about we use portray on the namespace, as pursues:

$ kubectl depict namespace/test

You'll take note of that we presently have a few qualities recorded in the amount segment and the points of confinement segment is as yet clear. We likewise have a Used segment, which tells us how near the points of confinement we are right now. We should attempt to turn up a couple of units utilizing the accompanying definition:

apiVersion: v1

kind: ReplicationController

metadata:

name: busybox-ns

namespace: test

names:

name: busybox-ns

spec:

copies: 4

selector:

name: busybox-ns

layout:

metadata:

names:

name: busybox-ns

spec:

compartments:

- name: busybox-ns

picture: busybox command:

- sleep

- "3600"

Posting 3-17: busybox-ns.yaml

You'll take note of that we are making four copies of this essential case. In the wake of utilizing create to fabricate this RC, run the depict command on the test namespace again. You'll see that the used qualities for cases and RCs are at their maximum. Nonetheless, we requested four copies and just observe three cases being used.

How about we see what's going on with our RC. You may endeavor to do that with the command here:

kubectl depict rc/busybox-ns

Notwithstanding, on the off chance that you attempt, you'll be disheartened to see a not discovered message from the server. This is on the grounds that we created this RC in another namespace and kubectl accept the default namespace if not determined. This implies we have to indicate - namepsace=test with each command when we wish to get to assets in the test namespace.

We can likewise set the current namespace by working with the setting settings. To start with, we have to locate our present setting, which is found with the accompanying command:

$ kubectl config see | grep current-setting

Next, we can take that specific circumstance and set the namespace variable like the accompanying:

$ kubectl config set-setting <Current Context> - namespace=test

Presently you can run the kubectl command without the need to determine the namespace. Make sure to switch back when you need to take a gander at the assets running in your default namespace.

Run the command with the namespace indicated. In the event that you've set your current namespace as exhibited in the tip box, you can leave off the - namespace contention:

$ kubectl depict rc/busybox-ns - namespace=test

As should be obvious in the previous picture, the initial three cases were effectively created, however, our last one comes up short with the Limited to 3 cases blunder.

This is a simple method as far as possible for assets parceled out at a network scale. Significantly, you can likewise set amounts for CPU, memory, constant volumes, and privileged insights. Also, limits work along these lines to share, however they set the breaking point for each unit or holder inside the namespace.

A note on asset utilization

As a large portion of the models in this book use GCP or AWS, it very well may be exorbitant to keep everything running. It's additionally simple to come up short on assets utilizing the default group size, particularly on the off chance that you keep each model running. In this manner, you might need to erase more seasoned cases, replication controllers, reproduction sets, and administrations intermittently. You can likewise pulverize the bunch and recreate utilizing Chapter 1, Introduction to Kubernetes as an approach to bring down your cloud supplier bill.

Summary

We investigated systems administration and administrations in Kubernetes. You should now understand how organizing correspondences are structured in K8s and feel great getting to your administrations inside and remotely. We perceived how kube-proxy adjusts traffic both locally and across the group. Also, we investigated the new Ingress assets that permit us better control of approaching traffic. We additionally took a gander at how DNS and administration disclosure is accomplished in Kubernetes. We polished off with brisk take a gander at namespace and separation for multitenancy.

Updates, Gradual Rollouts, And Autoscaling

This part will expand upon the center ideas, which tell you the best way to turn out updates and test new highlights of your application with insignificant disturbance to up-time. It will cover the nuts and bolts of doing application refreshes, progressive rollouts, and A/B testing. Likewise, we will take a gander at scaling the Kubernetes bunch itself.

This section will talk about the accompanying subjects:

Application scaling

Moving updates

A/B testing

Application autoscaling

Scaling up your group

Since form 1.2, Kubernetes has discharged a Deployments API. Arrangements are the prescribed method to manage scaling and application refreshes going ahead. Be that as it may, it is as yet thought to be beta at the hour of composing this book, while moving updates has been steady for a few renditions. We will investigate moving updates in this part as a prologue to the scaling idea and then plunge into the favored technique for utilizing arrangements in the following section.

Model set up

Before we start investigating the different capacities incorporated with Kubernetes for scaling and updates, we will require another model condition. We are going to utilize a variety of our past holder picture with a blue foundation (allude to the v0.1 and v0.2 (next to each other) picture, later in this part, for an examination). We have the accompanying code:

```
apiVersion: v1
kind: ReplicationController
metadata:
name: node-js-scale
names:
name: node-js-scale
spec:
copies: 1
selector:
name: node-js-scale
layout:
metadata:
names:
name: node-js-scale
spec:
compartments:
- name: node-js-scale
picture: jonbaier/unit scaling:0.1 ports:
```

- containerPort: 80

Posting 4-1: unit scaling-controller.yaml

apiVersion: v1

kind: Service

metadata:

name: node-js-scale

names:

name: node-js-scale

spec:

type: LoadBalancer

sessionAffinity: ClientIP

ports:

- port: 80 selector:

name: node-js-scale

Posting 4-2: unit scaling-service.yaml

Create these administrations with the accompanying commands:

$kubectl create - f unit scaling-controller.yaml

$kubectl create - f unit scaling-service.yaml

The open IP address for the administration may pause for a minute to create.

Scaling up

After some time, as you run your applications in the Kubernetes bunch, you will locate that a few applications need more assets, while others can make do with less assets. Rather than evacuating the whole RC (and related units), we need a progressively consistent approach to scale our application all over.

Fortunately, Kubernetes incorporates a scale command, which is fit explicitly for this reason. The scale command works both with Replication Controllers and the new Deployments deliberation. For the present, we will investigate the use with Replication Controllers. In our new model, we have just a single copy running. You can check this with a get units command:

$ kubectl get cases - l name=node-js-scale

How about we take a stab at scaling that up to three with the accompanying command:

$ kubectl scale - replicas=3 rc/node-js-scale

In the event that all goes well, you'll just observe the scaled word on the yield of your terminal window.

Alternatively, you can determine the - current-reproductions banner as a confirmation step. The scaling will possibly happen if the real number of reproductions presently running matches this check.

Subsequent to posting our units by and by, we should now observe three cases running with a name like node-js-scale-XXXXX, where the X characters are a random string.

You can likewise utilize the scale command to decrease the quantity of imitations. In either case, the scale command includes or expels the vital case reproductions, and the administration naturally updates and parities across new or remaining imitations.

Smooth updates

The scaling of our application all over as our asset demands change is helpful for some creation situations, yet shouldn't something be said about basic application refreshes? Any generation system will have code updates, fixes, and highlight increments. These could be happening month to month, week by week, or even every day. Ensuring that we have a solid method to push out these progressions without interference to our clients is a vital thought.

By and by, we profit by the long stretches of experience the Kubernetes system is based on. There is a worked in help for moving updates with the 1.0 form. The moving update command enables us to refresh whole RCs or simply the fundamental Docker picture utilized by every reproduction. We can likewise determine an update interim, which will enable us to refresh each case in turn and hold up until continuing to the following.

We should take our scaling model and play out a moving update to the 0.2 adaptation of our holder picture. We will utilize an update interim of 2 minutes, so we can watch the procedure as it occurs in the accompanying manner:

$kubectl moving update node-js-scale - image=jonbaier/unit scaling:0.2 - update-period="2m"

You should see some content about making another RC named node-js-scale-XXXXX, where the X characters will be a random series of numbers and letters. Likewise, you will see the start of a circle that is beginning one imitation of the new form and expelling one from the current RC. This procedure will proceed until the new RC has the full tally of copies running.

In the event that we need to track with continuously, we can open another terminal window and utilize the get units command, alongside a name channel, to perceive what's going on:

$ kubectl get units - l name=node-js-scale

This command will channel for units with node-js-scale in the name. On the off chance that you pursue this giving the moving update command, you should see a few cases running as it creates new forms and expels the old ones individually.

The full yield of the past moving update

As should be obvious here, Kubernetes is first making another RC named node-js-

scale-10ea08ff9a118ac6a93f85547ed28f6. K8s then circles through individually,

making another case in the new controller and expelling one from the old. This proceeds until the new controller has the full copy tally and the bygone one is at zero. After this, the old controller is erased and the enhanced one is renamed with the first controller name.

On the off chance that you run a get cases command now, you'll see that the cases still all have a more extended name. On the other hand, we could have indicated the name of another controller in the command, and Kubernetes will create another RC and units utilizing that name. By and by, the controller of the old name basically vanishes in the wake of refreshing is finished. I prescribe that you indicate another name for the refreshed controller to maintain a strategic distance from perplexity in your unit naming down the line. A similar update command with this strategy will resemble this:

$kubectl moving update node-js-scale node-js-scale-v2.0 - image=jonbaier/unit scaling:0.2 - update-period="2m"

Utilizing the static outer IP address from the administration we created in the main segment, we can open the administration in a program. We should see our standard holder data page. Be that as it may, you'll see that the title currently says Pod Scaling v0.2 and the foundation is light yellow:

It's important that, during the whole update process, we've just been taking a gander at cases and RCs. We didn't do anything with our administration, yet the administration is as yet running fine and now coordinating to the new form of our cases. This is on the grounds that our administration is utilizing mark selectors for enrollment. Since both our old and new imitations utilize similar marks, the administration has no issue utilizing the new cases to support demands. The updates are done on the units individually, so it's consistent for the clients of the administration.

Testing, discharges, and cutovers

The moving update highlight can function admirably for a straightforward blue-green sending situation. In any case, in a genuine blue-green arrangement with a heap of different applications, there can be an assortment of interdependencies that require top to bottom testing. The update-time frame command enables us to include a break banner where some testing should be possible, however this won't generally be agreeable for testing purposes.

Correspondingly, you may need fractional changes to continue for a more drawn out time and as far as possible up to the heap balancer or administration level. For instance, you may wish to run an A/B test on another UI highlight with a segment of your clients. Another model is running a canary discharge (an imitation for this situation) of your application on new foundation like a recently included bunch node.

How about we investigate an A/B testing model. For this model, we should create another help that utilizations sessionAffinity. We will set the liking to ClientIP, which will enable us to advance clients to the equivalent backend unit. This is a key on the off chance that we need a segment of our clients to see one adaptation while others see another:

apiVersion: v1

kind: Service

metadata:

name: node-js-scale-abdominal muscle

marks:

administration: node-js-scale-abdominal muscle

spec:

type: LoadBalancer

ports:

- port: 80 sessionAffinity: ClientIP selector:

administration: node-js-scale-abdominal muscle

Posting 4-3: case AB-service.yaml

Create this administration as normal with the create command, as pursues:

$ kubectl create - f case AB-service.yaml

This will create a help that will point to our cases running both adaptation 0.2 and 0.3 of the application. Next, we will create the two RCs that create two copies of the application. One set will have form 0.2 of the application, and the other will have adaptation 0.3, as appeared here:

apiVersion: v1

kind: ReplicationController

metadata:

name: node-js-scale-a

names:

name: node-js-scale-a

form: "0.2"

administration: node-js-scale-stomach muscle

spec:

copies: 2

selector:

name: node-js-scale-a

version: "0.2"

service: node-js-scale-ab

template:

metadata:

labels:

name: node-js-scale-a

version: "0.2"

service: node-js-scale-ab

spec:

containers:

-name: node-js-scale

image: jonbaier/pod-scaling:0.2 ports:

-containerPort: 80 livenessProbe:

#An HTTP health check httpGet:

path: /

port: 80

initialDelaySeconds: 30

timeoutSeconds: 5

readinessProbe:

#An HTTP health check httpGet:

path: /

port: 80 initialDelaySeconds: 30 timeoutSeconds: 1

Listing 4-4: pod-A-controller.yaml

apiVersion: v1

kind: ReplicationController

metadata:

name: node-js-scale-b

labels:

name: node-js-scale-b

version: "0.3"

service: node-js-scale-ab

spec:

replicas: 2

selector:

name: node-js-scale-b

version: "0.3"

service: node-js-scale-ab

template:

metadata:

```
labels:
name: node-js-scale-b
version: "0.3"
service: node-js-scale-ab
spec:
containers:
-name: node-js-scale
image: jonbaier/pod-scaling:0.3 ports:
- containerPort: 80 livenessProbe:
#An HTTP wellbeing check httpGet:
way:/
port: 80
initialDelaySeconds: 40
timeoutSeconds: 6
readinessProbe:
#An HTTP wellbeing check httpGet:
way:/
port: 80 initialDelaySeconds: 30 timeoutSeconds: 1
```

Posting 4-5: unit B-controller.yaml

Note that we have a similar assistance mark, so these imitations will likewise be added to the administration pool dependent on this selector. We likewise have livenessProbe and readinessProbe characterized to ensure that our new form is functioning true to form. Once more, utilize the create command to turn up the controller:

```
$kubectl create - f unit A-controller.yaml
$kubectl create - f unit B-controller.yaml
```

Presently we have an assistance adjusting to the two adaptations of our application. In a genuine A/B test, we would now need to begin gathering measurements on the visit to every adaptation. Once more, we have sessionAffinity set to ClientIP, so all solicitations will go to a similar case. A few clients will see v0.2, and some will see v0.3.

Since we have sessionAffinity turned on, your test will probably show a similar form without fail. This is normal, and you would need to endeavor an association from different IP delivers to see both client encounters with every form.

Since the adaptations are each alone case, one can without much of a stretch separate logging and even add a logging holder to the case definition for a sidecar logging design. For quickness, we won't cover that arrangement in this book,

We can begin to perceive how this procedure will be helpful for a canary discharge or a manual blue-green organization. We can likewise perceive that it is so natural to dispatch another variant and gradually change over to the new discharge.

How about we take a gander at an essential change rapidly. It's truly as straightforward as a couple of scale commands, which are as per the following:

$kubectl scale - replicas=3 rc/node-js-scale-b

$kubectl scale - replicas=1 rc/node-js-scale-a

$kubectl scale - replicas=4 rc/node-js-scale-b

$kubectl scale - replicas=0 rc/node-js-scale-a

Utilize the get cases command joined with the - l channel in the middle of the scale commands to watch the progress as it occurs.

Presently, we have completely changed over to rendition 0.3 (node-js-scale-b). All clients will currently observe the variant 0.3 of the site. We have four imitations of rendition 0.3 and none of 0.2. In the event that you run a get rc command, you will see that despite everything we have a RC for 0.2 (node-js-scale-a). As a last cleanup, we can evacuate that controller totally, as pursues:

$ kubectl erase rc/node-js-scale-a

Application autoscaling

An ongoing element expansion to Kubernetes is that of the Horizontal Pod Autoscaler. This asset type is extremely valuable as it gives us an approach to naturally set edges for scaling our application. At present, that help is just for CPU, yet there is alpha help for custom application measurements too.

How about we utilize the node-js-scale Replication Controller from the earliest starting point of the part and include an autoscaling segment. Before we start, we should ensure we are downsized down to one copy utilizing the accompanying command:

$ kubectl scale - replicas=1 rc/node-js-scale

Presently we can create a Horizontal Pod Autoscaler with the accompanying hpa definition:

apiVersion: autoscaling/v1

kind: HorizontalPodAutoscaler

metadata:

name: node-js-scale

spec:

minReplicas: 1

maxReplicas: 3

scaleTargetRef:

apiVersion: v1

kind: ReplicationController

name: node-js-scale

targetCPUUtilizationPercentage: 20

Posting 4-6. node-js-scale-hpa.yaml

Feel free to create this with the kubectl create - f command. Presently we can list the hpas and get a portrayal too:

$ kubectl get hpa

We can likewise create autoscaling in the command line with the kubectl autoscale command. The first YAML will resemble the accompanying:

$kubectl autoscale rc/node-js-scale - min=1 - max=3 - cpu-percent=20

This will show us an autoscaler on the node-js-scale Replication Controller with a Target CPU of 30%. Also, you will see that the base units is set to 1 and most extreme is 3:

How about we likewise inquiry our cases to perceive what number of are running at this moment:

$ kubectl get cases - l name=node-js-scale

We should see just a single node-js-scale case on the grounds that our HPA is demonstrating 0% usage, so we should create some heap. We will utilize the well known blast application normal in numerous holder demos. The accompanying posting will assist us with making nonstop burden until we can hit the CPU limit for autoscaler:

```
apiVersion: v1

kind: ReplicationController

metadata:

name: boomload

spec:

copies: 1

selector:

application: loadgenerator

layout:

metadata:

names:

application: loadgenerator

spec:

compartments:

- image: williamyeh/blast

name: blast

command: ["/receptacle/sh","- c"]

args: ["while genuine ; do blast http://node-js-scale/ - c 10 - n 100 ; rest 1 ; done"]
```

Posting 4-7. boomload.yaml

Utilize the kubectl create - f command with this posting and then be prepared to begin checking the hpa. We can do this with the kubectl get hpa command we utilized before.

It might take a couple of seconds, yet we should begin to see the present CPU usage increment.

When it goes over the 20% limit we set the autoscaler will kick in:

When we see this, we can run kubectl get unit again and see there are presently a few node-

js-scale cases:

$ kubectl get cases - l name=node-js-scale

We can tidy up now by executing our heap age unit:

$ kubectl erase rc/boomload

Presently in the event that we watch the hpa, we should begin to see the CPU use drop. It might take a couple of moments, however, in the long run, we will return down to 0% CPU burden.

Scaling a bunch

Every one of these procedures are incredible for the scaling of the application, yet shouldn't something be said about the group itself. Sooner or later, you will pack the nodes full and need more assets to plan new units for your outstanding tasks at hand.

Autoscaling

At the point when you create your group, you can customize the beginning number of nodes (cronies) with the NUM_MINIONS condition variable. Of course, it is set to 4.

Moreover, the Kubernetes group has begun to incorporate autoscaling ability with the bunch itself. At present, this is the main help on GCE and GKE, however work is being done on different suppliers. This ability uses the KUBE_AUTOSCALER_MIN_NODES,

KUBE_AUTOSCALER_MAX_NODES,and KUBE_ENABLE_CLUSTER_AUTOSCALER

condition

factors.

The accompanying model tells the best way to set the earth factors for autoscaling before running kube-up.sh:

$ send out NUM_MINIONS=5

$export KUBE_AUTOSCALER_MIN_NODES=2

$export KUBE_AUTOSCALER_MAX_NODES=5

$export KUBE_ENABLE_CLUSTER_AUTOSCALER=true

Additionally, remember that changing this after the bunch is begun will have no impact. You would need to tear down the group and create it by and by. Hence, this area will tell you the best way to add nodes to a current group without remaking it.

When you start a bunch with these settings, your group will consequently scale here and there with the base and most extreme points of confinement dependent on figure asset utilization in the group.

GKE groups likewise support autoscaling when propelled, when utilizing the alpha highlights. The first model will utilize a banner, for example, - empower

autoscaling - min-nodes=2 - max-nodes=5 in a command-line

dispatch.

Scaling up the group on GCE

In the event that you wish to scale out a current bunch, we can do it with a couple of steps. Physically scaling up your group on GCE is quite simple. The current pipes utilizes oversaw occasion bunches in GCE, which enable you to effectively include more machines of a standard arrangement to the gathering through a case format.

You can see this format effectively in the GCE comfort. To begin with, open the support; as a matter of course, this should open your default venture reassure. On the off chance that you are utilizing another venture for your Kubernetes group, essentially select it from the undertaking dropdown at the highest point of the page.

As an afterthought board, see under Compute and then Compute Engine, and select Instance formats. You should see a layout titled kubernetes-crony format. Note that the name could fluctuate marginally on the off chance that you've customized your group naming settings.

You'll see various settings, yet the meat of the format is under the Custom metadata. Here, you will see various condition factors and likewise a startup content that is pursued another machine case is created. These are the center segments that enable us to create new machines and have them naturally added to the accessible group nodes.

Since the layout for new machines is as of now created, it is extremely easy proportional out our bunch in GCE. Once in the Compute segment of the reassure, basically go to Instance bunches found right over the Instance layouts connect as an afterthought board. Once more, you should see a gathering titled kubernetes-crony gathering or something comparable.

You'll see a page with a CPU measurements chart and three cases recorded here. Naturally, the bunch creates three nodes. We can alter this gathering by tapping on the EDIT GROUP button at the highest point of the page:

You should see kubernetes-crony format chose in Instance layout that we checked on a minute back. You'll likewise observe an Autoscaling setting, which is Off as a matter of course and an example tally of 3. Basically, increase this to 4 and snap on Save. You'll be reclaimed to the gathering subtleties page and you'll see a spring up discourse indicating the pending changes.

You'll additionally observe some auto mending properties on the Instance Group alter page. This recreates bombed occurrences and enables you to set wellbeing checks just as an underlying postpone period before a move is made.

In no time flat, you'll have another case recorded on the subtleties page. We can test this is prepared utilizing the get nodes command from the command line:

$ kubectl get nodes

An expression of alert on autoscaling and scale down as a rule

To start with, on the off chance that we rehash the prior procedure and abatement the commencement to four, GCE will expel one node. In any case, it won't really be the node you just included. Fortunately cases will be rescheduled on the rest of the nodes. Be that as it may, it can just reschedule where assets are accessible. On the off chance that you are near full limit and shut down a node, there is a decent possibility that a few units won't have a spot to be rescheduled. What's more, this is certifiably not a live relocation, so any application state will be lost in the progress. Most importantly you ought to painstakingly think about the suggestions before downsizing or actualizing an autoscaling plan.

For more data on general autoscaling in GCE, allude to

the https://cloud.google.com/figure/docs/autoscaler/?hl=en_US#sc aling_based_on_cpu_utilization connect.

Scaling up the bunch on AWS

The AWS supplier code likewise makes it simple to scale up your bunch. Like GCE, the AWS arrangement utilizes autoscaling gatherings to create the default four flunky nodes. Later on, the autoscaling gatherings will ideally be coordinated into the Kubernetes bunch autoscaling usefulness. For the present, we will walk however a manual arrangement.

This can likewise be effectively adjusted utilizing the CLI or the web comfort. In the reassure, from the EC2 page, just go to the Auto Scaling Groups segment at the base of the menu on the left. You should see a name like kubernetes-flunky gathering

We can scale this gathering up effectively by tapping on Edit. At that point, change the Desired, Min, and Max esteems to 5 and snap on Save. In almost no time, you'll have the fifth node accessible. You can indeed check this utilizing the get nodes command.

Downsizing is a similar procedure, yet recall that we talked about similar contemplations in the past Scaling up the bunch on GCE area. Remaining tasks at hand could get abandoned or, at any rate, surprisingly restarted.

Scaling physically

For different suppliers, making new cronies may not be a computerized procedure. Contingent upon your supplier, you'll have to perform different manual advances. It tends to be useful to take a gander at the supplier explicit contents in the bunch catalog.

Summary

We should now be more OK with the essentials of use scaling in Kubernetes. We additionally took a gander at the inherent capacities so as to move refreshes just as a manual procedure for testing and gradually coordinating updates. We investigated how proportional the nodes of our basic group and increment the general limit with regards to our Kubernetes assets. At long last, we investigated a portion of the new auto scaling ideas for both the bunch and our applications themselves.

In the following part, we will take a gander at the most recent strategies for scaling and refreshing applications with the new arrangements asset type, just as a portion of different sorts of remaining tasks at hand we can run on Kubernetes.

5

Deployments, Jobs, and DaemonSets

This section will cover the different sorts of outstanding burdens that Kubernetes underpins. We will cover Deployments for applications that are normally refreshed and long running. We will likewise return to the points of use updates and steady rollouts utilizing Deployments. Also, we will see Jobs utilized for short-running undertakings. At long last, we will take a gander at DaemonSets, which enable projects to be run on each node in our Kubernetes bunch.

This section will talk about the accompanying:

Arrangements

Application scaling with arrangements

Application refreshes with arrangements

Jobs

DaemonSets

Organizations

In the past part, we investigated a portion of the center ideas for application refreshes utilizing the old moving update technique. Beginning with variant 1.2, Kubernetes included the Deployment build, which enhances the essential systems of moving update and Replication Controllers. As the name recommends, it gives us a better control of the code organization itself. Arrangements enable us to delay and resume application rollouts. Also, it keeps a background marked by past organizations and enables the client to effectively rollback to past variants.

In the accompanying, posting 5-1, we can see that the definition is fundamentally the same as a Replication Controller. The fundamental distinction is that we currently have a capacity to make changes and updates to the arrangement items and let Kubernetes oversee refreshing the hidden units and imitations for us:

apiVersion: augmentations/v1beta1

kind: Deployment

metadata:

name: node-js-convey

marks:

name: node-js-convey

spec:

reproductions: 1

format:

metadata:

marks:

name: node-js-convey

spec:

holders:

- name: node-js-convey

picture: jonbaier/case scaling:0.1 ports:

- containerPort: 80

Posting 5-1: node-js-deploy.yaml

We can run the comfortable create command with the discretionary - record banner so the making of the sending is recorded in the rollout history. Else, we will just observe resulting changes in the rollout history:

$ kubectl create - f node-js-deploy.yaml - record

You may need to include - validate=false if this beta kind isn't empowered on your bunch.

We should see a message about the organization being effectively created. After a couple of seconds, it will wrap up our unit, which we can check for ourselves with a get cases command. We add the - l banner to just observe the units applicable to this arrangement:

$ kubectl get units - l name=node-js-convey

We create an assistance similarly as we did with Replication Controllers. Coming up next is a Service definition for the arrangement we just created. We'll see that it is practically indistinguishable from the Services we created previously:

apiVersion: v1

kind: Service

metadata:

name: node-js-convey

marks:

name: node-js-convey

spec:

type: LoadBalancer

ports:

- port: 80 sessionAffinity: ClientIP selector:

name: node-js-convey

Posting 5-2. node-js-convey service.yaml

When this administration is created utilizing kubectl, you'll have the option to get to the sending cases through the administration IP or the administration name on the off chance that you are inside a unit on this namespace.

Scaling

The scale command works a similar route as it did in our Replication Controller. To scale up, we essentially utilize the organization name and indicate the new number of reproductions, as appeared here:

$ kubectl scale arrangement node-js-send - copies 3

In the event that all goes well, we'll essentially observe a message about the arrangement being scaled on the yield of our terminal window. We can check the quantity of running cases utilizing the get cases command from prior, again.

Updates and rollouts

Arrangements consider refreshing in a couple of different ways. To start with, there is the kubectl set command, which enables us to change the sending arrangement without redeploying physically. Right now, it takes into account refreshing the picture, however as new forms of our application or compartment picture are prepared, we should do this frequently.

We should investigate utilizing our organization from the past segment. We ought to have three reproductions running at the present time. Confirm this by running the get cases command with a channel for our arrangement:

$ kubectl get units - l name=node-js-send

Take one of the units recorded on our arrangement, supplant it in the accompanying command where it says {POD_NAME_FROM_YOUR_LISTING}, and run the command:

$ kubectl portray unit/{POD_NAME_FROM_YOUR_LISTING} | grep Image:

We should see a yield like the accompanying picture with the present picture form of 0.1:

Since we comprehend what our present sending is running, how about we attempt to refresh to the following form. This can be accomplished effectively utilizing the kubectl set command and indicating the new form, as appeared here:

$kubectl set picture sending/node-js-convey node-js-deploy=jonbaier/unit scaling:0.2

On the off chance that all goes well, we should see the content that says sending "node-js-convey" picture refreshed showed on the screen.

We can twofold check the status utilizing the accompanying rollout status command:

$ kubectl rollout status arrangement/node-js-send

We should see some content about the arrangement effectively turned out. In the event that you see any content about sitting tight for the rollout to complete, you may need to sit tight a minute for it to complete or on the other hand check the logs for issues.

When it's done, run the get units command as prior, again. This time we will see new units recorded:

By and by plug one of your case names into the depict command we ran before. This time we should see the picture has been refreshed to 0.2.

What occurred off camera is that Kubernetes has revealed another variant for us. It essentially creates another reproduction set with the new form. When this unit is on the web and sound it slaughters one of the more seasoned renditions. It proceeds with this conduct, scaling out the new form and downsizing the old renditions, until just the new cases are left.

It's important that the rollback definition enables us to control the case supplant strategy in our organization definition. There is a strategy.type field that defaults to RollingUpdate and the previous conduct. Alternatively, we can likewise determine Recreate as the substitution methodology and it will slaughter all the old units first before making the new forms.

History and rollbacks

One of the valuable highlights of the rollout programming interface is the capacity to follow the arrangement history. How about we do one more refresh before we check the history. Run the kubectl set command again and indicate adaptation 0.3:

$kubectl set picture arrangement/node-js-convey node-js-deploy=jonbaier/unit scaling:0.3

By and by we'll see message that says organization "node-js-send" picture refreshed showed on the screen. Presently run the get cases command again:

$ kubectl get units - l name=node-js-send

We should likewise investigate our arrangement history. Run the rollout history command:

$ kubectl rollout history sending/node-js-convey

As should be obvious, the history shows us the underlying organization creation, our first update to 0.2, and then our last update to 0.3. Notwithstanding status and history, the rollout command additionally underpins the delay, continue, and fix sub-commands. The rollout delay command enables us to stop a command while the rollout is still in progress. This can be valuable for investigating and likewise supportive for canary sort dispatches, where we wish to do last testing of the new form before turning out to the whole client base. At the point when we are prepared to proceed with the rollout, we can essentially utilize the rollout continue command.

Be that as it may, imagine a scenario in which something turns out badly. That is the place the rollout fix command and the rollout history itself is extremely handy. How about we recreate this by attempting to refresh to a variant of our unit that isn't yet accessible. We will set the picture to adaptation 42.0, which doesn't exist:

$kubectl set picture organization/node-js-convey node-js-deploy=jonbaier/case scaling:42.0

We should at present observe the content that says sending "node-js-convey" picture refreshed

shown on the screen. However, on the off chance that we check the status, we will see that it is as yet pausing:

$ kubectl rollout status sending/node-js-convey

We can press Ctrl + C to murder the status command and then run the get units command again:

$ kubectl get cases - l name=node-js-convey

As we expected, it can't pull the 42.0 rendition of the picture since it doesn't exist. We may likewise have issues with arrangements in the event that we come up short on assets on the group or hit constrains that are set for our namespace. Furthermore, the organization can fizzle for various application-related causes, for example, wellbeing check disappointment, consent issues, and application bugs, obviously.

At whatever point an inability to rollout occurs, we can without much of a stretch rollback to a past rendition utilizing the rollout fix command. This command will return our organization to the past rendition:

$ kubectl rollout fix sending/node-js-convey

From that point forward, we can run a rollout status command again and we should see everything turned out effectively. Run the rollout history command again and we'll see both our endeavor to rollout form 42.0 and the return to 0.3:

We can likewise indicate the - to-modification banner when running a fix to rollback to a particular adaptation. This can be handy for times when our rollout succeeds, yet we find legitimate mistakes not far off.

Autoscaling

As should be obvious, Deployments are an extraordinary improvement over Replication Controllers enabling us to flawlessly refresh our applications, while incorporating with different assets of Kubernetes similarly.

Another region that we found in the past part, and additionally upheld for Deployments, is Horizontal Pod Autoscalers (HPAs). As you may have speculated, this likewise coordinates consummately with Deployments. We will stroll through a fast change of the HPAs from the past part, this time utilizing the Deployments we have created up until now:

apiVersion: autoscaling/v1

kind: HorizontalPodAutoscaler

metadata:

name: node-js-convey

spec:

minReplicas: 3

maxReplicas: 6

scaleTargetRef:

apiVersion: v1

kind: Deployment

name: node-js-convey

targetCPUUtilizationPercentage: 10

Posting 5-3. node-js-convey hpa.yaml

We have brought down the CPU edge to 10% and changed our base and greatest cases to 3 and 6, separately. Create the former HPA with our trusty kubectl create - f command. After this is finished, we can watch that it's accessible with the kubectl get hpa command:

We can likewise watch that we have just 3 cases running with the kubectl get convey command. Presently we should add some heap to trigger the autoscaler:

apiVersion: augmentations/v1beta1

kind: Deployment

metadata:

name: boomload-convey

spec:

reproductions: 1

format:

metadata:

marks:

application: loadgenerator-convey

spec:

holders:

- image: williamyeh/blast

name: blast convey

command: ["/container/sh","- c"]

args: ["while genuine ; do blast http://node-js-convey/ - c 10 - n 100 ; rest 1 ;

done"]

Posting 5-4. boomload-deploy.yaml

Create posting 5-4 not surprisingly. Presently screen the HPA with the exchanging kubectl get

hpa and kubectl get send commands. After a couple of seconds, we should see the heap bounce above 10%. After a couple of more minutes, we ought to likewise observe the quantity of units increment as far as possible up to 6 imitations:

Once more, we can tidy this up by expelling our heap age case and holding up a couple of seconds:

$ kubectl erase convey boomload-send

Once more, on the off chance that we watch the HPA, we'll begin to see the CPU use drop. Following a couple of moments, we will return down to 0% CPU burden and then the Deployment will downsize to 3 reproductions.

Jobs

Organizations and Replication Controllers are an extraordinary method to guarantee long running applications are consistently up and ready to endure a wide exhibit of foundation disappointments. In any case, there are some utilization cases this doesn't address—explicitly short running, run once, errands just as routinely planned undertakings. In the two cases, we need the assignments to run until consummation, however then end and start again at the following booked interim.

To address this kind of outstanding task at hand, Kubernetes has included a Batch API, which incorporates the Job type. This sort will create 1 to n units and guarantee that they all rush to fulfillment with a fruitful exit. In light of restartPolicy, we can either enable cases to just come up short without retry (restartPolicy: Never) or retry when a units exits without fruitful finishing (restartPolicy: OnFailure). In this model, we will utilize the last strategy:

apiVersion: bunch/v1

kind: Job

metadata:

name: long-task

spec:

format:

metadata:

name: long-task

spec:

holders:

- name: long-task

picture: docker/whalesay

command: ["cowsay", "Completing that undertaking in a jiffy"]

restartPolicy: OnFailure

Posting 5-5: longtask.yaml

How about we feel free to run this with the accompanying command:

$ kubectl create - f longtask.yaml

On the off chance that all goes well, you'll see work "long-task" created imprinted on the screen.

This reveals to us the activity was created, yet doesn't let us know whether it finished effectively. To watch that, we have to inquiry the activity status with the accompanying command:

$ kubectl portray jobs/long-task

You should see that we had 1 errand that succeeded and in the Events logs, a SuccessfulCreate message. On the off chance that we use kubectl get cases command, we won't see our long-task cases in the rundown, yet we may see the message at the base if the posting states that there are finished jobs that are not appeared. We should run the command again with the - an or - show-all banner to see the long-task unit and the finished Job status.

How about we burrow somewhat more profound to demonstrate to ourselves the work was finished effectively. We could utilize the logs command to take a gander at the units logs. Be that as it may, we can likewise utilize the UI for this undertaking. Open a program and go to the accompanying UI URL: https://<your ace

ip>/ui/

Snap on Jobs and then long-task from the rundown, so we can see the subtleties. At that point, in the Pods area, click on the case recorded there. This will give us the Pod subtleties page. At the base of the subtleties, click on View Logs and we will see the log yield

As should be obvious in the former picture, the whalesay holder is finished with the ASCII craftsmanship and our custom message from the runtime parameters in the model.

Different sorts of jobs

While this model gives an essential prologue to short running jobs, it just tends to the utilization instance of once and done errands. In actuality, bunch work is often done in Parallel or as a major aspect of a routinely happening assignment.

Parallel jobs

Utilizing Parallel jobs, we might be snatching assignments from a continuous line or just running a set number of errands that are not subject to one another. On account of jobs pulling from a line, our application must know about the conditions and have the rationale to choose how assignments are prepared and what to deal with straightaway. Kubernetes is essentially planning the jobs.

You can take in progressively about parallel jobs from the Kubernetes documentation and bunch API reference

Planned jobs

For assignments that need to run intermittently, Kubernetes has likewise discharged a CronJob type in alpha. As we may expect, this sort of occupation utilizes the hidden cron arranging to determine a calendar for the assignment we wish to run. Naturally, our bunch won't have the alpha group highlights empowered, however we can take a gander at a model CronJob inclining to figure out how these kinds of remaining tasks at hand will work going ahead:

apiVersion: group/v2alpha1

kind: CronJob

metadata:

name: long-task-cron

spec:

plan: "15 10 * 6"

jobTemplate:

spec:

layout:

spec:

compartments:

- name: long-task-cron

picture: docker/whalesay

command: ["cowsay", "Designers! Designers! Designers!

\n\n Saturday task

complete!"]

restartPolicy: OnFailure

Posting 5-6. longtask-cron.yaml

As should be obvious, the calendar partition mirrors a crontab with the accompanying organization: minute hour day-of month day-of-week

In this model, 15 10 * 6 creates an errand that will run each Saturday at 10:15 am.

DaemonSets

While Replication Controllers and Deployments are extraordinary at ensuring that a particular number of utilization occurrences are running, they do as such with regards to the best fit. This implies the scheduler searches for nodes that meet asset prerequisites (accessible CPU, specific stockpiling volumes, and so on) and attempts to spread across the nodes and zones.

This functions admirably for making profoundly accessible and shortcoming tolerant applications, however shouldn't something be said about situations where we need a specialist to run on each and every node in the group? While the default spread attempts to utilize different nodes, it doesn't ensure that each node will have a copy and, for sure, will just fill various nodes comparable to the amount determined in the RC or Deployment detail.

To facilitate this weight, Kubernetes presented DaemonSet, which basically characterizes a case to run on each and every node in the group or a characterized subset of those nodes. This can be valuable for various creation related exercises, for example, checking and logging specialists, security operators, and file system daemons.

Truth be told, Kubernetes as of now utilizes this ability for a portion of its center system parts. In the event that we review from Chapter 1, Introduction to Kubernetes, we saw a node-issue finder running on the nodes. This unit is really running on each node in the group

as DaemonSet. We can see this by questioning DaemonSets in the kube-system namespace:

$ kubectl get ds - namespace=kube-system

You can discover more data about node-issue locator just as yaml in the accompanying posting at:

etector:

apiVersion: augmentations/v1beta1

kind: DaemonSet

metadata:

name: node-issue locator v0.1

namespace: kube-system

marks:

k8s-application: node-issue locator

rendition: v0.1

kubernetes.io/bunch administration: "genuine"

spec:

format:

metadata:

marks:

k8s-application: node-issue locator

rendition: v0.1

kubernetes.io/bunch administration: "genuine"

spec:

hostNetwork: genuine

holders:

- name: node-issue locator

picture: gcr.io/google_containers/node-issue detector:v0.1 securityContext:

advantaged: genuine assets:

limits: cpu: "200m" memory: "100Mi"

demands: cpu: "20m" memory: "20Mi"

volumeMounts:

- name: log

mountPath:/log

readOnly: genuine

volumes:

- name: log hostPath:

way:/var/log/

Posting 5-7. node-issue indicator definition

Node choice

As referenced already, we can plan DaemonSets to run on a subset of nodes too. This can be accomplished utilizing something many refer to as nodeSelectors. These enable us to oblige the nodes a cases runs on, by searching for explicit marks and metadata. They just match key-esteem combines on the marks for every node. We can include our very own names or utilize those that are relegated as a matter of course.

We are not constrained to DaemonSets, as nodeSelectors really work with Pod definitions also and are not restricted to DaemonSets. We should investigate work model (a slight alteration of our previous long-task model).

To begin with, we can see these on the nodes themselves. We should get the names of our nodes:

$ kubectl get nodes

Utilize a name from the yield of the past command and attachment it into this one:

$ kubectl portray node <node-name>

We should now add an epithet name to this node:

$ kubectl mark nodes <node-name> nodenickname=trusty-steve

On the off chance that we run the kubectl depict node command once more, we will see this mark recorded alongside the defaults. Presently we can plan remaining tasks at hand and determine this particular node. Here is an adjustment of our prior long-running assignment with nodeSelector included:

apiVersion: group/v1

kind: Job

metadata:

name: long-task-ns

spec:

layout:

metadata:

name: long-task-ns

spec:

compartments:

- name: long-task-ns

picture: docker/whalesay

command: ["cowsay", "Completing that assignment in a jiffy"]

restartPolicy: OnFailure

nodeSelector:

nodenickname: trusty-steve

Posting 5-8. longtask-nodeselector.yaml

Create the activity from this posting with kubectl create - f.

When that succeeds, it will create a case dependent on the former determination. Since we have characterized nodeSelector, it will attempt to run the unit on nodes that have coordinating marks and fizzle on the off chance that it finds no candidates. We can discover the unit by determining the activity name in our question, as pursues:

$ kubectl get units - a - l work name=long-task-ns

We utilize the - a banner to show all cases. Jobs are fleeting and once they enter the finished state, they won't appear in an essential kubectl get pods question. We additionally utilize the - l banner to determine units with the activity name=long-task-ns mark. This will give us the unit name which we can push into the accompanying command:

$ kubectl depict unit <Pod-Name-For-Job> | grep Node:

The outcome should show the name of the node this unit was run on. On the off chance that all has gone well, it should coordinate the node we named a couple of steps prior with the trusty-steve name.

Summary

Presently you ought to have a decent establishment of the center builds in Kubernetes. We investigated the new Deployment reflection and how it enhances the essential Replication Controller, taking into consideration smooth updates and strong coordination with administrations and autoscaling. We likewise took a gander at different sorts of remaining task at hand in jobs and DaemonSets. You figured out how to run short-running or bunch assignments just as how to run specialists on each node in our group. At last, we investigated node determination and how that can be utilized to channel the nodes in the bunch utilized for our remaining tasks at hand.

We will expand on what you realized in this section and take a gander at the Stateful applications in the following part, investigating both basic application segments and the information itself.

6

Storage and Running Stateful Applications

In this section, we will talk about how to connect persevering volumes and create stockpiling for stateful applications and information. We will stroll through capacity concerns and how we can continue information across units and the holder life cycle. We will investigate the PersistentVolumes types just as PersistentVolumeClaim. At long last, we will investigate the new StatefulSets discharge in adaptation 1.5.

This part will examine the accompanying points:

Relentless stockpiling

PersistentVolumes

PersistentVolumeClaims

StorageClasses

StatefulSets

Persevering stockpiling

Up until now, we just worked with outstanding tasks at hand that we could begin and stop freely, with no issue. In any case, true applications often convey state and record information that we like (even demand) not to lose. The transient idea of holders themselves can be a major test. In the event that you review our talk of layered file systems in Chapter 1, Introduction to Kubernetes, the top layer is writable. (It's additionally icing, which is delightful.) However, when the holder kicks the bucket, the information goes with it. The equivalent is valid for slammed holders that Kubernetes restarts.

This is the place volumes or circles become an integral factor. A volume that exists outside the compartment enables us to spare our significant information across holders blackouts. Further, in the event that we have a volume at the unit level, information can be shared between compartments in a similar application stack and inside a similar case.

Docker itself has some help for volumes, however Kubernetes gives us tireless stockpiling that keeps going past the lifetime of a solitary holder. The volumes are attached to units and live amazing those cases. Also, a case can have different volumes from an assortment of sources. We should investigate a portion of these sources.

Transitory plates

Perhaps the most straightforward approaches to accomplish improved ingenuity in the midst of compartment accidents and information sharing inside a case is to utilize the emptydir volume. This volume type can be utilized with either the capacity volumes of the node machine itself or a discretionary RAM plate for better.

Once more, we improve our tirelessness past a solitary holder, yet when a case is evacuated, the information will be lost. Machine reboot will likewise clear any information from RAM-type plates. There might be times when we simply need some common transitory space or have holders that procedure information and hand it off to another compartment before they kick the bucket. Whatever the case, here is a speedy case of utilizing this brief plate with the RAM-upheld alternative.

Open your preferred proofreader and create a file like the one in the accompanying Listing 6-1:

apiVersion: v1

kind: Pod

metadata:

name: memory-pd

spec:

holders:

- image: nginx:latest ports:

- containerPort: 80 name: memory-pd volumeMounts:

- mountPath:/memory-pd

name: memory-volume

volumes:

- name: memory-volume emptyDir:

medium: Memory

Posting 6-1: stockpiling memory.yaml

The previous model is most likely of natural at this point, however we will by and by issue a create command pursued by an executive command to see the envelopes in the holder:

$ kubectl create - f stockpiling memory.yaml

$ kubectl executive memory-pd - ls - lh | grep memory-pd

This will give us a slam shell in the holder itself. The ls command shows us a memory-pd organizer at the top level. We use grep to channel the yield, yet you can run the command without | grep memory-pd to see all organizers:

Once more, this envelope is very brief as everything is put away in the node's (minion's) RAM. At the point when the node gets restarted, every one of the files will be deleted. We will take a gander at an increasingly changeless model straightaway.

Cloud volumes

Numerous organizations will as of now have critical foundation running in general society cloud. Fortunately, Kubernetes has local help for the sturdy stockpiling gave by two of the most well known suppliers.

GCE steady plates

We have the accompanying from the GCE site:

Google Persistent Disk is solid and elite square stockpiling for the Google Cloud Platform. Persevering Disk give SSD and HDD stockpiling which can be connected to cases running in either Google Compute Engine or Google Container Engine.

Capacity volumes can be straightforwardly resized, immediately upheld up, and offer the capacity to help synchronous perusers. (you can allude to more insights regarding this in point 1 in the References segment toward the finish of the section)

How about we create another GCE constant circle.

1.From the comfort, in Compute Engine, go to Disks. On this new screen, click on the Create Disk button. We'll be given a screen like the accompanying GCE new constant circle picture.

2.Choose a name for this volume and give it a concise depiction. Ensure that Zone is equivalent to the nodes in your group. GCE PDs must be appended to machines in a similar zone.

3.Enter mysite-volume-1 in the Name field. Pick the zone coordinating in any event one node in your bunch. Pick None (clear circle) for Source type and give 10

(10 GB) as incentive in Size (GB). At long last, click on Create:

The decent thing about PDs on GCE is that they consider mounting to different machines (nodes for our situation). Be that as it may, when mounting to various machines, the volume must be in perused just mode. Along these lines, allows first mount this to a solitary case, so we can create a few files. Use Listing 6-2: stockpiling gce.yaml as pursues to create a unit that will mount the plate in read/compose mode:

apiVersion: v1

kind: Pod

metadata:

name: test-gce

spec:

holders:

- image: nginx:latest ports:

- containerPort: 80 name: test-gce volumeMounts:

- mountPath:/usr/share/nginx/html

name: gce-pd

volumes:

- name: gce-pd gcePersistentDisk:

pdName: mysite-volume-1

fsType: ext4

Posting 6-2: stockpiling gce.yaml

Initially, how about we issue a create command pursued by a depict command to discover which node it is running on:

$kubectl create - f stockpiling gce.yaml

$kubectl depict case/test-gce

Note the node and spare the case IP address for some other time. At that point, open a SSH session into that node:

$gcloud process - venture "<Your venture ID>" ssh - zone "<your gce zone>" "<Node running test-gce pod>"

Since we've just taken a gander at the volume from inside the running holder, how about we get to it legitimately from the node (follower) itself this time. We will run a df command to see where it is mounted, yet we should change to root first:

$ sudo su -

$ df - h | grep mysite-volume-1

As should be obvious, the GCE volume is mounted legitimately to the node itself. We can utilize the mount way recorded in the yield of the prior df command. Use album to change to the envelope now. At that point, create another file named index.html with your preferred supervisor:

$cd/var/lib/kubelet/modules/kubernetes.io/gce-pd/mounts/mysite-volume-1

$vi index.html

Enter a curious message, for example, Hello from my GCE PD!. Presently spare the file and leave the manager. In the event that you review from Listing 6-2, the PD is mounted straightforwardly to the Nginx HTML catalog. In this way, we should test this out while regardless we have the SSH session open on the node. Do a basic twist command to the unit IP we recorded before:

$ twist <Pod IP from Describe>

You should see Hello from my GCE PD! or on the other hand whatever message you spared in the index.html file. In a certifiable situation, we can utilize the volume for a whole site or some other focal stockpiling. How about we investigate running a lot of burden adjusted web servers all indicating a similar volume.

Initially, leave the SSH session with two leave commands. Before we continue, we should evacuate our test-gce unit with the goal that the volume can be mounted perused uniquely across various nodes:

$ kubectl erase case/test-gce

Presently we can create a RC that will run three web servers all mounting the equivalent persevering plate, as pursues:

apiVersion: v1

kind: ReplicationController

metadata:

name: http-pd

marks:

name: http-pd

spec:

imitations: 3

selector:

name: http-pd

format:

metadata:

name: http-pd

marks:

name: http-pd

spec:

holders:

- picture: nginx:latest

ports:

- containerPort: 80 name: http-pd volumeMounts:

- mountPath:/usr/share/nginx/html

name: gce-pd

volumes:

- name: gce-pd gcePersistentDisk:

pdName: mysite-volume-1

fsType: ext4

readOnly: genuine

Posting 6-3: http-pd-controller.yaml

How about we likewise create an outer help, so we can see it from outside the bunch:

apiVersion: v1

kind: Service

metadata:

name: http-pd

names:

name: http-pd

spec:

type: LoadBalancer

ports:

- name: http

convention: TCP

port: 80

selector:

name: http-pd

Posting 6-4: http-pd-service.yaml

Feel free to create these two assets now. Trust that the outside IP will get relegated. After this, a portray command will give us the IP we can use in a program:

$ kubectl depict administration/http-pd

On the off chance that you don't see the LoadBalancer Ingress field yet, it likely needs more opportunity to get allocated. Type the IP address from LoadBalancer Ingress into a program, and you should see your natural index.html file appear with the content we entered beforehand!

AWS Elastic Block Store

K8s likewise underpins AWS Elastic Block Store (EBS) volumes. Like the GCE PDs, EBS volumes are required to be joined to an example running in a similar accessibility zone. A further restriction is that EBS must be mounted to a solitary example at once.

For quickness, we won't stroll through an AWS model, yet an example YAML file is incorporated to kick you off. Once more, make sure to create the EBS volume before your case:

```
apiVersion: v1
kind: Pod
metadata:
name: test-aws
spec:
compartments:
- image: nginx:latest ports:
- containerPort: 80 name: test-aws volumeMounts:
- mountPath:/usr/share/nginx/html
name: aws-pd
volumes:
- name: aws-pd awsElasticBlockStore:
volumeID: aws://<availability-zone>/<volume-id>
fsType: ext4
```

Posting 6-5: stockpiling aws.yaml

Other stockpiling alternatives

Kubernetes underpins an assortment of different kinds of capacity volumes. A full rundown can be found here:

Here are a not many that might be exceptionally compelling:

nfs: This sort enables us to mount a Network File Share (NFS), which can be valuable for both enduring the information and sharing it across the foundation

gitrepo: As you may have speculated, this alternative clones a Git repo into another and void organizer

PersistentVolumes and StorageClasses

So far, we've seen instances of legitimately provisioning the capacity inside our unit definitions. This works very well in the event that you have full power over your group and foundation, yet at bigger scales, application proprietors will need to utilize capacity that is overseen independently. Commonly, a focal IT group or the cloud supplier itself will deal with the subtleties behind provisioning stockpiling and leave the application proprietors to stress over their essential concern, the application itself.

So as to suit this, we need some route for the application to determine and demand stockpiling without being worried about how that capacity is given. This is the place

PersistentVolumes and PersistentVolumeClaims come into play. PersistentVolumes are like volumes we created before, yet they are given by the bunch regulate and are not reliant on a specific case. This volume would then be able to be guaranteed by units utilizing PersistentVolumeClaims.

PersistentVolumeClaims enables us to indicate the subtleties of the capacity required. We can characterized the measure of capacity just as the entrance type, for example, ReadWriteOnce (peruse and compose by one node), ReadOnlyMany (read-just by numerous nodes), and ReadWriteMany (peruse and compose by numerous nodes). Obviously, which modes are bolstered is subject to the support stockpiling supplier. For instance, we found in the AWS EBS model that mounting to different nodes was impossible.

Furthermore, Kubernetes gives two different techniques to indicating certain groupings or sorts of capacity volumes. The first is the utilization of selectors as we have seen beforehand for case determination. Here, names can be applied to capacity volumes and then claims can reference these names to additionally channel the volume they are given. Second, Kubernetes has an idea of StorageClass which permits us determine a capacity provisioner and parameters for the sort of volumes it arrangements.

We will plunge into StorageClasses in the following segment, yet here is a speedy case of a PersistentVolumeClaims for delineation purposes. You can find in the comments that we demand 1Gi of capacity in ReadWriteOnce mode with a StorageClass of solidstate and mark of aws-stockpiling.

```
kind: PersistentVolumeClaim

apiVersion: v1

metadata:

name: demo-guarantee

explanations:

volume.beta.kubernetes.io/capacity class: "solidstate"

spec:

accessModes:

- ReadWriteOnce assets:

demands: stockpiling: 1Gi

selector:

matchLabels:

discharge: "aws-capacity"
```

Posting 6-6: pvc-example.yaml

StatefulSets

The reason for StatefulSets is to give some consistency and consistency to application organizations with stateful information. Up to this point, we have sent applications to the bunch characterizing free prerequisites around required assets, for example, PC and capacity. The group has booked our remaining task at hand on any node that can meet these prerequisites. While we can utilize a portion of these imperatives to send in a progressively unsurprising way, it will be useful on the off chance that we had a develop worked to assist us with giving this consistency.

StatefulSets were set to GA in 1.6 as we went to press. There were beforehand beta in rendition 1.5 and were known as PetSets preceding that (alpha in 1.3 and 1.4).

This is the place StatefulSets come in. StatefulSets furnish us first with numbered and dependable naming for both system access and capacity claims. The cases themselves are names with the accompanying show, where N is from 0 to the quantity of copies:

"Name of Set"- N

This implies a Statefulset called db with 3 reproductions will create the accompanying units:

db-0

db-1

db-2

This gives Kubernetes an approach to relate arrange names and PersistentVolumes with explicit cases. Moreover, it additionally serves to arrange creation and end of units. Unit will be begun from 0 to N and ended from N to 0.

A stateful model

We should investigate a case of a stateful application. To begin with, we will need to create and utilize a StorageClass as we talked about before. This will enable us to guide into the Google Cloud Persistent Disk provisioner. The Kubernetes people group is building provisioners for an assortment of StorageClasses including GCP and AWS. Every provisioner has its own arrangement of parameters accessible. Both GCP and AWS suppliers let you pick the kind of plate (strong state, standard, and so on) just as the flaw zone which is expected to coordinate the unit appending to it. AWS moreover enables you to determine encryption parameters just as IOPs for Provisioned IOPs volumes. There are various different provisioners underway including Azure and an assortment of non-cloud choices:

```
kind: StorageClass
apiVersion: storage.k8s.io/v1beta1
metadata:
name: solidstate
provisioner: kubernetes.io/gce-pd
parameters:
type: pd-ssd
zone: us-central1-b
```

Posting 6-7: solidstate-sc.yaml

Utilize the accompanying command with the former inclining to create a StorageClass sort of

SSD drives in us-central1-b:

```
$ kubectl create - f solidstate.yaml
```

Next, we will create a StatefulSet kind with our trusty httpwhalesay demo (you can allude to more insights regarding this in point 2 in the References segment toward the finish of the part). While this application includes any genuine state, we can see the capacity asserts and investigate the correspondence way:

```
apiVersion: applications/v1beta1
kind: StatefulSet
metadata:
name: whaleset
spec:
serviceName: sayhey-svc
reproductions: 3
```

```
layout:
metadata:
names:
application: sayhey
spec:
terminationGracePeriodSeconds: 10
compartments:
- name: sayhey
picture: jonbaier/httpwhalesay:0.2
command: ["node", "index.js", "Whale it up!."]
ports:
- containerPort: 80
name: web
volumeMounts:
- name: www
mountPath:/usr/share/nginx/html
volumeClaimTemplates:
- metadata:
name: www
comments:
volume.beta.kubernetes.io/capacity class: solidstate spec:
accessModes: [ "ReadWriteOnce" ]
assets:
demands:
capacity: 1Gi
```

Posting 6-8: sayhey-statefulset.yaml

Utilize the accompanying command to get the opportunity to begin the production of this StatefulSet. In the event that you watch case creation intently, you will see it create whaleset-0, whaleset-1, and whaleset-2 in progression:

$ kubectl create - f sayhey-statefulset.yaml

Following this, we can see our StatefulSet and the comparing units utilizing the well-known get subcommand:

$kubectl get statefulsets

$kubectl get units

Contingent upon your planning, the units may in any case be making. As should be obvious in the former picture, the third holder is as yet being spun up.

We can likewise observe the volumes the set has created and guarantee for each case. First PersistentVolumes themselves:

$ kubectl get pv

The first command should show the three PersistentVolumes named www-whaleset-N. We see the size is 1Gi and the entrance mode is set to ReadWriteOnce (RWO) similarly as we characterized in our StorageClass:

You'll see a great part of similar settings here likewise with the PVs themselves. You may likewise see the finish of the case name (or PV name in the past posting) looks like www-whaleset-N. www is the mount name we determined in the previous YAML definition. This is then affixed to the case name to create the real PV and PVC name. One more territory we can guarantee that the best possible circle is connected with it is coordinating case.

Another zone where this arrangement is significant is in the system correspondence. StatefulSets additionally give reliable naming here. Before we can do this, we should create a help endpoint so we have a typical passage point for approaching solicitations:

apiVersion: v1

kind: Service

metadata:

name: sayhey-svc

names:

application: sayhey

spec:

ports:

- port: 80

name: web

clusterIP: None

selector:

application: sayhey

Posting 6-9: sayhey-svc.yaml

$ kubectl create - f sayhey-svc.yaml

Presently we should open a shell in one of the cases and check whether we can speak with another in the set:

$ kubectl executive whaleset-0 - I - t slam

The former command gives us a slam shell in the first whaleset unit. We would now be able to utilize the Service name to make a basic HTTP demand. We can utilize both the short name, sayhey-

svc, and the completely qualified name, sayhey-svc.default.svc.cluster.local:

$ twist sayhey-svc

$ twist sayhey-svc.default.svc.cluster.local

You'll see a yield like the accompanying picture. The administration endpoint goes about as a typical correspondence point for every one of the three cases:

Presently we should check whether we can speak with a particular pod in the StatefulSet. As we saw before, the StatefulSet named the case in a methodical way. It additionally gives them hostnames along these lines so that there is a particular DNS passage for each unit in the set. Once more, we will see the show of "Name of Set"- N and then include the completely qualified assistance URL. The accompanying model shows this for whaleset-1, which is the second Pod in our set:

$ twist whaleset-1.sayhey-svc.default.svc.cluster.local

Running this command from our current Bash shell in whaleset-0 will show us the yield from whaleset-1:

You can exit out of this shell now with exit.

For learning purposes, it can likewise be informative to depict a portion of the things from this area in more detail. For instance, kubectl portray svc sayhey-svc will give all of us three case IP address in the administration endpoints.

Summary

In this section, we investigated an assortment of constant stockpiling alternatives and how to execute them with our units. We took a gander at PersistentVolumes and likewise PersistentVolumeClaims, which enable us to isolate capacity provisioning and application stockpiling demands.

Furthermore, we took a gander at StorageClasses for provisioning gatherings of capacity as indicated by a detail.

We additionally investigated the new StatefulSets reflection and figured out how we can send stateful applications in a steady and requested way. In the following section, we will see how to coordinate Kubernetes with Continuous Integration and Delivery pipelines.

Continuous Delivery

This part will tell the peruser the best way to coordinate their assemble pipeline and organizations with a Kubernetes bunch. It will cover the idea of utilizing Gulp.js and Jenkins related to your Kubernetes group.

This part will examine the accompanying themes:

Coordinating with nonstop organization pipeline

Utilizing Gulp.js with Kubernetes

Coordinating Jenkins with Kubernetes

Coordinating with nonstop conveyance pipeline

Persistent reconciliation and conveyance are key segments to present day improvement shops. Speed to market or interim to-income are urgent for any organization that is making their very own software. We'll perceive how Kubernetes can support you.

CI/CD (short for Continuous Integration/Continuous Delivery) often requires vaporous form and test servers to be accessible at whatever point changes are pushed to the code archive. Docker and Kubernetes are appropriate for this assignment, as it's anything but difficult to create compartments in no time flat and similarly as simple to expel them after forms are run. What's more, in the event that you as of now have a huge segment of foundation accessible on your bunch, it can bode well to use the inactive limit with respect to fabricates and testing.

In this article, we will investigate two prevalent instruments utilized in building and conveying software:

Gulp.js: This is a straightforward errand sprinter used to mechanize the fabricate procedure utilizing JavaScript and Node.js

Jenkins: This is a completely fledged nonstop joining server

Gulp.js

Gulp.js gives us the system to do Build as code. Like Infrastructure as code, this enables us to automatically characterize our construct procedure. We will stroll through a short guide to exhibit how you can create a total work process from a Docker picture work to the last Kubernetes administration.

Essentials

For this segment of the article, you will require a NodeJS domain introduced and prepared including the node bundle chief (npm). In the event that you don't as of now have these bundles introduced, you can discover directions for introducing them at

https://docs.npmjs.com/beginning/introducing node.

You can check whether NodeJS is introduced accurately with a node - v command.

You'll additionally require Docker CE and a DockerHub record to push another picture. You can discover guidelines to introduce Docker CE at https://docs.docker.com/establishment/.

You can without much of a stretch create a DockerHub account at https://hub.docker.com/.

After you have your qualifications, you can sign in with the CLI utilizing $ docker login command.

Swallow manufacture model

How about we start by making a venture catalog named node-swallow:

$mkdir node-swallow

$cd node-swallow

Next, we will introduce the swallow bundle and check whether it's prepared by running the npm command with the variant banner, as pursues:

$ npm introduce - g swallow

You may need to open another terminal window to ensure that swallow is on your way.

Likewise, try to explore back to your node-swallow catalog:

$ swallow - v

Next, we will introduce swallow locally in our venture envelope just as the swallow git and swallow shell modules, as pursues:

$npm introduce - spare dev swallow

$npm introduce swallow git - spare

$npm introduce - spare dev swallow shell

At long last, we have to create a Kubernetes controller and administration definition file, just as a gulpfile.js file, to run every one of our assignments. Once more, these files are accessible in the book file group, in the event that you wish to duplicate them. Allude to the accompanying code:

apiVersion: v1

kind: ReplicationController

metadata:

name: node-swallow

names:

name: node-swallow

spec:

reproductions: 1

selector:

name: node-swallow

layout:

metadata:

names:

name: node-swallow

spec:

compartments:

- name: node-swallow

picture: <your username>/node-gulp:latest

imagePullPolicy: Always ports:

- containerPort: 80

Posting 7-1: node-swallow controller.yaml

As should be obvious, we have an essential controller. You should supplant <your username>/node-gulp:latest with your Docker Hub username:

apiVersion: v1

kind: Service

metadata:

name: node-swallow

names:

name: node-swallow

spec:

type: LoadBalancer

ports:

- name: http

convention: TCP

port: 80

selector:

name: node-swallow

Posting 7-2: node-swallow service.yaml

Next, we have a basic help that chooses the units from our controller and creates an outside burden balancer for access, as prior:

```
var swallow = require('gulp');

var git = require('gulp-git');

var shell = require('gulp-shell');

/Clone a remote repo gulp.task('clone', function(){

return git.clone('https://github.com/jonbaierCTP/beginning with-kubernetes-s e.git', work (fail) {

in the event that (fail) toss blunder; });

});

/Update codebase gulp.task('pull', function(){

return git.pull('origin', 'ace', {cwd: './beginning with-kubernetes-se'}, work (fail) {

in the event that (fail) toss blunder; });

});

/Build Docker Image

gulp.task('docker-construct', shell.task([

'docker construct - t <your username>/node-swallow ./beginning with-

kubernetes-se/docker-picture source/compartment data/', 'docker push <your username>/node-swallow'

]));

/Run New Pod

gulp.task('create-kube-unit', shell.task([

'kubectl create - f node-swallow controller.yaml', 'kubectl create - f node-swallow service.yaml'

]));

/Update Pod

gulp.task('update-kube-unit', shell.task([

'kubectl erase - f node-swallow controller.yaml', 'kubectl create - f node-swallow controller.yaml'

]));
```

Posting 7-3: gulpfile.js

At last, we have the gulpfile.js file. This is the place all our manufacture undertakings are characterized. Once more, fill in your Docker Hub username in both the <your username>/node-swallow segments.

Glancing through the file, first, the clone task downloads our picture source code from GitHub. The force undertakings execute a git pull on the cloned archive. Next, the docker-manufacture command fabricates a picture from the holder data subfolder and drives it to DockerHub. At long last, we have the create-kube-unit and update-kube-case commands. As you can figure, the create-kube-unit command creates our controller and administration just because, while the update-kube-case command essentially replaces the controller.

How about we feel free to run these commands and see our start to finish work process:

$ swallow clone

$ swallow docker-manufacture

The first run through, you can run the create-kube-unit command, as pursues:

$ swallow create-kube-unit

This is the long and short of it. In the event that we run a snappy kubectl portray command for the node-swallow administration, we can get the outside IP for our new assistance. Peruse to that IP and you'll see the well-known compartment information application running. Note that the host begins with node-swallow, similarly as we named it in the recently referenced case definition:

On consequent updates, run the force and refresh kube-case commands, as appeared here:

$ swallow pull

$ swallow docker-construct

$ swallow update-kube-unit

This is an exceptionally basic model, however you can start to perceive that it is so natural to arrange your fabricate and sending start to finish with a couple of straightforward lines of code. Next, we will see how to utilize Kubernetes to really run assembles utilizing Jenkins.

Kubernetes module for Jenkins

One way we can utilize Kubernetes for our CI/CD pipeline is to run our Jenkins fabricate slaves in a containerized situation. Fortunately, there is as of now a module, composed via Carlos Sanchez, which enables you to run Jenkins slaves in Kubernetes' units.

Requirements

You'll require a Jenkins server handy for this next model. On the off chance that you don't have one you can use, there is a Docker picture accessible at https://hub.docker.com/_/jenkins/.

Running it from the Docker CLI is as straightforward as this:

docker run - name myjenkins - p 8080:8080 - v/var/jenkins_home Jenkins

Introducing modules

Sign in to your Jenkins server, and from your home dashboard, click on Manage Jenkins.

At that point, select Manage Plugins from the rundown.

A note for those introducing another Jenkins server: When you first sign in to the Jenkins server, it requests that you introduce modules. Pick the default ones or no modules will be introduced:

The certifications module is required, however ought to be introduced of course. We can check the

Introduced tab if all else fails

Next, we can tap on the Available tab. The Kubernetes module ought to be situated under Cluster Management and Distributed Build or Misc (cloud). There are numerous modules, so you can on the other hand scan for Kubernetes on the page. Check the case for Kubernetes Plugin and snap on Install without restart.

In the event that you wish to introduce a nonstandard form or simply prefer to tinker, you can alternatively download the modules. The most recent Kubernetes and Durable Task modules can be found here:

Kubernetes module:

https://wiki.jenkins-ci.org/show/JENKINS/Kubernetes+Plugin

Tough Task module:

https://wiki.jenkins-ci.org/show/JENKINS/Durable+Task+Plugin

Next, we can tap on the Advanced tab and look down to Upload Plugin. Explore to the tough task.hpi file and tap on Upload. You should see a screen that shows an introducing progress bar. Following a moment or two, it will refresh to Success.

At last, introduce the principle Kubernetes module. On the left-hand side, click on Manage Plugins and then the Advanced tab by and by. This time, transfer the kubernetes.hpi file and tap on Upload. Following a couple of moments, the establishment ought to be finished.

Designing the Kubernetes module

Snap on Back to Dashboard or the Jenkins connect in the upper left corner. From the primary dashboard page, click on the Credentials connect. Pick a space from the rundown; for my situation, I simply utilized the default Global certifications area. Snap on Add Credentials:

Leave Kind as Username with secret phrase and Scope as Global. Include your Kubernetes administrator certifications. Recall that you can discover these by running the config command:

$ kubectl config see

You can leave ID clear, give it a reasonable portrayal, and snap on the OK button.

Since we have our accreditations spared, we can include our Kubernetes server. Snap on the Jenkins connect in the upper left corner and then Manage Jenkins. From that point, select Configure System and look over right down to the Cloud area. Select Kubernetes from the Add another cloud dropdown and a Kubernetes area will show up

You'll have to determine the URL for your lord as https://<Master IP>/.

Next, pick the certifications we included starting from the drop list. Since Kubernetes utilize a self-marked testament of course, you'll likewise need to check the Disable https authentication check checkbox.

Snap on Test Connection and if all goes well, you should see Connection effective showing up by the catch.

In the event that you are utilizing a more established form of the module, you may not see the Disable https authentication check checkbox. If so, you should introduce oneself marked declaration straightforwardly on the Jenkins Master.

At long last, we will include a case format by picking Kubernetes Pod Template from the Add Pod Template dropdown alongside Images.

This will create another new area. Use jenkins-slave for the Name and Labels area. Snap on Add by Containers and again use jenkins-slave for the Name. Use

csanchez/jenkins-slave for the Docker Image and leave/home/jenkins for the

Working Directory.

Marks can be utilized later on in the assemble settings to constrain the work to utilize the Kubernetes bunch:

Snap on Save and you are good to go. Presently, new forms created in Jenkins can utilize the slaves in the Kubernetes case we just created.

Here is another note about firewalls. The Jenkins Master should be reachable by every one of the machines in your Kubernetes bunch, as the case could land anyplace. You can discover your port settings in Jenkins under Manage Jenkins and Configure Global Security.

Reward fun

Fabric8 charges itself as a joining stage. It incorporates an assortment of logging, observing, and ceaseless conveyance apparatuses. It additionally has a decent reassure, an API vault, and a 3D game that gives you a chance to take shots at your units. It's an extremely cool task, and it really runs on Kubernetes. Allude to http://fabric8.io/.

It's a simple single command to set up on your Kubernetes group, so allude to http://fabric8.io/direct/getStarted/gke.html.

Summary

We took a gander at two persistent mix devices that can be utilized with Kubernetes. We did a concise stroll through of conveying the Gulp.js task on our group. We additionally took a gander at another module used to coordinate Jenkins incorporate slaves with your Kubernetes bunch. You should now have a superior feeling of how Kubernetes can incorporate with your own CI/CD pipeline.

Monitoring and Logging

This section will cover the use and customization of both implicit and outsider monitoring apparatuses on our Kubernetes group. We will cover how to utilize the apparatuses to screen the wellbeing and execution of our group. Furthermore, we will take a gander at worked in logging, the Google Cloud Logging administration, and Sysdig.

This section will talk about the following themes:

How Kuberentes utilizes cAdvisor, Heapster, InfluxDB, and Grafana

Customizing the default Grafana dashboard

Using FluentD and Grafana

Installing and using logging apparatuses

Working with well known outsider devices, for example, StackDriver and Sysdig, to expand our monitoring abilities

Monitoring activities

True monitoring goes a long ways past checking whether a system is ready for action. Despite the fact that wellbeing checks, similar to those you learned in Chapter 2, Pods, Services, Replication Controllers, and Labels, in the Health checks segment, can assist us with isolating issue applications. Activity groups can best serve the business when they can envision the issues and relieve them before a system goes offline.

Best practices in monitoring are to gauge the exhibition and use of center assets and watch for patterns that stray from the ordinary baseline. Containers are not different here, and a key part to managing our Kubernetes group is having a reasonable view into execution and accessibility of the OS, arrange, system (CPU and memory), and capacity assets over all hubs.

In this part, we will examine a few choices to screen and quantify the presentation and accessibility of all our group assets. What's more, we will take a gander at a couple of choices for alerting and warnings when unpredictable patterns begin to develop.

Worked in monitoring

On the off chance that you review from Chapter 1, Introduction to Kubernetes, we noticed that our hubs were at that point running various monitoring administrations. We can see these indeed by running the get units command with the kube-system namespace determined as pursues:

$ kubectl get units - namespace=kube-system

Again, we see an assortment of administrations, yet how does this all fit together? In the event that you review the Node (some time ago minions) segment from Chapter 2, Pods, Services, Replication Controllers, and Labels, every hub is running a kublet. The kublet is the main interface for hubs to interact and refresh the API server. One such update is the measurements of the hub assets. The genuine reporting of the asset utilization is performed by a program named cAdvisor.

cAdvisor is another open-source venture from Google, which gives different measurements on container asset use. Measurements include CPU, memory, and system insights. There is no compelling reason to enlighten cAdvisor regarding individual containers; it gathers the measurements for all containers on a hub and reports this back to the kublet, which in go reports to Heapster.

Google's open-source ventures

Google has an assortment of open-source ventures identified with Kubernetes. Look at them, use them, and even contribute your very own code!

cAdvisor and Heapster are referenced in the following area:

cAdvisor: https://github.com/google/cadvisor

Heapster: https://github.com/kubernetes/heapster

Contrib is a trick for an assortment of segments that are not part of center

Kubernetes. It is found at:

https://github.com/kubernetes/contrib.

LevelDB is a key store library that was utilized in the production of InfluxDB. It is found at:

https://github.com/google/leveldb.

Heapster is one more open-source venture from Google; you may begin to see a topic emerging here (see the preceding information box). Heapster runs in a container on one of the minion hubs and totals the information from kublet. A basic REST interface is given to question the information.

When using the GCE arrangement, a couple of extra bundles are set up for us, which spares us time and gives us a total bundle to screen our container remaining tasks at hand. As should be obvious from the preceding System unit listing screen capture, there is another case with influx-grafana in the title.

InfluxDB is portrayed on its official site as pursues

An open-source circulated time arrangement database with no outer conditions.

InfluxDB depends on a key store bundle (allude to the past Google's open-source ventures information box) and is immaculate to store and question occasion—or time sensitive insights, for example, those gave by Heapster.

Finally, we have Grafana, which gives a dashboard and graphing interface for the information put away in InfluxDB. Using Grafana, clients can create a custom monitoring dashboard and get quick perceivability into the strength of their Kubernetes group and in this way their whole container infrastructure.

Exploring Heapster

How about we rapidly take a gander at the REST interface by running SSH to the hub with the Heapster unit.

In the first place, we can list the units to find the one running Heapster, as pursues:

$ kubectl get units - namespace=kube-system

The name of the unit should begin with monitoring-heapster. Run a depict command to see which hub it is running on, as pursues:

$ kubectl portray units/<Heapster monitoring Pod> - namespace=kube-system

From the yield in the following screen capture, we can see that the unit is running in kubernetes-minion-merd. Additionally note the IP for the unit, a couple of lines down, as we will require that in a minute:

Next, we can SSH to this container with the well-known gcloud ssh command, as pursues:

$gcloud figure - venture "<Your venture ID>" ssh - zone "<your gce zone>" "<kubernetes minion from describe>"

From here, we can get to the Heapster REST API legitimately using the case's IP address. Recall that case IPs are routable in the containers as well as on the hubs themselves. The Heapster API is listening on port 8082, and we can get a full rundown of measurements at/programming interface/v1/metric-trade pattern/.

How about we see the rundown now by issuing a twist command to the case IP address we spared from the depict command, as pursues:

$ twist - G <Heapster IP from describe>:8082/programming interface/v1/metric-send out construction/

We will see a listing that is very long. The main segment shows every one of the measurements accessible.

Customizing our dashboards

Since we have the fields, we can have a great time. Review the Grafana page we took a gander at in Chapter 1, Introduction to Kubernetes. We should pull that up again by going to our group's monitoring URL. Note that you may need to sign in with your group accreditations. Allude to the following arrangement of the link you have to utilize:

https://<your ace

IP>/programming interface/v1/intermediary/namespaces/kube-system/administrations/monitoring-grafana

We'll see the default Home dashboard. Snap on the down bolt beside Home and select Cluster. This shows the Kubernetes bunch dashboard, and now we can add our own measurements to the board. Look over right to the base and tap on Add a Row. This ought to create a space for another column and present a green tab on the left-hand side of the screen.

We should begin by adding a view into the filesystem use for every hub (minion). Snap on the green tab to expand and then select Add Panel and then diagram. An unfilled chart ought to show up on the screen alongside a question board for our custom diagram.

The main field in this board should show a question that starts with 'SELECT mean("value") FROM ...'. Snap on the A character beside this field to expand it. Leave the principal field beside FROM as default and then snap on the following field with the select estimation esteem. A dropdown menu will show up with the Heapster measurements we found in the past tables. Select filesystem/usage_bytes_gauge. Presently in the SELECT line, click on mean() and then on the x image to evacuate it. Next, click on the + image on the finish of the line and include selectors - > max. At that point, you'll see a GROUP BY push with time($interval) and fill(none). Cautiously click on fill and not on the (none) divide and again on x to expel it. At that point, click on the + image toward the finish of the line and select tag(hostname).

Next, how about we click on the Axes tab, with the goal that we can set the units and legend. Under Left Y Axis, click on the field alongside Unit and set it to information - > bytes and Label to Disk Space Used. Under Right Y Axis, set Unit to none - > none. Next, on the Legend tab, try to check Show in Options and Max in Values.

Presently, we should rapidly go to the General tab and pick a title. For my situation, I named mine Filesystem Disk Usage by Node (max).

We would prefer not to lose this pleasant new chart we've created, so how about we click on the spare symbol in the upper right corner. It would appear that a floppy plate (you can do a Google picture search on the off chance that you don't have a clue what this is).

After we click on the spare symbol, we will see a green exchange box that confirms the dashboard was spared. We would now be able to tap the x image over the diagram subtleties board and underneath the chart itself.

This will return us to the dashboard page. On the off chance that we look over right down, we will see our new chart. How about we add another board to this line. Again utilize the green tab and then select Add Panel - > singlestat. By and by, a vacant board will show up with a setting structure underneath it.

Suppose, we need to watch a specific hub and screen organize use. We can without much of a stretch do this by first going to the Metrics tab. At that point expand the inquiry field and set the second an incentive in the FROM field to arrange/rx. Presently we can indicate the WHERE statement by clicking the + symbol toward the finish of the line and choosing hostname from the dropdown. After hostname = click on select label esteem and pick one of the minion hubs from the rundown.

In the Options tab, ensure that Unit design is set to information - > bytes and check the Show box alongside Spark lines. The sparkline gives us a brisk history perspective on the ongoing variety in the worth. We can utilize Background mode to take up the whole foundation; of course, it utilizes the zone underneath the worth.

In Coloring, we can alternatively check the Value or Background box and pick Thresholds and Colors. This will enable us to pick different hues for the worth dependent on the edge level we indicate. Note that an unformatted form of the number must be utilized for edge esteems.

Presently, how about we return to the General tab and set the title as Network bytes got (Node35ao). Utilize the identifier for your minion hub. By and by, how about we spare our work and come back to the dashboard.

Grafana has various other board types you can play with, for example, Dashboard list, Plugin rundown, Table, and Text.

As should be obvious, it is truly simple to manufacture a custom dashboard and screen the wellbeing of our bunch initially.

FluentD and Google Cloud Logging

Looking back at the System unit listing screen capture toward the beginning of the part, you may have noticed various cases starting with the words fluentd-cloud-logging-kubernetes... . These pods show up when using the GCE supplier for your K8s bunch. A unit like this exists on each hub in our group and its sole reason for existing is to handle the processing of Kubernetes logs.

On the off chance that we sign in to our Google Cloud Platform account, we can see a portion of the logs handled there. Essentially utilize the left side, under Stackdriver select Logging. This will take us to a log listing page with various drop-down menus on the top. In the event that this is your first time visiting the page, the first dropdown will probably be set to Cloud HTTP Load Balancer.

In this drop-down menu, we'll see various GCE kinds of passages. Select GCE VM Instances and then the Kubernetes ace or one of the hubs. In the second dropdown, we can pick different log gatherings, including kublet. We can likewise channel by the occasion log level and date. Moreover, we can utilize the play catch to watch occasions stream in live:

FluentD

Presently we realize that the fluentd-cloud-logging-kubernetes units are sending the information to the Google Cloud, however for what reason do we need FluentD? Basically, FluentD is a gatherer. It very well may be designed to have different sources to gather and label logs, which are then sent to different yield points for investigation, alerting, or archiving. We can even change information using plugins before it is given to its destination.

Not all supplier arrangements have FluentD installed of course, however it is one of the prescribed ways to deal with give us more prominent adaptability for future monitoring tasks. The AWS Kubernetes arrangement likewise utilizes FluentD, however instead advances occasions to Elasticsearch.

Exploring FluentD

On the off chance that you are interested about the inner workings of the FluentD arrangement or simply need to alter the log assortment, we can investigate effectively using the kubectl executive command and one of the unit names from the command we ran before in the part.

In the first place, how about we check whether we can find the FluentD config file:

$kubectl executive fluentd-cloud-logging-kubernetes-minion-bunch r4qt - namespace=kube-system - ls/and so on/td-specialist

We will glance in the and so on organizer and then td-specialist, which is the familiar subfolder. While searching in this index, we should see a td-agent.conf file. We can see that file with a basic feline command, as pursues:

$kubectl executive fluentd-cloud-logging-kubernetes-minion-bunch r4qt - namespace=kube-system - feline/and so on/td-operator/td-agent.conf

We should see various sources including the different Kubernetes segments, Docker, and some GCP components.

While we can make changes here, recall that it is a running container and our progressions won't be spared if the unit bites the dust or is restarted. On the off chance that we truly need to alter, it's ideal to utilize this container as a base and assemble another container which we can push to a storehouse for later use.

Maturing our monitoring activities

While Grafana gives us an incredible begin to screen our container activities, it is as yet a work in progress. In this present reality of tasks, having a total dashboard see is incredible once we know there is an issue. Be that as it may, in ordinary situations, we'd like to be proactive and really get warnings when issues emerge. This kind of alerting ability is an unquestionable requirement to keep the activities group on the ball and out of receptive mode.

There are numerous arrangements accessible in this space, and we will investigate two specifically—GCE monitoring (StackDriver) and Sysdig.

GCE (StackDriver)

StackDriver is an extraordinary spot to begin for infrastructure in the general population cloud. It is really possessed by Google, so it's integrated as the Google Cloud Platform monitoring administration. Before your lock-in alerts start ringing, StackDriver likewise has strong integration with AWS. What's more, StackDriver has alerting ability with help for warning to an assortment of stages and webhooks for anything else.

Pursue GCE monitoring

In the GCE reassure, in the Stackdriver segment click on Monitoring. This will open another window, where we can pursue a free preliminary of Stackdriver. We would then be able to include our GCP venture and alternatively an AWS account also. This requires a couple of more advances, yet instructions are included on the page. Finally, we'll be given instructions on the most proficient method to install the operators on our group hubs. We can skirt this until further notice, yet will return to it in a minute.

Snap on Continue, set up your day by day alarms, and snap on Continue again.

Snap on Launch Monitoring to continue. We'll be taken to the main dashboard page, where we will see some fundamental measurements on our hub in the bunch. In the event that we select Resources from the side menu and, at that point Instances, we'll be taken to a page with every one of our hubs recorded. By clicking on the individual hub, we can again observe some essential information even without a specialist installed.

Stackdriver additionally offers monitoring and logging operators that can be installed on the hubs. In any case, it at present doesn't bolster the container OS that is utilized as a matter of course in the GCE kube-up content. You can even now observe the fundamental measurements for any hubs in GCE or AWS, however should utilize another OS on the off chance that you need the nitty gritty specialist install.

Alarms

Next, we can take a gander at the alerting arrangements accessible as a feature of the monitoring administration. From the instance subtleties page, click on the Create Alerting Policy button in the Incidents area at the highest point of the page.

We will tap on Add Condition and select a Metric Threshold. In the Target segment, set

Asset TYPE to Instance (GCE). At that point, set APPLIES to Group and kubernetes.

Leave CONDITION TRIGGERS IF set to Any Member Violates.

In the Configuration segment, leave IF METRIC as CPU Usage (GCE Monitoring) and CONDITION as above. Presently set THRESHOLD to 80 and set the time in FOR to 5 minutes.

Next, we will include a notice. In the Notification area, leave Method as Email and enter your email address.

We can avoid the Documentation area, however this is the place we can add content and formatting to alarm messages.

Finally, name the arrangement as Excessive CPU Load and tap on Save Policy.

Presently at whatever point the CPU from one of our instances goes over 80 percent, we will get an email warning. On the off chance that we ever need to audit our approaches, we can find them in the Alerting dropdown and then in Policies Overview at the menu on the left-hand side of the screen.

Past system monitoring with Sysdig

Monitoring our cloud systems is an extraordinary beginning, however shouldn't something be said about perceivability to the containers themselves? In spite of the fact that there are an assortment of cloud monitoring and perceivability instruments, Sysdig stands out for its capacity to plunge profound into system activities as well as explicitly containers.

Sysdig is open source and is charged as an all inclusive system perceivability instrument with local help for containers (you can allude to more insights concerning this in point 2 in the References area toward the finish of the section). It is a command-line apparatus, which gives insight into the zones we've taken a gander at before, for example, stockpiling, system, and system forms. What separates it is the degree of detail and perceivability it offers for these procedure and system exercises. Besides, it has local help for containers, which gives us a full image of our container tasks. This is an exceptionally prescribed device for your container tasks weapons store. The main site of Sysdig is http://www.sysdig.org/.

Sysdig Cloud

We will investigate the Sysdig instrument and a portion of the helpful command-line-based UIs in a minute. In any case, the group at Sysdig has additionally assembled a business item, named Sysdig Cloud, which gives the propelled dashboard, alerting, and warning administrations we talked about before in the section. Additionally, the differentiator here has high perceivability into containers, including some decent perceptions of our application topology.

In the event that you'd preferably skirt the Sysdig Cloud area and simply evaluate the command-line device, basically jump to the Sysdig command line segment later in this part.

On the off chance that you have not done so effectively, pursue Sysdig Cloud at http://www.sysdigcloud.com.

Subsequent to activating and logging in just because, we'll be taken to an invite page. Clicking on Next, we are indicated a page with different choices to install the sysdig operators. For our model condition, we will utilize the Kubernetes arrangement. Selecting Kubernetes will give you a page with your API key and a link to instructions. The instructions will walk you through how to create a Sysdig operator DaemonSet on your group. Remember to include the API Key from the install page.

We won't have the option to continue on the install page until the operators interface. Subsequent to creating the DaemonSet and waiting a minute, the page should continue to the AWS integration page. You can round this out in the event that you like, yet for this stroll through we will tap on Skip. At that point, click on Let's Get Started.

As of this writing, Sysdig and Sysdig Cloud were not completely good with the most recent container OS sent naturally in the GCE kube-up content, Container-Optimized OS from Google: https://cloud.google.com

/container-advanced os/docs.

We'll be taken to the main sysdig cloud dashboard screen. We should see at any rate two minion hubs show up under the Explore tab.

This page shows us a table view, and the links on the left given us a chance to investigate some key measurements for CPU, memory, networking, and so on. Despite the fact that this is an incredible beginning, the definite perspectives will give us an a lot further take a gander at every hub.

Point by point sees

We should investigate these perspectives. Select one of the minion hubs and then look down to the detail segment that shows up underneath. Of course, we should see the System: Overview by Process see (if it's not chosen, simply click on it from the rundown on the left-hand side). On the off chance that the diagram is difficult to peruse, basically utilize the boost symbol in the upper left corner of each chart for a bigger view.

There are an assortment of interesting perspectives to investigate. Just to get out a couple of others, Services | HTTP Overview and Hosts and Containers | Overview by Container give us some extraordinary diagrams for inspection. In the later view, we can see details for CPU, memory, system, and file use by container.

Topology views

Likewise, there are three topology sees at the base. These perspectives are ideal for helping us understand how our application is communicating. Snap on

Topology | Network Traffic and sit tight a couple of moments for the view to completely populate.

We note the view maps out the progression of correspondence between the minion hubs and the ace in the bunch. You may likewise take note of a + image in the top corner of the hub boxes. Snap on that in one of the minion hubs and utilize the zoom instruments at the highest point of the view zone to zoom into the subtleties

Note that we would now be able to see every one of the parts of Kubernetes running inside the ace. We can perceive how the different segments cooperate. We will see kube-intermediary and the kublet procedure running, just as various boxes with the Docker whale, which indicate that they are containers. On the off chance that we zoom in and utilize the in addition to symbol, we will see that these are the containers for our cases and center Kubernetes forms, as we found in the administrations running on the ace segment in Chapter 1, Introduction to Kubernetes.

Additionally, on the off chance that you have the ace included in your checked hubs, we can observe kublet initiate correspondence from a minion and tail it right through the kube-apiserver container in the ace.

We can even at times observe the instance correspondence with GCE infrastructure to refresh metadata. This view is incredible in request to get a psychological picture of how our infrastructure and underlying containers are talking to each other.

Measurements

Next, how about we switch over to the Metrics tab in the left-hand menu by Views. Here, there are additionally an assortment of supportive perspectives.

We should take a gander at capacity.estimated.request.total.count in System. This view shows us a gauge of what number of solicitations a hub is fit for handling when completely stacked. This can be extremely valuable for infrastructure planning:

Alerting

Since we have this extraordinary information, how about we create a few notices. Look back up to the highest point of the page and find the chime symbol by one of your minion sections. This will open a Create Alert discourse. Here, we can set manual cautions like what we did before in the part. Be that as it may, there is additionally the choice to utilize BASELINE and HOST COMPARISON.

Using the BASELINE choice is amazingly useful as Sysdig will watch the recorded examples of the hub and caution us at whatever point one of the measurements strays outside the normal metric limits. No manual settings are required, so this can truly spare time for the warning arrangement and help our tasks group to be proactive before issues emerge.

The HOST COMPARISON alternative is additionally an incredible assistance as it enables us to contrast measurements and different has and alert at whatever point one host has a metric that varies fundamentally from the gathering. An incredible use case for this is monitoring asset use crosswise over minion hubs to guarantee that our scheduling constraints are not creating a bottleneck some place in the group.

You can pick whichever alternative you like and give it a name and warning level. Empower the notice strategy. Sysdig underpins email, SNS (short for Simple Notification Service), and PagerDuty as warning techniques. You can alternatively empower Sysdig Capture to gain further insight into issues. When you have everything set, simply click on Create and you will begin to get cautions as issues come up.

The sysdig command line

Regardless of whether you just utilize the open-source instrument or you are trying out the full Sysdig Cloud bundle, the command-line utility is an incredible ally to need to find issues or get a more profound understanding of your system.

In the center instrument, there is the main sysdig utility and likewise a command-line style UI named csysdig. How about we investigate a couple of helpful commands.

Find the applicable install instructions for your OS here:

http://www.sysdig.org/install/

Once installed, allows first take a gander at the procedure with the most system action by issuing the following command:

$ sudo sysdig - pc - c topprocs_net

This is an interactive view that will show us a top procedure regarding system action. Likewise, there are a plenty of commands to use with sysdig. A couple of other helpful commands to give a shot include the following:

$sudo sysdig - pc - c topprocs_cpu

$sudo sysdig - pc - c topprocs_file

$sudo sysdig - pc - c topprocs_cpu container.name=<Container Name NOT ID>

More models can be found at

http://www.sysdig.org/wiki/sysdig-models/.

The csysdig command-line UI

Since we are in a shell on one of our hubs doesn't mean we can't have a UI. Csysdig is an adjustable UI to investigate every one of the measurements and insight that Sysdig gives. Essentially type csysdig at the brief:

$ csysdig

Subsequent to entering csysdig, we see an ongoing listing of all procedures on the machine. At the base of the screen, you'll note a menu with different choices. Snap on Views or press F2 in the event that you love to utilize your console. On the left-hand menu, there are an assortment of choices, yet we'll take a gander at strings. Double tap to choose Threads.

On some operating systems and with some SSH customers, you may have issues with the Function keys. Check the settings on your terminal and ensure the capacity keys are using the VT100+ groupings.

We can see every one of the strings at present running on the system and some information about the asset use. Of course, we see a major rundown that is updating often. On the off chance that we click on the Filter, F4 for the mouse tested, we can thin down the rundown.

Type kube-apiserver, on the off chance that you are on the ace, or kube-intermediary, in the event that you are on a hub (minion), in the channel box and press Enter.

On the off chance that we need to inspect somewhat further, we can essentially choose one of the strings in the rundown and snap on Dig or press F6. Presently we see an itemized listing of system calls from the command continuously. This can be an extremely helpful apparatus to gain profound insight into the containers and processing running on our group.

Snap on Back or press the Backspace key to return to the past screen. At that point, go to Views again. This time, we will take a gander at the Containers see. By and by, we can channel and additionally utilize the Dig view to get more top to bottom perceivability into what's going on at a system call level.

Another menu thing you may note here is Actions, which is accessible in the most up to date discharge. These highlights enable us to go from process monitoring to activity and reaction. It enables us to play out an assortment of activities from the different procedure sees in csysdig. For instance, the container see has activities to drop into a slam shell, slaughter containers, inspect logs, and more. It merits getting to know the different activities and hotkeys and even include your own custom hotkeys for regular tasks.

Prometheus

A newcomer to the monitoring scene is an open-source instrument called Prometheus. Prometheus is an open-source monitoring apparatus that was worked by a group at SoundCloud. You can find progressively about the task from https://prometheus.io.

Their site offers the following highlights (you can allude to more insights regarding this in point 3 in the References segment toward the finish of the section):

A multi-dimensional information model (time arrangement distinguished by metric name and key/esteem sets)

An adaptable inquiry language to use this dimensionality

No dependence on appropriated capacity; single server hubs are self-ruling

Time arrangement assortment happens by means of a force model over HTTP

pushing time arrangement is upheld by means of an intermediary passage

Targets are found by means of administration disclosure or static design Multiple methods of graphing and dashboard support

CoreOS has a decent blog entry on setting up Prometheus with Kubernetes here:

https://coreos.com/blog/monitoring-kubernetes-with-prometheus.html

Summary

We investigated monitoring and logging with Kubernetes. You should now be comfortable with how Kubernetes utilizes cAdvisor and Heapster to gather measurements on every one of the assets in a given bunch. Besides, we perceived how Kubernetes spares us time by providing InfluxDB and Grafana set up and arranged out of the container. Dashboards are effectively adjustable for our regular operational needs.

Moreover, we took a gander at the inherent logging abilities with FluentD and the Google Cloud Logging administration. Likewise, Kubernetes gives us incredible time savings by setting up the essentials for us.

Finally, you found out about the different outsider choices accessible to screen our containers and groups. Using these instruments will enable us to gain significantly more insight into the wellbeing and status of our applications. Every one of these devices combine to give us a strong toolset to oversee everyday activities.

In the following section, we will investigate the new group league capacities. Still for the most part in beta, this usefulness will enable us to run various bunches in different datacenters and even mists, however oversee and circulate applications from a single control plane.

Cluster Federation

This part will examine the new organization capacities and how to utilize them to deal with different groups crosswise over cloud suppliers. We will likewise cover the united variant of the center builds. We will walk you through combined Deployments, ReplicaSets, ConfigMaps, and Events.

This part will talk about the following themes:

Federating bunches

Federating different groups

Inspecting and controlling assets over different groups

Launching assets over different groups

Introduction to organization

While organization is still new in Kubernetes, it lays the preparation for the exceptionally looked for cross-cloud supplier arrangement. Using alliance, we can run different Kubernetes groups on-premise and in at least one open cloud suppliers and oversee applications utilizing the whole arrangement of all our authoritative assets.

This begins to create a way for avoiding cloud supplier lock-in and profoundly accessible sending that can put application servers in numerous bunches and take into account correspondence to different administrations situated in single points among our united groups. We can improve detachment on blackouts at a specific supplier or geographic area while providing more prominent adaptability for scaling and utilizing all out infrastructure.

At present, the league plane backings these assets (ConfigMap, DaemonSets, Deployment, Events, Ingress, Namespaces, ReplicaSets, Secrets, and Services). Note that league and its parts are in alpha and beta periods of discharge, so usefulness may in any case be somewhat touchy.

Setting up league

While we can utilize the bunch we had running for the remainder of the models, I would profoundly prescribe that you start new. The default naming of the bunches and settings can be risky for the organization system. Note that the - bunch setting and - mystery name banners are there to assist you with working around the default naming, yet for first-time alliance, it can even now be confusing and not exactly clear.

Henceforth, starting crisp is the means by which we will stroll through the models in this section. Either utilize new and separate cloud supplier (AWS and/or GCE) records or tear down the present bunch and reset your Kubernetes control condition by running the following commands:

$kubectl config unset settings

$kubectl config unset groups

Twofold watch that nothing is recorded using the following commands:

$kubectl config get-settings

$kubectl config get-bunches

Next, we will need to get the kubefed command on our way and make it executable. Explore back to the envelope where you have the Kubernetes download extricated. The kubefed command is situated in the/kubernetes/customer/bin envelope. Run the following commands to get in the bin organizer and change the execution authorizations:

$sudo cp kubernetes/customer/bin/kubefed/usr/nearby/bin

$sudo chmod +x/usr/nearby/bin/kubefed

Settings

Settings are utilized by the Kubernetes control plane to keep confirmation and bunch setup put away for various groups. This enable us to get to and deal with numerous bunches available from the equivalent kubectl. You can generally observe the settings accessible with the get-settings command that we utilized before.

New bunches for alliance

Again, ensure you explore to any place Kubernetes was downloaded and move into the bunch sub-organizer:

$ compact disc kubernetes/group/

Before we continue, ensure you have the GCE command line and the AWS command line installed, confirmed, and arranged. Allude to Chapter 1, Introduction to Kubernetes, on the off chance that you need help doing so on another container.

In the first place, we will create the AWS bunch. Note that we are adding a situation variable named OVERRIDE_CONTEXT that will enable us to set the setting name to something that follows the DNS naming standards. DNS is a basic segment for organization as it enables us to do cross-group revelation and administration correspondence. This is significant in a unified reality where groups might be in different server farms and even suppliers.

Run these commands to create your AWS group:

$export KUBERNETES_PROVIDER=aws

$export OVERRIDE_CONTEXT=awsk8s

$./kube-up.sh

Next, we will create a GCE group, by and by using the OVERRIDE_CONTEXT condition variable:

$export KUBERNETES_PROVIDER=gce

$export OVERRIDE_CONTEXT=gcek8s

$./kube-up.sh

In the event that we investigate our settings now, we will see both the awsk8s and the gcek8s that we just created. The star before gcek8s means that it's the place kubectl is at present pointing and executing against:

$ kubectl config get-settings

Initializing the league control plane

Since we have two bunches, we should set up the alliance control plane in the GCE group. To begin with, we'll have to ensure that we are in the GCE setting, and then we will initialize the alliance control plane:

$ kubectl config use-setting gcek8s

$kubefed init ace control - have group context=gcek8s - dns-zone-name="mydomain.com"

The preceding command creates another setting only for league called ace control. It utilizes the gcek8s bunch/setting to have the league segments, (for example, API server and controller). It accept GCE DNS as the organizations DNS administration. You'll have to refresh dns-zone-name with a domain addition you oversee.

As a matter of course, the DNS supplier is GCE. You can utilize - dns-provider="aws-route53" to set it to AWS route53; be that as it may, out of the crate execution still has issues for some clients.

On the off chance that we check our settings by and by we will presently observe three settings:

$ kubectl config get-settings

How about we ensure we have all the organization segments running before we continue. The league control plane uses the alliance system namespace. Utilize the kubectl get cases command with the namespace determined to screen the advancement. When you see two API server cases and one controller unit you ought to be set:

$ kubectl get cases - namespace=federation-system

Since we have the league parts set fully operational, we should change to that setting for the subsequent stages:

$ kubectl config use-setting expert control

Adding bunches to the league system

Since we have our league control plane we can add the bunches to the alliance system. To begin with, we will join the GCE group and then the AWS bunch:

$kubefed join gcek8s - have bunch context=gcek8s - mystery name=fed-mystery gce

$kubefed join awsk8s - have bunch context=gcek8s - mystery name=fed-mystery aws

Unified assets

Unified assets enable us to convey over different groups and/or locales. As of now, adaptation 1.5 of Kubernetes bolster various center asset types in the alliance API, including ConfigMap, DaemonSets, Deployment, Events, Ingress, Namespaces, ReplicaSets, Secrets, and Services.

How about we investigate a Federated Deployment that will enable us to plan units crosswise over both

AWS and GCE:

apiVersion: augmentations/v1beta1

kind: Deployment

metadata:

name: hub js-convey

marks:

name: hub js-convey

spec:

imitations: 3

format:

metadata:

marks:

name: hub js-convey

spec:

containers:

- name: hub js-convey

picture: jonbaier/case scaling:latest ports:

- containerPort: 80

Listing 9-1. hub js-convey fed.yaml

Create this organization with the following command:

$ kubectl create - f hub js-convey fed.yaml

Presently how about we have a go at listing the cases from this organization:

$ kubectl get units

We should see a message like the preceding one portrayed. This is on the grounds that we are as yet using the ace control or organization setting, which doesn't itself run cases. We will, in any case, see the organization in the alliance plane and in the event that we inspect the occasions we will see that the sending was in certainty created on both our united groups:

$ kubectl get arrangements

$ kubectl portray arrangements hub js-convey

We should see something like the following. Notice that the Events: segment shows arrangements in both our GCE and AWS settings:

We can likewise observe the combined occasions using the following command:

$ kubectl get occasions

It might pause for a minute for every one of the three cases to run. When that occurs, we can change to each bunch setting and see a portion of the units on each. Note that we would now be able to utilize get units since we are on the individual groups and not on the control plane:

$kubectl config use-setting awsk8s

$kubectl get units

$kubectl config use-setting gcek8s

$kubectl get units

We should see the three units spread over the groups with two on one and a third on the other. Kubernetes has spread it over the group with no manual intervention. Any cases that bomb will be restarted, yet now we have the additional repetition of two cloud suppliers.

Unified designs

In present day software advancement, it isn't unexpected to isolate setup factors from the application code itself. In this manner it is simpler to make updates to support URLs, accreditations, regular ways, and so on. Having these qualities in outer arrangement files implies we can undoubtedly refresh setup without rebuilding the whole application.

This partition takes care of the initial issue, yet obvious transportability comes when you can expel the reliance from the application totally. Kubernetes offers a design store for precisely this reason. ConfigMaps are straightforward builds that store key-esteem sets.

Kubernetes likewise bolsters Secrets for increasingly touchy arrangement information. This will be shrouded in more detail in Chapter 10, Container Security. You can utilize the model there in both single bunches or on the league control plane as we are demonstrating with ConfigMaps here.

How about we investigate a model that will enable us to store some setup and then expend it in different cases. The following listings will work for both combined and single bunches, however we will continue using a united arrangement for this model.

The ConfigMap kind can be created using strict qualities, level files and registries, and finally

YAML definition files. The following listing is a YAML definition file:

apiVersion: v1

kind: ConfigMap

metadata:

name: my-application-config

namespace: default

information:

backend-service.url: my-backend-administration

Listing 9-2: configmap-fed.yaml

Allows first switch back to our alliance plane:

$ kubectl config use-setting expert control

Presently, create this listing with the following command:

$ kubectl create - f configmap-fed.yaml

How about we show the configmap object that we just created. The - o yaml banner encourages us show the full information:

$ kubectl get configmap my-application-config - o yaml

Since we have a ConfigMap object, how about we fire up a united ReplicaSet that can utilize the ConfigMap. This will create copies of cases over our bunch that can get to

the ConfigMap object. ConfigMaps can be gotten to through condition factors or mount volumes. This model will utilize a mount volume that gives an envelope chain of command and the files for each key with the substance representing the qualities:

```
apiVersion: augmentations/v1beta1
kind: ReplicaSet
metadata:
name: hub js-rs
spec:
imitations: 3
selector:
matchLabels:
name: hub js-configmap-rs
format:
metadata:
marks:
name: hub js-configmap-rs
spec:
containers:
- name: configmap-case
picture: jonbaier/hub express-info:latest
ports:
- containerPort: 80
name: web
volumeMounts:
- name: configmap-volume
mountPath:/and so forth/config
volumes:
- name: configmap-volume configMap:
name: my-application-config
```

Listing 9-3: configmap-rs-fed.yaml

Create this case with kubectl create - f configmap-rs-fed.yaml. After creation, we

should change settings to one of the bunches where the cases are running. You can pick either, however we will utilize the GCE setting here:

$ kubectl config use-setting gcek8s

Since we are on the GCE group explicitly, we should check the configmaps here:

$ kubectl get configmaps

As should be obvious, the ConfigMap is spread locally to each bunch. Next, how about we find a case from our combined ReplicaSet:

$ kubectl get cases

How about we take one of the hub js-rs case names from the listing and run a slam shell with kubectl executive:

$ kubectl executive - it hub js-rs-6g7nj slam

At that point change registries to the/and so forth/config organizer that we set up in the case definition. Listing this index uncovers a single file with the name of the ConfigMap we defined before:

$cd/and so on/config

$ls

In the event that we, at that point show the substance of the files with the following command, we should see the worth we entered before: my-backend-administration:

$ reverberation $(cat backend-service.url)

If we somehow happened to glance in any of the units over our combined group we would see similar qualities. This is an extraordinary method to decouple arrangement from an application and appropriate it over our armada of bunches.

Other unified assets

So far we saw unified Deployments, ReplicaSets, Events, and ConfigMaps in

activity. DaemonSets, Ingress, Namespaces, Secrets, and Services are additionally upheld. Your particular arrangement will fluctuate and you may have a lot of bunches that vary from our model here. As referenced before, these assets are still in beta, so it merits spending some an opportunity to explore different avenues regarding the different asset types and understand how well the league develops are upheld for your specific blend of infrastructure.

Genuine multi-cloud

This is an exciting space to watch. As it develops it gives us a great beginning to doing multi-cloud usage and providing excess crosswise over districts, server farms, and even cloud suppliers.

While Kubernetes provides a simple and exciting way to multi-cloud infrastructure, note that generation multi-cloud requires significantly more than dispersed organizations. A full arrangement of abilities from logging and monitoring to consistence and host-hardening, there is a lot to oversee in a multi-supplier arrangement.

Genuine multi-cloud selection will require a well-arranged design, and Kubernetes steps forward in pursuing this objective.

Summary

In this section, we took a gander at the new league abilities in Kubernetes. We perceived how we can send groups to various cloud suppliers and oversee them from a single control plane. We additionally conveyed an application crosswise over groups in both AWS and GCE. While these highlights are new and still mainly in alpha and beta, we should now have the right stuff to use them as they advance and become some portion of the standard Kubernetes operating model.

In the following part, we will investigate another propelled point, security. We will cover the nuts and bolts for secure containers and likewise how to verify your Kubernetes group. We will likewise take a gander at the Secrets build, which gives us the capacity to store touchy setup information like our preceding ConfigMap model.

Container Security

This section will examine the essentials of holder security from the compartment runtime level to the host itself. We will talk about how to apply these ideas to remaining tasks at hand running in a Kubernetes bunch and a portion of the security concerns and practices that relate explicitly to running your Kubernetes group.

This part will examine the accompanying themes:

Fundamental holder security

Holder picture security and ceaseless powerlessness filtering

Kubernetes bunch security

Kubernetes mysteries

Nuts and bolts of holder security

Holder security is a profound branch of knowledge and in itself can fill its very own book. Having said this, we will cover a portion of the elevated level concerns and give a beginning stage to consider this zone.

In the A short diagram of holders area of Chapter 1, Introduction to Kubernetes, we took a gander at a portion of the center segregation includes in the Linux part that empower compartment innovation. Understanding the subtleties of how compartments work is the way to getting a handle on the different security worries in overseeing them.

Keeping compartments contained

One of the most clear highlights talked about in the paper is that of getting away from the seclusion/virtualization of the compartment develop. Current holder usage watch against this utilizing namespaces to detach forms just as permitting control of the Linux abilities accessible to a compartment. Also, there is an expanded move towards secure default arrangements of the out-of-the-case compartment condition. For instance,

Docker as a matter of course just empowers a little arrangement of capacities (you can allude to more subtleties about this in point 2 in the References segment toward the finish of the section). Systems administration is another road of break and it very well may be trying since there are an assortment of system

choices that fitting in to most present day holder arrangements.

The following zone examined in the paper is that of assaults between two holders. The User namespace model gives us included assurance here by mapping the root client inside the holder to a lower level client on the host machine. Systems administration is obviously still an issue and something that requires appropriate constancy and consideration while choosing and actualizing your holder organizing arrangement.

Assaults inside the holder itself are another vector and likewise with past concerns, namespaces and organizing are critical to security here. Another perspective that is imperative in this situation is simply the application security. The code still needs to pursue secure coding rehearses and the software ought to be stayed up with the latest and fixed consistently. At long last, the productivity of holder images has an additional advantage of contracting the assault surface. The images ought to be worked with just the bundles and software essential.

Asset fatigue and arrangement security

Like the Denial of Service assaults, we've seen in different territories of figuring that asset weariness is especially a relevant worry in the holder world. While cgroups give a few impediments on asset use for things, for example, CPU, memory, and plate use, there are as yet substantial assault roads for asset depletion. Devices, for example, Docker offer some beginning defaults to the cgroups confinements, and Kubernetes likewise offers extra restricts that can be set on gatherings of compartments running in the bunch. It's essential to understand these defaults and change for your organizations.

While the Linux part and the highlights that empower holders give us some type of detachment, they are genuinely new to the Linux working system. All things considered, despite everything they contain their own bugs and vulnerabilities. The inherent systems for abilities and namespaces can and do have issues and it is critical to follow these as a feature of your protected holder activities.

The last region shrouded in the NCC paper is simply the assault of the compartment the board layer itself. The Docker motor, picture repositories, and arrangement instruments are largely huge vectors of assault and ought to be viewed as when building up your methodology. We'll glance more inside and out at how we can address the repositories and Kubernetes as a coordination layer in the following areas.

In case you're keen on find out about the particular security highlights of Docker's execution, investigate:

https://docs.docker.com/motor/security/security/.

Picture repositories

Helplessness the executives is a basic segment of any cutting edge IT activity. Zero-day vulnerabilities are on the ascent and even those vulnerabilities with patches can be unwieldy to remediate. To start with, application proprietors must be made mindful of their vulnerabilities and potential patches. At that point these patches must be coordinated into systems and code and often this requires extra arrangements or support windows. In any event, when there is perceivability to vulnerabilities, there is often a slack in remediation, often taking enormous associations a while to fix.

While holders significantly improve the way toward refreshing applications and limiting personal time, there still stays a test innate in weakness the executives. Particularly since an aggressor just needs to uncover one such weakness; making anything short of 100% of systems fixed is a hazard for bargain.

What's required is a quicker criticism circle in addressing vulnerabilities. Constant filtering and integrating with the software arrangement life cycle is critical to speeding the data and remediation of vulnerabilities. Fortunately, this is actually the methodology being incorporated with the most recent holder the board and security tooling.

Persistent helplessness examining

One such open-source venture that has developed in this space is Clair. We become acquainted with this from the Clair GitHub page: Clair is an open source venture for the static investigation of vulnerabilities in appc and docker holders.

You can visit Clair at the accompanying connection:

https://github.com/coreos/clair.

Clair examines your code against Common Vulnerabilities and Exploits (CVEs). It tends to be coordinated into your CI/CD pipeline and run as a reaction to new forms. In the event that vulnerabilities are discovered, they can be taken as input into the pipeline, even stop arrangement, and bomb the construct. This powers designers to know about and remediate vulnerabilities during their typical discharge process.

Clair can be incorporated with various compartment picture repositories and CI/CD pipelines.

Clair can even be sent on Kubernetes: https://github.com/coreos/clair#kubernetes.

Clair is additionally utilized as the filtering system in CoreOS's Quay picture store. Quay offers various undertaking highlights including ceaseless helplessness checking:

https://quay.io/

Both Docker Hub and Docker Cloud bolster security checking. Once more, compartments that are pushed to the storehouse are consequently filtered against CVEs and warnings of vulnerabilities are sent because of any discoveries. Also, parallel examination of the code is performed to coordinate the mark of the segments with that of known renditions.

There are an assortment of other checking instruments that can be utilized also for filtering your picture repositories including OpenSCAP just as Twistlock and AquaSec

Picture marking and check

Regardless of whether you are utilizing a private picture vault in-house or an open repo, for example, Docker Hub, realize that you are running just the code that your engineers have composed. The potential for pernicious code or man-in-the-center assaults on downloads is a significant factor in securing your compartment images.

Accordingly, both rkt and Docker bolster the capacity to sign images and confirm that the substance have not changed. Distributers can utilize keys to sign the images when they are pushed to the repositories and clients can confirm the mark on the client-side when downloading for use:

From the rkt documentation:

"Before executing a remotely brought ACI, rkt will confirm it dependent on appended marks produced by the ACI maker."

https://coreos.com/rkt/docs/most recent/subcommands/trust.ht ml

https://coreos.com/rkt/docs/most recent/marking and-verifica tion-guide.html

From the Docker documentation:

"Content trust enables you to confirm both the honesty and the distributer of the considerable number of information got from a library over any channel."

https://docs.docker.com/motor/security/trust/content_t rust/

From the Docker Notary GitHub page:

"The Notary venture includes a server and a client for running and collaborating with confided in assortments."

https://github.com/docker/public accountant

Kubernetes group security

Kubernetes has kept on including various security includes in their most recent discharges and has a balanced arrangement of control focuses that can be utilized in your bunch; everything from secure node correspondence to unit security and even capacity of delicate design information.

Secure API calls

During each apus call, Kubernetes applies various security controls.

After secure TLS correspondence is built up, the API server goes through Authorization and Authentication. At long last, an Admission Controller circle is applied to the solicitation before it arrives at the API server.

Secure node correspondence

Kubernetes bolsters the utilization of secure correspondence channels between the API server and any client including the nodes themselves. Regardless of whether it's a GUI or command-line utility, for example, kubectl, we can utilize authentications to speak with the API server. Consequently, the API server is the focal communication point for any progressions to the group and is a basic part to verify.

In organizations, for example, GCE, the kubelet on every node is conveyed for secure correspondence as a matter of course. This arrangement utilizes the TLS bootstrapping and the new testaments' API to set up a protected association with the API server utilizing TLS client endorsements and a Certificate Authority (CA) bunch.

Approval and validation modules

The module systems for validation and approval in Kubernetes are in their early stages. Be that as it may, these highlights likewise keep on creating in the following barely any discharges. There are likewise outsider suppliers that incorporate with the highlights here.

Verification is at present bolstered as tokens, passwords, and authentications with plans to include the module ability at a later stage. OpenID Connect tokens are upheld and a few outsider usage, for example, Dex from CoreOS and aser record and validation from Cloud Foundry, are accessible.

Approval as of now underpins three modes. The full RBAC (short for Role-Based Access Control)mode is as yet a work in advance and will in the end bring a develop job based confirmation from Kubernetes itself. Quality Based Access Control (ABAC) is as of now upheld and gives a client a chance to characterize benefits by means of traits in a file. At long last, a webhook system is bolstered, which considers mix with outsider approval by means of REST web administration calls.

Get familiar with every territory here:

http://kubernetes.io/docs/administrator/approval/http://kubernetes.io/docs/administrator/verification/

Confirmation controllers

Kubernetes likewise gives a system to coordinating with extra check as a last advance. This could be as picture examining, signature checks, or anything that can react in the predetermined style. At the point when an API call is made, the snare is called and that server can run its confirmation. Confirmation controllers can likewise be utilized to change asks for and include or modify the first solicitation. When the tasks are run, a reaction is then sent back with a status that teaches Kubernetes to permit or deny the call.

This can be particularly useful for checking or testing images as we referenced in the last area. The ImagePolicyWebhook module gives a confirmation controller that takes into account joining with extra picture assessment.

For more data, visit the Using Admission Controller page in the accompanying documentation:

https://kubernetes.io/docs/administrator/affirmation controllers/.

Case security strategies and setting

Probably the most recent expansion to the Kubernetes' security munititions stockpile is that of Pod security approaches and settings. These enable clients to control clients and gatherings for holder forms and appended volumes, limit the utilization of host systems or namespaces, and even set the root filesystem to peruse as it were. Furthermore, we can confine the capacities accessible and likewise set SELinux alternatives for the names that are applied to the holders in each unit.

Notwithstanding SELinux, Kubernetes likewise included help for utilizing AppArmor with your cases utilizing comments. For more data, allude to the accompanying documentation page:

https://kubernetes.io/docs/administrator/apparmor/.

We'll stroll through a case of utilizing a case security setting to add a few imperatives to our units. Since the usefulness is still in beta, we'll have to empower the beta augmentations API and likewise add PodSecurityPolicy to the rundown of affirmation controllers being used.

Empowering beta APIs

To start with, you'll have to SSH into your lord node, change to a root client, and then alter the

/and so forth/kubernetes/shows/kube-apiserver.manifest file in your favored supervisor. Once more, we can SSH by means of the Google Cloud CLI or utilize the Google Cloud Console, which has a worked in SSH client on the VM occasions page.

The best practice isn't to SSH onto the nodes themselves. Notwithstanding, we have done as such at a few points in this book for illustrative purposes. It's imperative to understand how things are running on the nodes themselves and can here and there be essential both for learning and investigating. Having said this, utilization the instruments, for example, kubectl executive when you essentially need to run a command from inside the bunch or a unit.

Look down to the command segment and we should see something like the accompanying posting:

"canister/sh",

"- c",

"/usr/neighborhood/canister/kube-apiserver - v=2 - cloud-config=/and so on/gce.conf -

address=127.0.0.1 - permit

privileged=true - approval strategy file=/and so on/srv/kubernetes/abac-authz-policy.jsonl - essential auth-file=/and so on/srv/kubernetes/basic_auth.csv - cloud-provider=gce - client-ca-file=/and so on/srv/kubernetes/ca.crt - etcd-servers=http://127.0.0.1:2379 - etcd-servers-overrides=/events#http://127.0.0.1:4002 - secure-port=443 - tls-cert-file=/and so forth

/srv/kubernetes/server.cert - tls-private-key-

file=/and so forth/srv/kubernetes/server.key - token-auth-

file=/and so forth/srv/kubernetes/known_tokens.csv - capacity backend=etcd2 - target-

slam mb=180 - administration group ip-range=10.0.0.0/16 - etcd-majority read=false

- affirmation

control=NamespaceLifecycle,LimitRanger,ServiceAccount,PersistentVolumeLabel

,DefaultStorageClass,ResourceQuota

- approval mode=ABAC - permit privileged=true 1>>/var/log/kube-apiserver.log 2>&1"

Your posting may shift, so simply include the parameters featured in striking as pursues. Additionally, duplicate the first posting as a reinforcement so you can reestablish it if necessary later on:

"container/sh",

"- c",

"/usr/neighborhood/container/kube-apiserver - v=2 - cloud-config=/and so forth/gce.conf - address=127.0.0.1

- permit privileged=true - approval arrangement

file=/and so forth/srv/kubernetes/abac-authz-policy.jsonl - fundamental auth-

file=/and so forth/srv/kubernetes/basic_auth.csv - cloud-provider=gce - client-ca-

file=/and so forth/srv/kubernetes/ca.crt - etcd-servers=http://127.0.0.1:2379 -

etcd-servers-overrides=/events#http://127.0.0.1:4002 - secure-port=443 -

tls-cert-file=/and so forth/srv/kubernetes/server.cert - tls-private-key-

file=/and so forth/srv/kubernetes/server.key - token-auth-

file=/and so forth/srv/kubernetes/known_tokens.csv - capacity backend=etcd2 - target-

slam mb=180 - administration group ip-range=10.0.0.0/16 - etcd-majority read=false

- affirmation

control=NamespaceLifecycle,LimitRanger,ServiceAccount,PersistentVolumeLabel

,DefaultStorageClass,ResourceQuota,PodSecurityPolicy - approval

mode=ABAC - permit privileged=true - runtime-

config=extensions/v1beta1=true,extensions/v1beta1/podsecuritypolicy=true

1>>/var/log/kube-apiserver.log 2>&1"

Spare the file and exit sudo on the off chance that you have a root shell. In the event that all goes well, Kubernetes should see the show changes and restart the API Server. This may take a couple of moments and during reboot, kubectl may get lethargic. I for the most part watch this with the accompanying command:

$ kubectl get cases - namespace=kube-system

Watch the STATUS and AGE sections. Once the restart is fruitful, we'll have a STATUS of Running and an AGE on the request for a couple of moments or less.

On the off chance that we had any grammatical errors with the show, we may see blunders in STATUS or even get a for all time inert kubectl. On the off chance that this occurs, we'll have to reestablish our prior parameters. As a last resort, you can reboot the case. The default for GCE arrangements has a boot content that will supplant the show with the default settings.

When your API server is refreshed and running, we can include a security approach and run a unit with a case security setting characterized. The arrangement runs at the bunch level and implements the strategy for all units. The unit security setting is set in the case definition and applies just to that case.

Making a PodSecurityPolicy

Since we've included the PodSecurityPolicy confirmation controller, we'll have to include a case security approach before we can create our model in posting 10-2 further down.

Once more, the case security approach applies group wide:

{

"kind": "PodSecurityPolicy",

"apiVersion":"extensions/v1beta1",

"metadata": {

"name": "default"

},

"spec": {

"special": bogus,

```
"seLinux": {
"rule": "RunAsAny"
},
"supplementalGroups": {
"rule": "RunAsAny"
},
"runAsUser": {
"rule": "RunAsAny"
},
"fsGroup": {
"rule": "RunAsAny"
},
"volumes": ["*"],
"readOnlyRootFilesystem": genuine
}
}
```

Posting 10-1: default-security-policy.json

Create this with the accompanying:

```
$ kubectl create - f default-security-policy.json
```

The previous default approach doesn't enable compartments to run in special mode. It permits any seLinux names, any supplemental gathering IDs, any client to run the main procedure, and any gathering ID for the filesytems. It additionally bolsters a wide range of volumes.

Since we have a fundamental approach for the group, how about we create a Pod. To start with, we will create a Pod with our node-express-information compartment:

```
apiVersion: v1
kind: Pod
metadata:
name: node-js-nopsc
```

spec:

holders:

- name: node-js-nopsc

picture: jonbaier/node-express-info:latest ports:

- containerPort: 80

Posting 10-2: nodejs-case nopsc.yaml

Create the case with the former posting. At that point utilize the kubectl executive command to get a shell inside the case. Next, we will endeavor to create a file utilizing the touch command:

$kubectl executive - it node-js-nopsc slam

root@node-js-nopsc:/src# contact file.txt

We ought to get a blunder like touch: can't contact 'file.txt': Read-just file system. This is on the grounds that we set the ReadOnlyFileSystem property to genuine, so all holders (unit security setting characterized or not) are currently run with read-just root filesystems. Type exit to leave this case.

Making a case with a PodSecurityContext

Since we have seen the impacts of the unit security strategy, we should investigate the case security setting. Here we can characterize seLinuxOptions that let us characterize the name setting for the holders in the unit. We can likewise characterize runAsUser to indicate the UID with which every compartment will run and the runAsNonRoot banner that will basically anticipate beginning holders that run as UID 0 or root. We can likewise determine the Group (GID) for the primary procedure in every holder with supplementalGroup. At long last, we can indicate the Group (GID) for filesystem proprietorship and new files with fsGroup.

Posting 10-4 is a rendition of our past node-express-information unit with the runAsNonRoot set to genuine. Understand that root (UID 0) is the default client if none is characterized in the Dockerfile. Posting 10-3 shows the Dockerfile for our node-express-information compartment. We have not characterized the USER mandate and along these lines it will run as root:

FROM node:latest

Include src//src

WORKDIR/src

RUN npm introduce

ENV PORT=80

CMD ["node", "index.js"]

Posting 10-3: node-express-data Dockerfile

apiVersion: v1

kind: Pod

metadata:

name: node-js-case

spec:

holders:

- name: node-js-case

picture: jonbaier/node-express-info:latest ports:

- containerPort: 80

securityContext:

runAsNonRoot: genuine

Posting 10-4: nodejs-case psc.yaml

Understanding the connection between the security setting and how the holders are fabricated is significant. On the off chance that we attempt to create the former Listing 10-4 with kubectl create - f nodejs-case psc.yaml, we will see that it never starts and gives us

VerifyNonRootError:

Understanding that running holders safely is anything but a simply an assignment of executives including imperatives is significant. The work must be done as a team with engineers who will appropriately create the images.

Tidy up

The arrangement we have set up might be unreasonably prohibitive for learning and improvement, so you may wish to expel it. You can do as such with the accompanying command:

$ kubectl erase psp default

You'll likewise need to fix the progressions to /and so on/kubernetes/shows/kube-apiserver.manifest that we did on the Kubernetes ace toward the start of this segment. In particular, you should expel the PodSecurityPolicy from the rundown of the confirmation control area.

Extra contemplations

Notwithstanding the highlights we just assessed, Kubernetes has various different develops that ought to be considered in your general bunch solidifying process. Prior in the book, we took a gander at namespaces that give a legitimate partition to multi-tenure. While the namespaces themselves don't segregate the real system traffic, a portion of the system modules, for example, Calico and Canal, give extra ability to organize approaches. We additionally took a gander at portions and constrains that can be set for each namespace and ought to be utilized to keep a solitary occupant or undertaking from expending such a large number of assets inside the bunch.

Verifying touchy application information (insider facts)

At times, our application needs to hold touchy data. This can be qualifications or tokens to sign in to a database or administration. Putting away this delicate data in the picture itself is something to be kept away from. Here, Kubernetes gives us an answer in the develop of insider facts.

Privileged insights give us an approach to store touchy data without incorporating plaintext forms in our asset definition files. Privileged insights can be mounted to the cases that need them and then got to inside the unit as files with the mystery esteems as substance. On the other hand, you can likewise uncover the privileged insights through condition factors.

We can without much of a stretch create a mystery either with YAML or on the command line. Privileged insights do should be base-64 encoded, however on the off chance that we utilize the kubectl command line, this encoding is accomplished for us.

How about we start with the accompanying Secret:

$kubectl create mystery conventional mystery phrases - from-literal=quiet-phrase="Shh! Dont' tell"

We would then be able to check for the Secret with this command:

$ kubectl get insider facts

Since we have effectively created the Secret, how about we make a case that can utilize the mystery. Privileged insights are devoured in units by method for joined volumes. In the accompanying Listing 10-5, you'll see that we use volumeMount to mount the key to an organizer in our compartment:

apiVersion: v1

kind: Pod

metadata:

name: mystery case

spec:

holders:

- name: mystery case

picture: jonbaier/node-express-info:latest ports:

- containerPort: 80

name: web

volumeMounts:

- name: mystery volume

mountPath:/and so forth/mystery phrases

volumes:

- name: mystery volume mystery:

secretName: mystery phrases

Posting 10-5: mystery pod.yaml

Create this case with kubectl create - f mystery pod.yaml. Once created, we can get a slam shell in the unit with kubectl executive and then change indexes to the/and so on/mystery phrases envelope that we set up in the case definition. Posting this catalog uncovers a solitary file with the name of the mystery that we created before:

$kubectl executive - it mystery case slam

$cd/and so forth/mystery phrases

$ls

On the off chance that we, at that point show those substance, we should see the expression we encoded beforehand, Shh!

Dont' tell:

$ feline calm expression

Normally, this would be utilized for a username and secret word to a database or administration, or any delicate accreditations and arrangement information.

Remember that privileged insights are still in their beginning times, however they are an indispensable segment for creation activities. There are a few upgrades arranged here for future discharges. Right now, mysteries are still put away in plaintext in the etcd server. Be that as it may, the privileged insights develop allows us to control which units can get to it and it stores the data on the tmpfs, yet doesn't store it very still for each case. You'll likely need more security set up for a generation prepared system.

Summary

We investigated fundamental holder security and some basic territories of thought. We additionally addressed essential picture security and consistent helplessness checking. Later in this section, we took a gander at the general security highlights of Kubernetes including insider facts for putting away touchy setup information, secure API calls, and in any event, setting up security arrangements and settings for cases running on our group.

You should now have a strong beginning stage for verifying your group and moving towards creation. Keeping that in mind, the following section will cover a general technique for moving towards generation and will likewise take a gander at some outsider merchants that offer instruments to fill in the holes and help you in transit.

Extending Kubernetes with OCP, CoreOS, and Tectonic

The primary portion of this part will cover how open standards empower a differing ecosystem of compartment usage. We'll take a gander at the Open Container Initiative (OCI) and its crucial give an open holder determination also. The second 50% of this section will cover CoreOS and its preferences as a host OS, including execution and backing for different compartment usage. Additionally, we'll investigate the Tectonic undertaking offering from CoreOS.

This section will talk about the accompanying subjects:

Why standards matter?

The Open Container Initiative and Cloud Native Computing Foundation

Compartment details versus usage

CoreOS and its points of interest

Structural

The significance of standards

In the course of recent years, containerization innovation has had an enormous development in fame. While Docker has been at the focal point of this ecosystem, there is an expanded number of players in the compartment space. There is as of now various options in contrast to the containerization and Docker execution itself (rkt, Garden, and so on). Also, there is a rich ecosystem of outsider apparatuses that upgrade and praise your holder framework. Kubernetes lands unequivocally on the organization side of this ecosystem, however most importantly every one of these apparatuses structure the premise to construct cloud-local applications.

As we referenced at the absolute starting point of the book, a most alluring aspect concerning compartments is their capacity to bundle our application for sending across different condition levels (that is, improvement, trying, and generation) and different foundation suppliers (GCP, AWS, On-premise, and so on).

To genuinely bolster this sort of organization dexterity, we need not just the compartments themselves to have a typical stage, yet in addition the fundamental details to pursue a typical arrangement of standard procedures. This will take into consideration executions that are both adaptable and profoundly specific. For instance, a few remaining tasks at hand may should be run on a profoundly secure execution. To give this, the execution should settle on increasingly purposeful choices about certain parts of usage. In either case, we will have greater nimbleness and opportunity if our compartments are based on some normal structures that all usage concur on and support.

The Open Container Initiative

One of the principal activities to increase boundless industry commitment is the OCI. Among the 36 business partners are Docker, Red Hat, VMware, IBM, Google, and AWS, and they are recorded on the OCI site at:

https://www.opencontainers.org/.

The motivation behind the OCI is to part executions, for example, Docker and rkt, from a standard particular for the configuration and runtime of containerized remaining tasks at hand. By their very own terms, the objective of the OCI particular has three fundamental tenets(you can allude to more insights regarding this in point 1 in the References area toward the finish of the section):

Making a proper determination for holder picture positions and runtime, which will enable an agreeable compartment to be compact across all major, consistent working systems and stages without fake specialized hindrances.

Tolerating, keeping up, and propelling the ventures related with these standards (the Projects). It will hope to concur on a standard arrangement of compartment activities (start, executive, pause,....) just as runtime condition related with compartment runtime.

Blending the already referenced standard with other proposed standards, including the appc particular.

Cloud Native Computing Foundation

A second activity that additionally has a far reaching industry acknowledgment is the Cloud Native Computing Foundation (CNCF). While still centered around containerized outstanding burdens, the CNCF works somewhat higher up the stack at an application configuration level. The reason for existing is to give a standard arrangement of instruments and innovations to manufacture, work, and coordinate cloud-local application stacks. Cloud has given us access to an assortment of new advances and practices that can improve and advance our exemplary software structures. This is additionally especially centered at the new worldview of microservice-arranged improvement.

As an establishing member in CNCF, Google has given the Kubernetes open-source venture as the initial step. The objective will be to expand interoperability in the ecosystem and bolster better incorporation with ventures. CNCF is now facilitating an assortment of undertakings in arrangement, logging, checking, following, and application strength.

For more data on CNCF, allude to https://cncf.io/.

Standard holder determination

A center aftereffect of the OCI exertion is the creation and improvement of the all-encompassing holder detail. The determination has five center standards for all compartments to pursue, which I will quickly summarize (you can allude to more insights regarding this in point 2 in the References area toward the finish of the section):

The holder must have standard tasks to create, start, and stop compartments across all executions.

The compartment must be content-freethinker, which implies that kind of utilization inside the holder doesn't change the standard tasks or distributing of the holder itself.

The compartment must be foundation skeptic too. Versatility is principal; in this manner, the holders must have the option to work simply in GCE as in your organization's datacenter or on a designer's PC.

A holder should likewise be intended for computerization, which enables us to robotize across the manufacture, refreshing, and arrangement pipelines. While this standard is somewhat dubious, the compartment execution ought not require difficult manual strides for creation and discharge.

At long last, the usage must help modern evaluation conveyance. Indeed, addressing the fabricate and arrangement pipelines and requiring a streamlined proficiency to the versatility and travel of the compartments among foundation and organization levels.

The particular likewise characterizes center standards for holder groups and runtimes. You can peruse increasingly about the particulars on the GitHub venture at https://github.com/opencontainers/specs.

While the center determination can be somewhat dynamic, the runC usage is a solid case of the OCI specs as a compartment runtime and picture position. Once more, you can peruse a greater amount of the specialized subtleties on the runC site and GitHub at the accompanying URLs: https://github.com/opencontainers/runc https://runc.io/

The sponsorship group and runtime for an assortment of well known compartment apparatuses is runC. It was given to OCI by Docker and was created from a similar pipes work utilized in the Docker stage. Since its discharge, it has had an invite take-up by various undertakings.

Indeed, even the prevalent open source PaaS, Cloud Foundry reported that it will utilize runC in Garden. Nursery gives the containerization pipes to Deigo, which goes about as a coordination layer like Kubernetes.

The rkt execution was initially founded on the appc particular. The appc particular was really a previous endeavor by the people at CoreOS to frame a typical determination around containerization. Presently that CoreOS is taking an interest in OCI, they are attempting to help blend the appc determination into OCI; it should bring about a more significant level of similarity across the holder ecosystem.

CoreOS

While the details give us a shared opinion, there are additionally a few patterns developing around the decision of OS for our compartments. There are a few tailor-fit OSes that are being grown explicitly to run holder outstanding tasks at hand. In spite of the fact that usage differ, they all have comparative qualities. Concentrate on a thin establishment base, nuclear OS refreshing, and marked applications for productive and secure activities.

One OS that is picking up ubiquity is CoreOS. CoreOS offers significant benefits for both security and asset usage. It gives asset usage by expelling bundle conditions totally from the image. Rather, CoreOS runs all applications and administrations in compartments. By giving just a little arrangement of administrations required to help running compartments and bypassing the need of hypervisor utilization, CoreOS gives us a chance to utilize a bigger bit of the asset pool to run our containerized applications. This enables clients to increase a better from their framework and better compartment to node (server) use proportions.

More holder OSes

There are a few other holder streamlined OSes that have risen as of late.

Red Hat Enterprise Linux Atomic Host centers around security with SELinux empowered as a matter of course and Atomic updates to the OS like what we saw with CoreOS. Allude to the accompanying connection:

https://access.redhat.com/articles/rhel-nuclear beginning

Ubuntu Snappy additionally benefits from the productivity and security increases of isolating the OS segments from the structures and applications. Utilizing application images and check marks, we get a proficient Ubuntu-based OS for our holder remaining tasks at hand at http://www.ubuntu.com

/cloud/instruments/smart.

Ubuntu LXD runs a compartment hypervisor and gives a way to moving Linux-based VMs to holders effortlessly:

https://www.ubuntu.com/cloud/lxd.

VMware Photon is another lightweight compartment OS that is enhanced explicitly for vSphere and the VMware stage. It runs Docker, rkt, and Garden and additionally has a few images that you can run on the well known open cloud suppliers. Allude to the accompanying connection:

https://vmware.github.io/photon/.

At long last, CoreOS has some additional preferences in the domain of security. First off, the OS can be refreshed as one entire unit rather than by means of individual bundles (allude to the previous figure). This keeps away from numerous issues that emerge from halfway updates. To accomplish this, CoreOS utilizes two allotments—one as the dynamic OS parcel and an auxiliary one to get a full update. When updates are finished effectively, a reboot advances the auxiliary segment. In the case of anything turns out badly, the first parcel is accessible for failback.

The system proprietors can likewise control when those updates are applied. This gives us the adaptability to organize basic updates while working with genuine planning for the more typical updates. Likewise, the whole update is marked and transmitted through SSL for included security across the whole procedure.

rkt

A focal bit of the CoreOS ecosystem is its very own holder runtime, named rkt. As we referenced before, rkt is another execution with a particular spotlight on security. The principle preferred position of rkt is in running the motor without a daemon as root, the manner in which Docker does today. At first, rkt likewise had a favorable position in setting up a trust for holder images. Be that as it may, late updates to Docker have made incredible steps with the new Content Trust include.

Most importantly rkt is as yet an execution concentrated on security to run holders underway. rkt uses a picture design named ACI, yet it additionally bolsters running Docker-based images. Over the previous year, rkt has experienced huge updates and is currently at form 1.24.0. It has increased a lot of energy as an approach to run Docker images safely underway.

Also, CoreOS is working with Intel® to incorporate the new Intel® Virtualization Technology, which enables compartments to run in more elevated levels of segregation. This equipment improved security enables the holders to be run inside a Kernel-based Virtual Machine (KVM) process giving segregation from the piece like what we see with hypervisors today.

etcd

Another focal piece in the CoreOS ecosystem worth referencing is their open-source etcd venture. etcd is a conveyed and predictable key-esteem store. A RESTful API is utilized to interface with etcd, so it's anything but difficult to incorporate with your task.

On the off chance that it sounds natural, this is on the grounds that we saw this procedure running in Chapter 1, Introduction to Kubernetes, in the Services running on the ace area. Kubernetes really uses etcd to monitor group setup and current state. K8s utilizes it for the administration disclosure capacities also. For more subtleties, allude to https://github.com/coreos/etcd.

Kubernetes with CoreOS

Since we understand the benefits, we should investigate a Kubernetes bunch utilizing CoreOS. The documentation underpins various stages, however one of the least demanding to turn up is AWS with the CoreOS CloudFormation and CLI contents.

On the off chance that you are keen on running Kubernetes with CoreOS on different stages, you can discover more subtleties in the CoreOS documentation at

https://coreos.com/kubernetes/docs/most recent/.

We can locate the most recent guidelines for AWS at https://coreos.com/kubernetes/docs/most recent/ kubernetes-on-aws.ht ml.

You can adhere to the guidelines referenced before to turn up Kubernetes on CoreOS. You'll have to create a key pair on AWS and likewise determine a district, group name, bunch size, and DNS to continue.

Also, we should create a DNS passage and will require an assistance, for example, Route53 or a generation DNS administration. When adhering to the guidelines, you'll need to set the DNS to a space or sub-area, where you have authorization to establish up a precedent. We should refresh the record after the bunch is ready for action and has a powerful endpoint characterized.

There you have it! We presently have a bunch running CoreOS. The content creates all the fundamental AWS assets, for example, Virtual Private Clouds (VPCs), security gatherings, and IAM job. Since the bunch is going we can get the endpoint with the status command and update our DNS record:

$ kube-aws status

Duplicate the section recorded alongside Controller DNS Name and then alter your DNS records to point the area or sub-space you indicated prior to point to this heap balancer.

In the event that you overlook which space you determined or need to keep an eye on the design you can glance in the produced kubeconifg file with your preferred supervisor. It will look something like this:

apiVersion: v1

kind: Config

bunches:

- bunch:

authentication authority: qualifications/ca.pem

server: https://coreos.mydomain.com

name: kube-aws-my-coreos-bunch group

settings:

- setting:

bunch: kube-aws-my-coreos-group bunch

namespace: default

client: kube-aws-my-coreos-bunch administrator

name: kube-aws-my-coreos-bunch setting

clients:

- name: kube-aws-my-coreos-bunch administrator

client:

client-authentication: qualifications/admin.pem

client-key: accreditations/administrator key.pem

current-setting: kube-aws-my-coreos-bunch setting

For this situation, the server line will have your area name.

On the off chance that this is a crisp box, you should download kubectl independently as it isn't packaged with kube-aws:

$ wget

https://storage.googleapis.com/kubernetes-discharge/discharge

/v1.0.6/container/linux/amd64/kubectl

We would now be able to utilize kubectl to see our new group:

$ ./kubectl - kubeconfig=kubeconfig get nodes

We should see a solitary node recorded with the EC2 interior DNS as the name. Note kubeconfig, this reveals to Kubernetes the way to utilize the setup file for the group that was simply created. This is likewise helpful on the off chance that we need to deal with various bunches from a similar machine.

Tectonic

Running Kubernetes on CoreOS is an extraordinary beginning, however you may find that you need a more elevated level of help. Enter Tectonic, the CoreOS venture offering for running Kubernetes with CoreOS. Tectonic uses a significant number of the segments we previously talked about. CoreOS is the OS and both Docker and rkt runtimes are upheld. Likewise, Kubernetes, etcd, and wool are bundled together to give a full heap of group coordination. We talked about wool quickly in Chapter 3, Networking, Load Balancers, and Ingress. It is an overlay arrange that uses a model like the local Kubernetes model, and it utilizes etcd as a backend.

Offering a help bundle like Red Hat, CoreOS likewise gives 24x7 help to the open-source software that Tectonic is based on. Tectonic additionally gives ordinary group refreshes and a pleasant dashboard with sees for every one of the segments of Kubernetes. CoreUpdate enables clients to have more control of the programmed updates. Likewise, it ships with modules for observing, SSO, and other security highlights.

You can discover more data and the most recent guidelines to introduce here:

https://coreos.com/tectonic/docs/most recent/introduce/aws/index.html.

Tectonic is presently commonly accessible and the dashboard as of now has some pleasant highlights.

Another pleasant element is the Events page. Here, we can watch the occasions live, respite, and channel dependent on occasion seriousness and asset type:

A helpful component to peruse anyplace in the dashboard system is the Namespace: sifting alternative. Just snap on the dropdown by the word Namespace: at the highest point of any page that shows assets, and we can channel our perspectives by namespace. This can be useful on the off chance that we need to sift through the Kubernetes system cases or take a gander at a specific assortment of assets:

Summary

In this part, we took a gander at the developing standards bodies in the compartment network and how they are molding the innovation for the better with open particulars. We additionally investigated CoreOS, a key player in both the holder and the Kubernetes people group. We investigated the innovation they are creating to upgrade and praise holder coordination and saw direct how to utilize some of it with Kubernetes. At last, we took a gander at the bolstered venture offering of Tectonic and a portion of the highlights that are accessible at this point.

In the following part, which is the last one, we will investigate the more extensive Kubernetes ecosystem and the apparatuses accessible to move your group from advancement and testing into out and out creation.

Towards Production Ready

In this part, we'll see contemplations to move to creation. We will likewise show some supportive devices and outsider undertakings accessible in the Kubernetes people group everywhere and where you can go to get more help.

This part will talk about the accompanying subjects:

Creation attributes

The Kubernetes ecosystem

Where to find support?

Prepared for creation

We strolled through various run of the mill activities utilizing Kubernetes. As we saw, K8s offers an assortment of highlights and reflections that facilitate the weight of everyday administration for compartment arrangements.

There are numerous attributes that characterize a creation prepared system for holders.

We perceived how the center ideas and deliberations of Kubernetes address a couple of these worries. The administration reflection has worked in administration disclosure and wellbeing checking at both the administration and application level. We additionally get consistent application updates and adaptability from the replication controller and arrangement develops. All the center reflections of administrations, replication controllers, copy sets, and cases work with a center planning and proclivity rulesets and give us simple help and application structure.

There is worked in help for an assortment of tireless stockpiling alternatives, and the systems administration model gives sensible system tasks choices to work with other outsider suppliers. Likewise, we investigated CI/CD incorporation with a portion of the prominent instruments in the commercial center.

Besides, we have worked in system occasions following, and with the significant cloud suppliers, an out-of-the-container arrangement for observing and logging. We additionally perceived how this can be stretched out to outsider suppliers, for example, StackDriver and Sysdig. These administrations likewise address in general node wellbeing and proactive pattern deviation cautions.

The center develops likewise assist us with addressing high accessibility in our application and administration layers. The scheduler can be utilized with autoscaling systems to give this at a node level. At that point there is support for making the Kubernetes ace itself profoundly accessible. In Chapter 9, Cluster Federation, we investigated the new organization capacities that which guarantee a multi-cloud and multi-datacenter model for what's to come.

We at long last investigated another type of working systems that give us a thin base to expand on and secure update instruments for fixing and updates. The thin base, together with planning, can assist us with effective asset use. Also, we saw some solidified concerns and investigated the picture trust and check devices accessible. Security is a wide theme and abilities network exist for this point alone.

Prepared, set, go

While there are still a few holes, an assortment of the rest of the security and activity concerns are effectively being tended to by outsider organizations, as we will find in the accompanying segment. Going ahead, the Kubernetes venture will proceed to advance, and the network of tasks and accomplices around K8s and Docker will likewise develop. The people group is shutting the rest of the holes at a remarkable pace.

Outsider organizations

Since the Kubernetes task's underlying discharge, there has been a developing ecosystem of accomplices. We took a gander at CoreOS, Sysdig, and numerous others in the past sections, yet there are an assortment of undertakings and organizations in this space. We will feature a not many that might be helpful as you move towards generation. This is in no way, shape or form a thorough rundown and it is just intended to give some intriguing beginning stages.

Private libraries

Much of the time, associations won't have any desire to put their applications and/or protected innovation in open repositories. For those cases, a private vault arrangement is useful in safely incorporating organizations start to finish.

Google Cloud offers the Google Container

Vault at https://cloud.google.com/compartment library/.

Docker has its very own Trusted Registry

offering at https://www.docker.com/docker-trusted-library.

Quay.io additionally gives secure private libraries, powerlessness examining, and originates from the CoreOS group at https://quay.io/.

Google Container Engine

Google was the primary creator of the first Kubernetes venture and is as yet a significant giver. In spite of the fact that this book has for the most part centered around running Kubernetes all alone, Google is additionally offering a completely overseen compartment administration through the Google Cloud Platform.

Discover more data on the Google Container Engine (GKE) site at https://cloud.google.com/compartment motor/.

Kubernetes will be introduced on GCE and will be overseen by Google engineers. They additionally furnish private libraries and incorporation with your current private systems.

Create your first GKE group

From the GCP support, in Compute, click on Container Engine, and then on Container Clusters.

On the off chance that this is your first time making a bunch, you'll have a data confine the center of the page. Snap on the Create a compartment bunch button. Pick a name for your bunch and the zone. You'll likewise have the option to pick the machine type (occasion size) for your nodes and what number of nodes (group size) you need in your bunch. You'll additionally observe a decision for node picture, which gives you a chance to pick the base OS and machine picture for the nodes themselves. The ace is overseen and refreshed by the Google group themselves. Leave Stackdriver Logging and

Stackdriver Monitoring checked. Snap on Create, and in almost no time, you'll have another bunch prepared for use.

You'll require kubectl that is incorporated with the Google SDK to start utilizing your GKE group. Allude to Chapter 1, Introduction to Kubernetes, for subtleties on introducing the SDK. When we have the SDK, we can arrange kubectl and the SDK for our bunch utilizing the means laid out at https://cloud.google.com/holder motor/docs/before-you-begin# install_kubectl.

Sky blue Container Service

Another cloud-oversaw offering is Microsoft's Azure Container Service (ACS). ACS is extremely decent in light of the fact that it enables you to look over industry standard apparatuses, for example, Docker Swarm, Kubernetes, and Mesos. It at that point creates an oversaw group for you, yet utilizes one of these apparatus sets as the establishment. The favorable position is that you can in any case utilize the device's local API and the executives devices, yet leave the administration of the cloud foundation to Azure.

Discover increasingly about ACS at https://azure.microsoft.com/en-us/administrations/holder administration/.

ClusterHQ

ClusterHQ gives an answer for bringing stateful information into your containerized applications. They give Flocker, an instrument for overseeing relentless stockpiling volumes with compartments, and FlockerHub which gives a capacity vault to your information volumes.

It would be ideal if you allude to the ClusterHQ site for more data at https://clusterhq.com/.

Portworx

Portworx is another player in the extra room. It gives answers for carrying industriousness stockpiling to your compartments. Moreover, it has highlights for snapshotting, encryption, and even multi-cloud replication.

If you don't mind allude to the portworx site for more data at https://portworx.com/.

Shippable

Shippable is a constant joining, persistent sending, and discharge computerization stage that has worked in help for an assortment of current compartment conditions. The item touts supporting any language with a uniform help for bundling and test.

If it's not too much trouble allude to the Shippable site for more data at https://app.shippable.com/.

Twistlock

Twistlock.io is a powerlessness and solidifying apparatus customized for compartments. It gives the capacity to implement strategies, solidifies as indicated by CIS standards, and sweeps images in any famous library for vulnerabilities. It likewise furnishes check joining with famous CI/CD devices and RBAC answers for some, organization apparatuses, for example, Kubernetes.

If you don't mind allude to the Twistlock site for more data at https://www.twistlock.io/.

AquaSec

AquaSec is another security device giving an assortment of highlights. Picture checking with famous libraries, arrangement requirement, client get to control, and compartment solidifying are altogether secured. Also, AquaSec makes them intrigue usefulness in arrange division.

Kindly allude to the Aqua's site for more data at https://www.aquasec.com/.

Mesosphere (Kubernetes on Mesos)

Mesosphere itself is building a monetarily bolstered item (DCOS) around the open-source Apache Mesos venture. Apache Mesos is a group the board system that offers planning and asset sharing somewhat like Kubernetes itself, yet at an a lot more significant level. The open-source venture is utilized by a few surely understood organizations, for example, Twitter and AirBnB.

Get more data on the Mesos OS venture and the Mesosphere offerings at these locales:

http://mesos.apache.org/

https://mesosphere.com/

Mesos by its tendency is particular and permits the utilization of different systems for an assortment of stages. A Kubernetes structure is presently accessible, so we can exploit the group overseeing in Mesos while as yet keeping up the helpful application-level reflections in K8s. Allude to the accompanying connection:

https://github.com/kubernetes-hatchery/kube-mesos-system

Deis

The Deis venture gives an open-source Platform as a Service (PaaS) arrangement dependent on and around Kubernetes. This enables organizations to send their very own PaaS on-premise or on the general population cloud.

Deis gives apparatuses to application organization and arrangement, bundle the board (at the unit level), and administration handling.

You can allude to the accompanying site for more data on Deis:

https://deis.com/.

OpenShift

Another PaaS arrangement is OpenShift from Red Hat. The OpenShift stage utilizes the Red Hat Atomic stage as a safe and thin OS for running holders. In adaptation 3, Kubernetes has been included as the arrangement layer for all holder tasks on your PaaS. This is an extraordinary blend to oversee PaaS establishments at an enormous scale.

More data on OpenShift can be found at

https://enterprise.openshift.com/.

Where to find out additional?

The Kubernetes venture is an open-source exertion, so there is an expansive network of benefactors and aficionados. One extraordinary asset so as to discover more help is the Kubernetes Slack channel:

http://slack.kubernetes.io/

There is additionally a Kubernetes bunch on Google gatherings. You can go along with it at

https://groups.google.com/gathering/#!forum/kubernetes-clients.

Summary

We left a couple of breadcrumbs to control you on your proceeded with venture with Kubernetes. You ought to have a strong arrangement of generation attributes to kick you off. There is a wide network in both the Docker and Kubernetes world. There are likewise a couple of extra assets that we gave in the event that you need an amicable face en route.

At this point, we have seen the full range of holder activities with Kubernetes. You ought to be increasingly positive about how Kubernetes can streamline the administration of your holder arrangements and how you can plan to move compartments off the designer workstations onto creation servers. Presently get out there and start transporting your compartments!

Handling the kubernetes Package manager

In this part, we are going to investigate Helm, the Kubernetes bundle chief. Each fruitful and non-minor stage must have a decent bundling system.

Helm was created by Deis (procured by Microsoft 04/2017) and later added to the Kubernetes venture legitimately. We will begin by understanding the inspiration for Helm, its engineering, and its segments. At that point, we'll get hands-on and perceive how to utilize Helm and its graphs inside Kubernetes. That incorporates discovering, introducing, modifying, erasing, and overseeing graphs. To wrap things up, we'll spread how to create your very own graphs and handle forming, conditions, and templating.

The themes we will cover are as per the following:

- Understanding Helm
- Using Helm
- Creating your very own diagrams

Understanding Helm

Kubernetes gives numerous approaches to compose and coordinate your compartments at runtime, however it comes up short on a more elevated level association of collection sets of images together. This is the place Helm comes in. In this segment, we'll go over the inspiration for Helm, its design and parts, and talk about what has changed in the progress from Helm Classic to Helm.

The inspiration for Helm

Helm offers help for a few significant use cases:

•Managing unpredictability

•Easy redesigns

•Simple sharing

•Safe rollbacks

Outlines can depict even the most unpredictable applications, give repeatable application establishment, and fill in as a solitary purpose of power. Set up overhauls and custom snares take into consideration simple updates. It's easy to share graphs that can be formed and facilitated on open or private servers. At the point when you have to rollback late redesigns, Helm gives a solitary command to rollback a strong arrangement of changes to your foundation.

The Helm design

Helm is intended to play out the accompanying:

•Create new outlines without any preparation

•Package outlines into diagram file (tgz) files

•Interact with outline repositories where diagrams are put away

•Install and uninstall outlines into a current Kubernetes bunch

•Manage the discharge cycle of outlines that have been introduced with Helm utilizes a customer server design to accomplish these objectives

Helm segments

Helm has a server segment that sudden spikes in demand for your Kubernetes bunch and a customer part that you run on a neighborhood machine.

The Tiller server

The server is liable for overseeing discharges. It collaborates with the Helm customers just as the Kubernetes API server. Its fundamental capacities are as per the following:

•Listening for approaching solicitations from the Helm customer

•Combining an outline and arrangement to fabricate a discharge

•Installing outlines into Kubernetes

•Tracking the ensuing discharge

•Upgrading and uninstalling outlines by collaborating with Kubernetes

The Helm customer

You introduce the Helm customer on your machine. It is answerable for the accompanying:

•Local outline advancement

•Managing repositories

•Interacting with the Tiller server

•Sending outlines to be introduced

•Asking for data about discharges

•Requesting redesigns or uninstallation of existing discharges

Helm versus. Helm-exemplary

Helm was initially created by Deis until adaptation 0.70. From that point forward, the first Helm has been branded Helm-great. The main motivation to utilize Helm-exemplary is in the event that you as of now have existing diagrams and you're

not prepared to update. Helm great is accessible here:

https://github.com/helm/helm-classic.git.

Utilizing Helm

Helm is a rich bundle the executives system that gives you a chance to play out all the fundamental strides to deal with the applications introduced on your group. How about we focus in and get moving.

Introducing Helm

Introducing Helm includes introducing the customer and the server. Helm is actualized in Go, and a similar double executable can fill in as either customer or server.

Introducing the Helm customer

You should have Kubectl arranged appropriately to converse with your Kubernetes group on the grounds that the Helm customer utilizes the Kubectl arrangement to converse with the Helm server (Tiller)

Helm gives parallel discharges to all stages here: https://github.com/kubernetes/helm/discharges/most recent.

For Windows, it is your solitary choice.

For Mac OSX and Linux, you can introduce the customer from a content:

$ twist https://raw.githubusercontent.com/kubernetes/helm/ace/contents/get > get_helm.sh

$ chmod 700 get_helm.sh

$ ./get_helm.sh

On Mac OSX, you can likewise utilize Homebrew:

mix introduce kubernetes-helm

Introducing the Tiller server

Tiller ordinarily runs inside your group. For improvement, it is now and again simpler to run Tiller locally.

Introducing Tiller in-bunch

The most effortless approach to introduce Tiller is from a machine where the Helm customer is introduced. Run the accompanying command: helm init.

This will instate both the customer just as the Tiller server on the remote Kubernetes bunch. At the point when the establishment is done, you will have a running Tiller unit in the kube-system namespace of your group:

$ kubectl get po - namespace=kube-system - l name=tiller

NAMEREADYSTATUSRESTARTSAGE

tiller-convey 3210613906-2j5sh1/1Running01m

You can likewise run helm variant to look at both the customer's and the server's form:

$ helm form

Customer: &version.Version{SemVer:"v2.2.3", GitCommit:"1402a4d6ec9fb349e17b 912e32fe259ca21181e3", GitTreeState:"clean"}

Server: &version.Version{SemVer:"v2.2.3", GitCommit:"1402a4d6ec9fb349e17b 912e32fe259ca21181e3", GitTreeState:"clean"}

Introducing Tiller locally

In the event that you need to run Tiller locally, you have to assemble it first. This is bolstered on Linux

and Mac OSX:

$ disc $GOPATH

$ mkdir - p src/k8s.io

$ disc src/k8s.io

$ git clone https://github.com/kubernetes/helm.git

$ disc helm

$ make bootstrap construct

The bootstrap target will endeavor to introduce conditions, remake the merchant/tree, and approve design.

The fabricate target will arrange Helm and spot it in canister/helm. Tiller is additionally arranged and is set in canister/tiller.

Presently you can simply run container/tiller. Tiller will interface with the Kubernetes bunch by means of your Kubectl setup.

You have to advise the Helm customer to associate with the neighborhood Tiller server. You can do it by setting a situation variable:

$ send out HELM_HOST=localhost:44134

Or then again you can pass it as a command-line contention, - have localhost:44134.

Discovering diagrams

So as to introduce valuable applications and software with Helm, you have to discover their graphs first. This is the place the helm search command comes in. Helm, as a matter of course, look through the official Kubernetes diagram store, which is called stable:

$ helm search

NAMEVERSION DESCRIPTION

stable/chaoskube0.5.0Chaoskube intermittently executes random cases in you...

stable/cockroachdb0.2.2CockroachDB is an adaptable, survivable, unequivocally...

stable/dokuwiki0.1.3DokuWiki is a standards-agreeable, easy to us...

stable/jenkins0.3.1Open source constant joining server. It s...

stable/kapacitor motor. It ca...0.2.2InfluxDB's local information handling

stable/kube-lego declarations from Let's

...0.1.8Automatically demands

stable/kube-operations see read-just system ...0.2.0Kubernetes Operational View -

stable/kube2iam dependent on annota...0.2.1Provide IAM certifications to cases

The official archive has a rich library of outlines that speak to all cutting edge open source databases, checking systems, Kubernetes-explicit aides, and a huge number of different offerings, for example, a Minecraft server. You can scan for explicit outlines. For instance, how about we scan for graphs that contain kube in their name or depiction:

$ helm search kube

NAMEVERSION DESCRIPTION

stable/chaoskube0.5.0Chaoskube intermittently slaughters random units in you...

stable/kube-lego0.1.8Automatically demands testaments from Let's ...

stable/kube-operations view0.2.0Kubernetes Operational View - read-just system ...

stable/kube2iam0.2.1Provide IAM accreditations to units dependent on annota...

stable/sumokube0.1.1Sumologic Log Collector

stable/etcd-operator0.2.0CoreOS etcd-administrator Helm diagram for Kubernetes

stable/nginx-lego0.2.1Chart for nginx-entrance controller and kube-lego

stable/openvpn1.0.1A Helm diagram to introduce an openvpn server insid...

stable/spartakus1.1.1Collect data about Kubernetes bunches t...

stable/traefik1.1.2-h A Traefik based Kubernetes entrance controller w...

How about we attempt another inquiry:

$ helm search mysql

NAMEVERSION DESCRIPTION

stable/mysql0.2.5Fast, solid, adaptable, and simple to utilize open-

...

stable/mariadb0.5.14Fast, solid, adaptable, and simple to utilize open-

...

What was the deal? For what reason does mariadb appear in the outcomes? The explanation is that mariadb (which is a fork of MySQL) makes reference to MySQL in its portrayal, despite the fact that you can't see it in the truncated yield. To get the full depiction, utilize the helm examine command:

$ helm assess stable/mariadb

portrayal: Fast, solid, versatile, and simple to utilize open-source social database

system. MariaDB Server is planned for crucial, overwhelming burden generation systems

just as for installing into mass-conveyed software. motor: gotpl

home: https://mariadb.org

symbol: https://bitnami.com/resources/stacks/mariadb/img/mariadb-stack-220x234.png

watchwords:

- mariadb

- mysql

- database

- sql maintainers:

- email: containers@bitnami.com name: Bitnami

name: mariadb sources:

- https://github.com/bitnami/bitnami-docker-mariadb rendition: 0.5.14

Introducing bundles

Alright. You've discovered the bundle you had always wanted. Presently, you most likely need to introduce it on your Kubernetes group. At the point when you introduce a bundle, Helm creates a discharge

that you can use to monitor the establishment progress. We should introduce MariaDB utilizing the helm introduce command. How about we go over the yield in detail. The initial segment of the yield records the name of the discharge - alert-panda for this situation (you can pick your very own with the - name banner), the namespace, and the arrangement status:

$ helm introduce stable/mariadb NAME:alert-panda

LAST DEPLOYED: Sat Apr1 18:39:47 2017

NAMESPACE: default STATUS: DEPLOYED

The second piece of the yield records every one of the assets created by this outline. Note that the asset names are altogether gotten from the discharge name.

Assets:

==> v1/PersistentVolumeClaim

NAMESTATUSVOLUMECAPACITYACCESSMODESAGE

alert-panda-mariadbPending1s

==> v1/Service

NAME

Bunch IP

Outer IP

PORT(S)AGE

alert-panda-mariadb10.3.245.245<none>3306/TCP1s

==> augmentations/v1beta1/Deployment

NAMEDESIREDCURRENTUP-TO-DATEAVAILABLEAGE

alert-panda-mariadb11101s

==> v1/Secret NAME

TYPE

Information

AGE

alert-panda-mariadbOpaque21s

==> v1/ConfigMap

NAMEDATAAGE

alert-panda-mariadb11s

The last part is takes note of that give straightforward directions on the most proficient method to utilize MariaDB in the substance of your Kubernetes bunch. NOTES:

MariaDB can be gotten to by means of port 3306 on the accompanying DNS name from inside your bunch:

alert-panda-mariadb.default.svc.cluster.local

To associate with your database:

1.Run a case that you can use as a customer:

kubectl run alert-panda-mariadb-customer - rm - tty - I - picture bitnami/mariadb - command - slam

2.Connect utilizing the mysql cli, at that point give your secret phrase:

$ mysql - h alert-panda-mariadb

Checking establishment status

Helm doesn't trust that the establishment will finish since it might take some time. The helm status command shows the most recent data on a discharge in a similar configuration as the yield of the underlying helm introduce command. In the yield of the introduce command you can see that the tireless volume guarantee had a pending status. We should look at it now:

$ helm status alert-panda | grep Persist - A 3

==> v1/PersistentVolumeClaim

NAMESTATUS VOLUMECAPACITY ACCESSMODESAGE

alert-panda-mariadbBoundpvc-41... 0156 8GiRWO10m

Yippee! It is bound now, and there is a volume joined with 8 GB limit.

We should attempt to interface and check mariadb is in fact available. We should alter the recommended commands a smidgen from the notes to interface. Rather than running slam and then running mysql, we can legitimately run the mysql command on the compartment:

$ kubectl run alert-panda-mariadb-customer - rm - tty - I - picture bitnami/mariadb - command - mysql - h al

ert-panda-mariadb

On the off chance that you don't see a command brief, take a stab at squeezing enter.

MariaDB [(none)]> show databases;

| Database|

| information_schema |

| mysql|

| performance_schema |

3 lines in set (0.00 sec)

Modifying a graph

Frequently as a client, you need to redo or design the graphs you introduce. Helm completely bolsters customization by means of config files. To find out about conceivable customizations you can utilize the helm examine command once more, yet this time center around the qualities.

Here is a halfway yield:

$ helm investigate values stable/mariadb ## Bitnami MariaDB picture adaptation

ref: https://hub.docker.com/r/bitnami/mariadb/labels/##

Default: none

picture: bitnami/mariadb:10.1.22-r1

Specify an imagePullPolicy (Required)

It's prescribed to change this to 'Consistently' if the picture tag is 'most recent'

ref: http://kubernetes.io/docs/client direct/images/#updating-images imagePullPolicy: IfNotPresent

Specify secret phrase for root client

##ref: https://github.com/bitnami/bitnami-docker-mariadb/mass/ace/README.md#setting-the-root-secret phrase on-first-run

##

mariadbRootPassword:

Create a database client

##ref: https://github.com/bitnami/bitnami-docker-mariadb/mass/ace/README.md#creating-a-database-client on-first-run

##

mariadbUser:

mariadbPassword:

Create a database

##ref: https://github.com/bitnami/bitnami-docker-mariadb/mass/ace/README.md#creating-a-database-on-first-run

##

mariadbDatabase:

For instance, on the off chance that you need to set a root secret key and create a database when introducing mariadb, you can create the accompanying YAML file and spare it as mariadb-config.yaml:

mariadbRootPassword: supersecret mariadbDatabase: awesome_stuff

At that point, run helm and pass it the yaml file: helm introduce - f config.yaml stable/mariadb

You can likewise set individual qualities on the command line with - set. In the event that both - f and - set attempt to set similar qualities, at that point - set comes first. For instance, for this situation the root secret key will be evenbettersecret:

Helm introduce - f config.yaml - set mariadbRootPassword=evenbettersecret stable/mariadb

You can indicate numerous qualities utilizing comma-isolated records: - set a=1,b=2.

Extra establishment choices

The helm introduce command can introduce from a few sources:

- A diagram storehouse (as we've seen)
- A neighborhood graph document (helm introduce foo-0.1.1.tgz)
- An unloaded diagram catalog (helm introduce way/to/foo)
- A full URL (helm introduce https://example.com/diagrams/foo-1.2.3.tgz)

Updating and moving back a discharge

You might need to update a bundle you introduced to the best in class adaptation. Helm give the redesign command, which works wisely and just updates things that have changed. For instance, how about we check the present estimations of our mariadb establishment:

$ helm get values alert-panda mariadbDatabase: awesome_stuff mariadbRootPassword: evenbettersecret

Presently, we should run, overhaul, and change the name of the database:

$ helm overhaul alert-panda - set mariadbDatabase=awesome_sauce stable/mariadb

$ helm get values alert-panda mariadbDatabase: awesome_sauce

Note that we've lost our root secret phrase. All the current qualities are supplanted when you overhaul. Alright, allow's move to back. The helm history command gives all of us the accessible updates we can move back to:

$ helm history alert-panda

REVISION	STATUS	CHART	DESCRIPTION
1	SUPERSEDED	mariadb-0.5.14	Install complete
2	SUPERSEDED	mariadb-0.5.14	Upgrade complete
3	SUPERSEDED	mariadb-0.5.14	Upgrade complete
4	DEPLOYED	mariadb-0.5.14	Upgrade complete

Let's roll back to revision 3:

$ helm rollback alert-panda 3

Rollback was a success! Happy Helming!

$ helm history alert-panda

REVISION	STATUS	CHART	DESCRIPTION
1	SUPERSEDED	mariadb-0.5.14	Install complete
2	SUPERSEDED	mariadb-0.5.14	Upgrade complete
3	SUPERSEDED	mariadb-0.5.14	Upgrade complete
4	SUPERSEDED	mariadb-0.5.14	Upgrade complete
5	DEPLOYED	mariadb-0.5.14	Rollback to 3

Let's verify our changes were rolled back:

$ helm get values alert-panda mariadbDatabase: awesome_stuff mariadbRootPassword: evenbettersecret

Summary

In this section, we investigated Helm, the Kubernetes bundle chief. Helm enables Kubernetes to oversee muddled software made out of numerous Kubernetes assets with between conditions. It fills a similar need as an OS bundle administrator. It sorts out bundles and gives you a chance to look through diagrams, introduce and redesign graphs, and offer outlines with teammates. You can build up your outlines and store them in repositories.

Now, you ought to understand the significant job that Helm serves in the Kubernetes ecosystem and network. You ought to have the option to utilize it beneficially and even create and share your own outlines.

Don't miss out!

Visit the website below and you can sign up to receive emails whenever Jordan Lioy publishes a new book. There's no charge and no obligation.

https://books2read.com/r/B-A-GYIX-ELRGC

BOOKS 2 READ

Connecting independent readers to independent writers.

Also by Jordan Lioy

Docker & Kubernetes

Docker: The Complete Guide to the Most Widely Used Virtualization Technology. Create Containers and Deploy them to Production Safely and Securely.

Kubernetes: Build and Deploy Modern Applications in a Scalable Infrastructure. The Complete Guide to the Most Modern Scalable Software Infrastructure.

Standalone

Software Containers: The Complete Guide to Virtualization Technology. Create, Use and Deploy Scalable Software with Docker and Kubernetes. Includes Docker and Kubernetes.

www.ingramcontent.com/pod-product-compliance
Lightning Source LLC
LaVergne TN
LVHW080012210926
848481LV00011B/3005